# First Italian Reader

# First Italian Reader

## A Dual-Language Book

Edited and Translated by
**STANLEY APPELBAUM**

DOVER PUBLICATIONS, INC.
Mineola, New York

## Bibliographical Note

This Dover edition, first published in 2008, is a new selection of excerpts from 55 Italian authors (reprinted from standard texts) writing between ca. 1300 and ca. 1920 (the latest original publication date is 1921; see Introduction for data on individual authors), together with new English translations by Stanley Appelbaum, who made the selection and wrote the Preface and Introduction.

## Library of Congress Cataloging-in-Publication Data

First Italian reader : a dual-language book / edited and translated by Stanley Appelbaum.
    p. cm.
Italian and English.
ISBN-13: 978-0-486-46535-7
ISBN-10: 0-486-46535-7
    1. Italian language—Readers. 2. Italian language—Textbooks for foreign speakers—English. I. Appelbaum, Stanley.

PC1115.F57 2008
458.2'421—dc22

2007041872

Manufactured in the United States by LSC Communications
46535706     2017
www.doverpublications.com

# PREFACE

This is not a book for children or for absolute beginners in Italian: the material is adult (though not in the scabrous sense), and a good grounding in Italian grammar is needed for the fullest enjoyment of the passages in the original. This is a "first reader" in the sense of an introductory anthology of the whole span of Italian literature from ca. 1300 to ca. 1920. (Drama is excluded at the publisher's request, but a few major playwrights are represented by work in other genres.) The excerpts are totally unadulterated, not "retold" or simplified pabulum. Self-contained, this book can be used with or without an instructor. It should appeal to anyone interested in a rapid survey of a vital, energetic body of writing, and one of the great cultural legacies.

The 55 authors (or works: two are anonymous) include a host of the greatest names in the field, including many of world renown, and three Nobel laureates. The facing English translations, prepared specially for this volume, are complete, and as faithful as the differences between Italian and English allow; they obviate the use of reference books for unfamiliar words and grammatical forms, etc. The average length of the authors' contributions is about two pages (per language), but a few poets are given only one-half to one-and-a-half pages, and two or three prose writers are allotted up to three pages (Boccaccio!) to avoid truncating a good story or train of thought.

It would be impossible to compile for such literatures as English, German, and French (for instance) an anthology like this which reaches back into the thirteenth century and can be readily understood; Italian is fortunate in having remained fundamentally stable since then, except for relatively superficial changes. (Of course, this anthology, which has sought to include only very lucid and self-explanatory selections, has avoided the very rich literature in dialect; anyway, lucidity is often more a feature of a given author's style than of his date.) Nevertheless, some readers may wish to begin with the eighteenth- or nineteenth-century material for greater familiarity.

Italian literature has often been highly influential on the rest of Europe (for instance, this reader includes excerpts from three stories that inspired Shakespearean plays); from roughly 1300 to 1600 it often led the way. The present volume is particularly strong on the glorious sixteenth century. It also pays particular attention (in the area of prose) to the magnificent Italian storytelling tradition of the late Middle Ages and Renaissance, and (in the area of verse) to the sonnet, which was a thirteenth-century Italian invention.

The excerpts are chronological by authors' years of birth (or, where these are unknown, by the approximate date of the work). They include not only poetry and fiction, but also history, philosophy, and other expository prose; the reader can sample the surprising writing ability of men renowned for other talents, such as Michelangelo and Galileo. There is also much humor and fun, including the world-famous *Pinocchio*. This book will be welcome to all who have wished for a taste of the original wording of such writers as Dante, Manzoni, and Pirandello; of such works as the *Decameron, The Prince,* and *The Courtier.*

To avoid further breaking up of the already choppy pages, no footnotes have been used; thus, it is highly advisable to consult the numbered portions of the Introduction corresponding to the excerpts being read. There is extremely little duplication of material already in previous Dover dual-language books; and even in those few cases, the translations here are new. No attempt has been made to regularize such permissible variations in accenting as *ú/ù*, *í/ì*, or *-io/-ìo*. The excerpts here follow the source texts in each case (this is true of the orthography in general).

# CONTENTS

# INTRODUCTION

## Commentary on the Selections

**1.** *Novellino.* Anonymous; written between 1281 and 1300; first published 1525; the most important Italian story collection before Boccaccio's *Decameron*. This collection was dubbed *Novellino* by Giovanni Della Casa (see No. 23); earlier it had been called *Cento novelle antiche* (A Hundred Old Stories) or *Libro del bel parlar gentile* (Book of Comely Gentle Speech). Written by one or more Florentines or northern Italians, it combined entertainment with social "wisdom." Its stories are very brief, and are derived from a variety of sources; our selection B is a variation of a tale included in Petronius's *Satyricon;* C is obviously from Aesop. All three tales reprinted here are complete, except for their long, summarizing titles.

**2.** Dante Alighieri (1265–1321). Usually considered the greatest Italian author (he also wrote many other verse and prose works in Italian and Latin), Dante, after turbulent civic activities, was in permanent exile from his native city-state Florence when he composed his *Commedia* (called *Divina* in a 1555 edition), probably beginning about 1306. "Midway through life" (that is, at 35, with reference to the biblical life span of 70) he allegorically finds himself in a forest of moral confusion, attacked by wild animals emblematic of his vices, until rescued by the voice of reason in the guise of the great ancient Roman poet Vergil (our selection is the very opening of the *Inferno,* the first part of the *Commedia*). The fame of Dante, Petrarca (No. 3), and Boccaccio (No. 4) led to the acceptance of Tuscan as the chief literary dialect (see No. 14) and the basis of standard Italian.

**3.** Francesco Petrarca (1304–1374; often called Petrarch in English). A pioneer of humanism (the revival of Greco-Roman culture), Petrarca wrote voluminously in Italian and Latin, but was most lastingly influential as the perfecter of the sonnet (317 out of the 366 Italian lyric poems in his *Canzoniere* [Songbook] are sonnets, out-

standing for their virtuosity and sincerity; they were published by
1554). The sonnets, five of which are reprinted here, idealize his love
for the dead "Laura," whom he met in Avignon in 1327. The "vanity"
referred to in selection A is his love for Laura; D was written on Good
Friday of 1338; in E, his "master" is Love. Petrarca has been called
"Italy's greatest lyric stylist and poet."

**4.** Giovanni Boccaccio (1313–1375). A humanist and friend of
Petrarca, Boccaccio wrote many Italian and Latin works, but is best
known as "possibly the greatest storyteller of all time" in his hundred-
tale *Decameron* (Ten Days), written ca. 1349–1351. Our selection is
the complete seventh tale of Day Four (minus title). Fleeing the
plague of 1348, several young Florentines assemble in a rural villa and
tell stories of all kinds (the risqué element has helped make the collection perennially popular). The story included here is based on one
of the bawdy French *fabliaux* (short narrative poems of the twelfth
and thirteenth centuries).

**5.** Franco Sacchetti (ca. 1330–1400). His *Trecentonovelle* (Three
Hundred Tales; only 223 are extant) was perhaps written between
1385 and 1392, but not published until 1724. The excerpt in this volume is the beginning of his story 48, based on a universal folk motif of
which a prime example occurs in the *Arabian Nights* (Note that the
*podestà*, or chief magistrate, of Florence was regularly chosen from
another city.) Sacchetti also wrote poetry and religious works in addition to this major story collection, which affords a panorama of the
society of his day.

**6.** *I fioretti di San Francesco*. This anonymous collection of legends
concerning Saint Francis of Assisi (ca. 1181–1226) was based on earlier accounts in Latin. One reference work gives the date of writing as
ca. 1370–1390; many others offer no dates. The language is deliciously
simple, befitting the delicate, tender subject matter. Our selection is
the entire famous chapter devoted to the wolf of Gubbio, typical of
the saint's special rapport with animals.

**7.** Ser Giovanni Fiorentino (Master John of Florence; no dates
known). Though this author's life remains a mystery, his fifty-story collection *Pecorone*, written from 1378 to beyond 1400, makes him one
of the central figures in the development of the Italian tale after
Boccaccio. *Pecorone*, literally "ram," is also slang for a coward or a
fool; it has been rendered as *Numbskull*, and is said to refer to the
great number of foolish characters in the stories. Our selection is the
beginning of the second story, which later develops into one of
the sources of Shakespeare's *Merchant of Venice*, supplying the

"pound of flesh" theme and the appellation Belmonte. Tanais is the ancient name of Azov, at the mouth of the Don in Russia.

**8.** Luigi Pulci (1432–1484). In *Morgante,* an epic poem in octaves (eight-line stanzas; *ottava rima*) written between 1461 and 1483 (based on an anonymous fourteenth-century ballad) and first published in its entirety in 1483, Pulci, a friend of the Medici family, whom he served as a diplomat, created the first of the great Italian historical/fantastical epics of the Renaissance. In our selection, stanzas 19–27 of the first canto, Orlando (Charlemagne's nephew Roland, hero of the *Chanson de Roland*) is just leaving his uncle's court in a fit of pique; he encounters the giant Morgante, who will be converted to Christianity and will become his squire. (The memory of old wars against "Saracens" had been aroused by the fall of Constantinople in 1453.)

**9.** Matteo Maria Boiardo (1441–1494). We give the very opening of his epic poem *Orlando innamorato* (begun in the 1470s; Books I and II were published in 1483; Book III was left unfinished at his death and published with the rest in 1495). Boiardo, a member of the Este court in Ferrara, injected Arthurian-cycle romantic love into the martial tradition of epics about Charlemagne. Here, Orlando falls in love with the Cathayan enchantress Angelica when she comes to his uncle's court. Turpin was the legendary author of earlier Roland epics; Durindana was Orlando's sword; Baiardo was Rinaldo's steed.

**10.** Lorenzo de' Medici, the Magnificent (1449–1492), became head of state in Florence in 1469. An outstanding politician, cultural figure, and patron of the arts, he left behind a wide variety of writings. Of the two complete poems reprinted here, A is a *canzone a ballo* (dance song); B, a *canto carnascialesco* (Carnival-procession song); both were written before the dire 1478 conspiracy that shattered the author's merry frame of mind, but some critics find they are already nervous and pessimistic even as they invite the listener to "seize the day." (*Trionfo* may specifically designate the processional float.)

**11.** Poliziano (Politian; 1454–1494; pseudonym, based on his Tuscan hometown Montepulciano, of Angelo [Agnolo] Ambrogini). An eminent humanist, a protégé of Lorenzo the Magnificent, Poliziano wrote a vast amount in Italian and Latin, but all of his Italian verse seems to have been written in the decade 1470–1480. Of our two complete lyric poems, B is a *canzone a ballo* on the fleetingness of beauty, while A is an excerpt from the *Favola* (or *Festa*) *d'Orfeo* (Play [or Festival] of Orpheus; Mantua, 1480), a lyrical pastoral in dramatic form (a pioneering secular pageant with music, in which classi-

cal mythology replaces the biblical subject matter of earlier religious works).

**12.** Jacopo Sannazaro (1455–1530). A Neapolitan who served the Aragonese court there, he wrote varied works, some in Latin. We give one complete poem from *Arcadia*, written between 1480 and 1500 (definitive publication, 1504), a brief pastoral novel in prose and verse that was enormously influential throughout Europe for some two hundred years (it has been called "the most successful vernacular work of the Quattrocento"). Itself linking up with the classical bucolic tradition of Theocritus and Vergil, it influenced such authors as Garcilaso, Montemayor, Lope, Cervantes, d'Urfé, and Opitz, and, in England, Lodge and Sidney. It celebrates the sadness of love amid edenic surroundings. In the reference to the sun having guarded flocks, the sun is identified with the myths surrounding Apollo.

**13.** Niccolò Machiavelli (1469–1527). This Florentine statesman and widely traveled diplomat has left us many political and historical works, in addition to the play *La mandragora* (The Mandrake). In his first major work, his most famous, *Il principe* (written 1513, published 1532), of which we reprint one full chapter, he proclaims Italy's need for an absolute monarchy possessing sufficient territory to have its own army with which to resist foreign invaders. His admiration for strongmen and his relegation of conventional morality to a secondary, sometimes merely utilitarian, status led to his acquiring a demonic reputation.

**14.** Pietro Bembo (1470–1547). This humanist, courtier, cardinal, and friend of Ariosto and Castiglione, hailed Dante, Petrarca, and Boccaccio as the founders of the Italian literary language. His own first major work, written between 1497 and 1505, and published in the latter year, was called *Gli Asolani* (The Asolo Discourses) because it is set in Asolo (near Treviso in the Veneto), where Bembo had visited the villa of Catarina Cornaro, queen of Cyprus, in 1495. Of the three speakers in the work, the first is entirely in favor of human love; the second, entirely hostile to it. The third, Lavellino (from whose discourse, representing the author's views, our excerpt is taken), calls for a "Platonic" love, a desire for heavenly things sparked only initially by human desire. The work (in the vernacular, unusual for a philosophical opus at this time) was dedicated to Lucrezia Borgia, whom Bembo loved.

**15.** Ludovico Ariosto (1474–1533). In *Orlando furioso*, one of the several attempted continuations of Boiardo's unfinished *Orlando innamorato* (see No. 9), Ariosto, a courtier of the Estes in Ferrara from

1503 (he addresses Ippolito d'Este), produced the greatest Italian epic poem, full of ironically recounted adventures; our excerpt is the very opening. The writing probably began in 1504, and the work was published in stages in 1516, 1521, and 1532. The poem has been called "the highest literary achievement" of its day. Ariosto also wrote lyric verse, plays, and other works.

**16.** Michelangelo Buonarroti (1475–1564). The great sculptor, painter, and architect (see No. 25) was also a significant poet, whose works were published posthumously as *Rime* (Rhymes) in 1623 by a grand-nephew. Influenced by Dante, Petrarca, the Florentine circle around Lorenzo de' Medici, and the Roman noble poets of his own day, Michelangelo's verse is nevertheless stubbornly original. We give two sonnets.

**17.** Baldesar Castiglione (1478–1529). *Il cortegiano,* which has been termed the greatest of all "courtesy books," and which was widely imitated in Europe, was written between 1513 and 1518, according to some; between 1508 and 1524, according to others; it was definitely published in 1528. (From 1504 to 1513, the author attended the court of the city-state Urbino.) The book is in dialogue form (extremely popular in the Renaissance), the speakers being Urbino courtiers. The subject matter is the perfect courtier (male and female), ideal in every sense of the word. Was Castiglione describing himself in the male role?

**18.** Francesco Guicciardini (1483–1540). Largely in retirement after the disastrous sack of Rome in 1527, this former politician, diplomat, and soldier, a friend of Machiavelli, devoted himself chiefly to the writing of history. Our excerpt A is from his *Storie fiorentine* (written 1508 and 1509; left incomplete; not published until 1859); the excerpt discusses the famous reformer Girolamo Savonarola (1452–1498), who set up an austere theocracy in Florence. Excerpt B, from the *Storia d'Italia* (written between 1535 and 1540, published in 1561 and 1564, it covers events from 1490 to 1534), concerns the discovery and exploitation of the New World. Guicciardini, the greatest historian of the Italian Renaissance, is objective, balanced, and lucid, "a forerunner of modern methods of research."

**19.** Matteo Bandello (1484–1561). Courtier, diplomat, Dominican friar, bishop, poet, Bandello continued Italy's narrative traditions into the High Renaissance with his *Novelle,* the most important sixteenth-century story collection. In four books, with a total of 214 tales (definitive publication, 1573), the *Novelle,* varied in themes and tone, supplied Shakespeare with the plots for *Romeo and Juliet* (but see No.

20!), *Twelfth Night*, and *Much Ado About Nothing*. Our excerpt is the beginning of story 4.

**20.** Luigi Da Porto (1485–1529). At the court of Urbino from 1503 to 1505, a soldier until 1511, this friend of Bembo, historian and poet, is chiefly renowned for his "Istoria novellamente ritrovata di due nobili amanti con la loro pietosa morte, intervenuta già nella città di Verona nel tempo del signor Bartolomeo Dalla Scala" ("Newly Rediscovered History of Two Noble Sweethearts, with Their Pitiful Death, Which Occurred in the Past in the City of Verona in the Time of Its Lord Bartolomeo Dalla Scala [1301–1304]"). Written by 1524, it was published in 1531 and 1539. Based on material in the 1475 story collection *Novellino* by Masuccio Salernitano (ca. 1410–1475), where the locale is Siena, the story was in turn the source for Bandello's version.

**21.** Gian Francesco Straparola (ca. 1490–ca. 1557). One of the most celebrated Italian story collections, *Le piacevoli notti* (often called *The Nights of Straparola* in English) was published in 1550 and 1553. Its 75 tales, told by ten women during thirteen nights in the presence of Bembo, are largely folktales, including animal fables and stories derived from the Orient; one of them is the earliest known version of what we know as "Puss in Boots." In the story whose beginning we give here, the envious neighbor does not get *gold* from the doll; Adamantina becomes queen after saving the king from a particularly violent attack by the doll.

**22.** Benvenuto Cellini (1500–1571). The sculptor, goldsmith, medalist, and author of treatises on his craft is most famous for the autobiography (reaching the year 1562) that he dictated between 1558 and 1566. With "consummate skill as a storyteller," and in vigorous, spontaneous language, the boastful, aggressive artist reveals himself openly. Our excerpt A recounts part of an incident typical of his brawls and arrests; B refers to his work for French king François I at Fontainebleau between 1540 and 1545. The *Vita* wasn't published until 1728.

**23.** Giovanni Della Casa (1503–1556) added a word to the Italian vocabulary with this book: *galateo* is used to mean etiquette, or a book on etiquette (the increasingly refined Renaissance courts gave more and more importance to "good manners"). The original of the character Galateo, who is introduced in our excerpt, was Galeazzo Florimonte, bishop of Sessa Aurunca in the Campania region of Italy. The humanist Della Casa, papal nuncio to Venice from 1544 to 1549, retired in that city from 1551 to 1555, and wrote the *Galateo* there; it was published in 1558.

**24.** Cinzio (pseudonym of Giambattista [or Giovan Battista] Giraldi, 1504–1573, often called *Cinthio* in English), was a professor of philosophy and rhetoric, and wrote tragedies and literary theory. The 113 stories in his *Hecatommiti* (published 1565) include the source of Shakespeare's *Measure for Measure*, as well as the source story for *Othello*, the opening of which is included here.

**25.** Giorgio Vasari (1511–1574). A painter and architect, and pupil of Michelangelo, whom he idolized, Vasari is the author of *Le vite de' più eccellenti architetti, pittori, e scultori italiani* (The Lives of the Most Excellent Italian Architects, Painters, and Sculptors), 158 biographies from Cimabue to Vasari himself. Written between 1542 and 1550, and published in 1550 and 1568, it is considered as the founding work in the modern history of art. Excerpt A is from the Introduction; Totila was an Ostrogoth king who came to Rome in 546. Excerpt B is from the life of Michelangelo (see No. 16).

**26.** Gaspara Stampa (ca. 1523–1554). Sincere in a mannered era, Stampa, muse of a literary salon in Venice, left us, in her works inspired by her love for a nobleman, "the foremost poetic production by any woman of the Renaissance period." Her *Canzionere*, its 300 or so poems mainly sonnets, was published posthumously in 1554.

**27.** Torquato Tasso (1544–1595) wrote lyric poems, the verse play *Aminta* (Amyntas), and much more, but his major work, written between 1559 and 1575, and published in 1581, was the last great Italian epic poem, *Gerusalemme liberata,* based not on legends of Charlemagne, but on the historical First Crusade (though it contains plenty of fantasy and fiction). In our excerpt, from Canto VII, the heathen princess Erminia, wearing full armor, is fleeing the Crusaders when she finds herself in an idyllic pastoral setting. (Unlike the rollicking earlier epics, Tasso's is tinged by the more serious Counter-Reformation and renewed Turkish aggressivity.) Mentally unstable from 1577 on, the poet was kept in seclusion from 1579 to 1586.

**28.** Giordano Bruno (1548–1600). A heretic monk who wandered through Italy and many other countries, Bruno was tried by the Roman Inquisition from 1592 on for his beliefs in the heliocentric and atomic-materialistic theories, and in a world-soul; he was burned in 1600. The "last great metaphysician of the Renaissance," he wrote and published his *Dialoghi* at Oxford in 1584 and 1585. In our excerpt from the fifth, titled *De la causa, principio e uno,* he waxes truly dithyrambic on the subject of the oneness of the universe. Bruno also wrote Latin poems and an important Italian play.

**29.** Galileo Galilei (1564–1642). Outstanding in physics and astronomy, Galileo was also an excellent writer, and not in scientific Latin, but in "the best prose tradition of the Florentine Renaissance." *Il saggiatore* (written from 1618 to 1621; published 1623; on the interpretation of comets) has been named "a veritable masterpiece of polemics."

**30.** Tommaso Campanella (1568–1639). A Dominican friar, Campanella was tried four times for heresy, and spent much of his life in prison: from 1599 to 1626 in Naples for trying to set up an ideal republic (like the one in *La città del sole*) in his native Calabria; from 1626 to 1629 in Rome. His utopian magnum opus, the *Città*, was written from 1602 to 1611, and published in Germany in 1623. It takes the form of a dialogue between a Knight Hospitaler and a Genoese seaman who had sailed with Columbus. Features of the utopia are collective education and labor, and communal possession of property and women. Campanella also wrote important verse.

**31.** Giambattista (or Giovan Battista) Marino (1569–1625). The most famous and influential Italian poet of the seventeenth century, known for his delight in the senses and his mannered "conceits," Marino also wrote the longest Italian poem: the more than 40,000-line *L'Adone*, published 1623 in Paris. A rambling retelling of the loves of Venus and Adonis (our excerpt is from the long description of their pleasure garden), it displays a "dazzling technical mastery of rhetorical devices and phonic value."

**32.** Giambattista (or Giovanbattista) Vico (1668–1744), historian, jurist, philosopher, social scientist, and autobiographer, is best remembered as a precursor of the philosophy of history in *Princìpi di una Scienza nuova d'intorno alla comune natura delle nazioni* (Principles of a New Science Concerning the Common Nature of Nations; published 1725, 1730, and 1744). This comparative method for studying the rise and fall of nations, with its cyclical view of history, is written in short aphoristic sections that begin with an "axiom" (*degnità*). Of our four excerpts, the first three are complete sections, whereas the fourth begins partway into the discussion.

**33.** Pietro Metastasio (pseudonym of Pietro Trapassi, 1698–1782). Metastasio was the greatest eighteenth-century opera librettist, beginning this activity in 1724. Some of his librettos were used many times, even after Metastasio's death, by different composers; Haydn and Mozart set Metastasio texts. From 1729 Metastasio resided in Vienna, working for the Austrian court. The first of the two sonnets reprinted here was written in 1733. In the second, Penthesilea was an

Amazon queen living by the river Thermodon in Asia Minor; the wife of Ninus was the Assyrian queen Semiramis.

**34.** Gasparo Gozzi (1713–1786) was a prominent figure in Enlightenment Italy. A journalist in Venice (he edited the *Gazzetta veneta* and the *Osservatore veneto*), he was a satirist, a writer of essays, stories, and verse. He was the elder brother of the vigorously imaginative playwright Carlo Gozzi.

**35.** Giuseppe Parini (1729–1799). A notable Enlightenment poet and satirist, Parini is best known for his four-part blank-verse poem *Il giorno* (The Day), about the frivolity and idleness of Milanese high society. The sonnet reprinted here was found to be "picturesque" by Foscolo (see No. 38), who included it in an 1816 historical study of the Italian sonnet.

**36.** Vittorio Alfieri (1749–1803). The greatest Italian writer of classical verse tragedy also wrote some three hundred lyric poems in a Petrarchan vein, which were published in 1789 and 1804. Many reflect his wide travels in almost a dozen countries from 1766 on. Of the three sonnets by which he is represented here, A is dated January 13, 1778; B is dated August 9 and 10, 1784, in the South Tyrol (Alto Adige); and C was first published in October of 1784. An ardent rebel against tyranny, Alfieri was to influence the later Risorgimento.

**37.** Vincenzo Monti (1754–1828). Poet, dramatist, translator (especially of the *Iliad*), Monti was very changeable in his politics: after being the protégé of churchmen, he openly favored democracy as the official poet of Napoleonic Italy, only to become a placid neoclassicist under Austrian rule. The first of the two sonnets reprinted here was read in 1784 before the famous Roman literary society Arcadia. The second dates from 1822; the portrait painter was Filippo Agricola (1776–1857).

**38.** Ugo Foscolo (1778–1827). A major early Romantic poet, novelist, translator, and literary critic, long a wanderer over the face of the earth (he died near London), Foscolo wrote twelve sonnets (not counting juvenilia) said to be "among the most felicitous and moving of the romantic period." They were all included in his 1803 volume *Poesie*, though some had been published separately earlier. Of the five reprinted here, A was perhaps written 1802 or 1803, published 1803; B was written between 1797 and 1802, published 1802 and 1803 (full of conscious literary reminiscences: its first two lines are a paraphrase from the Latin poet Maximian of the sixth century; line 13, from Ovid); C was probably written in 1801, published 1802 and 1803; D was written 1802 or 1803, published 1803 (Zacinto=Zakynthos=

Zante, the island in the Ionian Sea where Foscolo was born); E was written 1802, published 1803, revised 1816 (the poet's brother killed himself in 1801, plagued by debts).

**39.** Alessandro Manzoni (1785–1873). His great historical novel *I promessi sposi* (inspired by Sir Walter Scott; called "the highest achievement of Italian Romanticism") was basically written between 1821 and 1823 and published in 1827, but was revised to make it more Tuscan, and definitively published in 1842. It concerns Lombard peasants in the years 1628–1631, when Milan was under Spanish domination. (This reflects the author's lifelong desire for the freedom and unification of Italy.) The young heroine puts her trust in a Capuchin monk named Cristoforo; our excerpt is part of the story of how, while still the layman Lodovico, he became a monk after engaging in a street brawl. Manzoni also wrote verse (especially religious verse), plays, history, philosophy, and criticism. It was on the occasion of Manzoni's death that Verdi composed his famous *Requiem*.

**40.** Silvio Pellico (1789–1854). A playwright and journalist, friend of Monti and Foscolo in Milan, Pellico was an inmate of three Austrian prisons (in Milan, Venice, and Moravia) from 1820 to 1830 because of his connection with the revolutionary society known as the Carbonari. He recounted his experiences lucidly and dispassionately in *Le mie prigioni*, published 1832, a widely read and influential work that has been called a masterpiece of Romantic literature. His lack of rancor vexed some of his revolutionary associates, but attracted other Europeans to the Italian cause. Our selection is the entire first chapter and the beginning of the second.

**41.** Giacomo Leopardi (1798–1837) has been termed "the dominant figure of Italian lyric poetry of all ages." A nobleman, always sickly (perhaps from having long been shut in at home, studying too hard), he is the poet of pessimism and unfulfilled hopes. Poem A (complete) was written in 1819; Poem B (we give the first part only), in 1829 ("a magnificent lyrical compendium of the poet's affective life"). Leopardi's poems, the *Canti*, were published in 1831, 1835, and 1845. He also wrote important prose.

**42.** Francesco De Sanctis (1817–1883). A major critic and historian of literature, a professor of Italian in Naples, De Sanctis was arrested in the revolution year 1848, and spent years of exile in Turin and Zurich, returning to Naples in 1859; in the periods 1861–1862 and 1879–1881 he served as Minister of Education. His *Storia della letteratura italiana*, written 1869–1871, made him "the founder of mod-

ern literary criticism in Italy" and "gave Italy an organic and enduring system of aesthetics." Our excerpt is part of the discussion of Metastasio (see No. 33).

**43.** Carlo Collodi (pseudonym of Carlo Lorenzini, 1826–1890). *Le avventure di Pinocchio: storia di un burattino* (The Adventures of Pinocchio: History of a Marionette) is beloved worldwide as the foremost Italian children's book. Collodi, a political journalist, novelist, and playwright who began to write for children in 1875 (*Pinocchio* was serialized in a periodical in 1881 and published as a volume in 1883), took his pseudonym from the Tuscan village where his mother was born. "Pinocchio" means pine seed. This book, from which we give the entire first chapter and the opening of the second, has been called "the masterwork of Tuscan literature after Galileo."

**44.** Ippolito Nievo (1831–1861). Nievo, a member of Garibaldi's famous 1859–1860 expedition of "a thousand men," was lost in a shipwreck when returning from Sicily. He had been a novelist, poet, and story writer. *Le confessioni di un italiano* (known variously in English as *The Confessions of an Italian, The Confessions of an Octogenarian*, and *The Castle of Fratta*) was written in 1857 and 1858, and published in 1867. We give the very beginning, with its extremely famous first sentence. Recounting the struggle for Italian unity and independence as reflected in a fictional autobiography, it has been called "the novel of the most extraordinary vitality and freshness in nineteenth-century Italy."

**45.** Giosuè Carducci (1835–1907), the first Italian to win a Nobel Prize for literature (1906), also a critic and a professor, was one of the three great poets of the late nineteenth century, along with Pascoli and D'Annunzio. The first of the two complete poems reprinted here, addressed to the poet's dead son, was included in the section "Rime nuove (1861–1887)" of Carducci's collected verse (published 1901); the second, reflecting a vacation in the Val d'Aosta, in the section "Rime e ritmi" [1890s]. The prose poem on the cicadas is from the volume *Prose*. Carducci was a republican in politics, a noble, moral classicist in his writing.

**46.** Giovanni Verga (1840–1922), outstanding Sicilian novelist, story writer, and dramatist, known for his earthy, headstrong characters, serialized *Mastro-don Gesualdo* in 1888 and brought it out in volume form in 1889. The title figure is a social-climbing stonemason whose life is ruined after he marries into the decaying nobility. The appellation "Mastro-don" combines the notions of artisan and gentleman. This novel was the second of a planned cycle that was to have

been called *I vinti* (The Vanquished). Verga's *verismo* was based on Flaubert's Realism and Zola's Naturalism.

**47.** Arrigo Boito (1842–1918) is best remembered for his extremely literate librettos for his own operas and those of other composers (especially Verdi's *Otello* and *Falstaff*), but he was also a writer of poems and stories, a member of the Milanese decadent, antibourgeois literary movement of the 1860s known as *scapigliatura* (bohemianism). We give the opening of his story "L'alfier nero," published in a periodical in 1867. Gall is the German creator of phrenology Franz Joseph Gall (1758–1828); Morant Bay is in Jamaica.

**48.** Antonio Fogazzaro (1842–1911). *Malombra* (this is the heroine's family name, connoting "evil shadows") was his first novel, begun in 1872, published in 1881. Called "his most interesting" (the very beginning is reprinted here), it's a Gothic romance (unusual in Italy) about a secluded noblewoman who believes she's the reincarnation of an ancestress. Fogazzaro is perhaps best known for his 1895 novel *Piccolo mondo antico* (Little World of the Past).

**49.** Giovanni Pascoli (1855–1912). A pupil of Carducci (No. 45), a poet, teacher, essayist, and critic, the great stylist Pascoli usually struck an elegiac, pastoral chord. Some of his poems (not the three reprinted here in their entirety) are notorious for their odd mixture of diction. He is said to have "contributed more than any other poet of the time . . . to the renewal of Italian poetry in the twentieth century." All three of our poems are from the collection *Myricae* (Latin for "tamarisks," emblems of humble beauty in Vergil's verse), various editions of which appeared between 1891 and 1903.

**50.** Italo Svevo (pseudonym of Ettore Schmitz, 1861–1928); the pseudonym (Italian Swabian) refers to his mixed ancestry. He worked in a bank in his native Trieste from 1880 to 1899, when he went into his brother-in-law's business. After his meeting with James Joyce, ca. 1905, and the 1923 publication of a new, acclaimed novel, his earlier, hitherto unnoticed novels were rediscovered and he enjoyed literary fame until his death in a car accident. *Senilità*, begun in 1892 and published in 1898, has been titled *As a Man Grows Older* in English, but this is misleading: the hero is thirty-five, and his "old age," or "senility," reflects his inability to love and live fully, and his too ready acceptance of an everyday existence. Our excerpt is the very beginning. The book has been called "the only Italian turn-of-century modern love story."

**51.** Gabriele D'Annunzio (1863–1938). Practically deified in the Mussolini era (after his work was all but over, when he was living in

seclusion), D'Annunzio had been a firebrand, not only in his sensual verse and drama, but also as a soldier and adventurer with an extravagant life style (he ruled the city of Fiume—now Rijeka in Croatia—for sixteen months after the First World War). Our selections are part of a poem, from the 1893 volume *Poema paradisiaco,* and two passages from the 1892 novel *L'innocente* (sometimes called *The Intruder* in English). D'Annunzio also produced journalism and film scenarios.

**52.** Benedetto Croce (1866–1952). Influenced by Vico (No. 32) and De Sanctis (No. 42), Croce dominated Italian cultural thought in the first half of the twentieth century with his philosophical, historical, critical, and political writings, and with his courageous anti-Fascist stance. Our excerpt is the very beginning of his *Breviario di estetica* (published in 1913), the Italian-language original of lectures he had been invited to write for the 1912 opening of the Rice Institute in Houston, Texas. Used for high-school reading for decades in Italy, this book contains "some of Croce's best pages."

**53.** Luigi Pirandello (1867–1936). This world-famous playwright, known for his ironic paradoxes, also wrote great stories and novels. His works reflect the fundamental relativity of human events and the impossibility of real communication between people. It is said that he wrote his best-known novel, *Il fu Mattia Pascal* (published 1904), to aid his family after his father's Sicilian sulfur mines were flooded. The hero, thought dead, thinks he can start a new life but is hampered because he now has no juridical identity. Our excerpt is the second half of Chapter I and the first half of Chapter II. Pirandello won the Nobel Prize for literature in 1934.

**54.** Grazia Deledda (1871–1936), the second Italian to become a Nobel laureate for literature (1926), wrote novels, stories, and essays. Self-taught, she combines the *verismo* of Verga (No. 46) with the symbolism and decadentism of D'Annunzio (No. 51) in her tales of sin, love, and death. In *Canne al vento* (periodical and volume publication, both in 1913), a work of her full maturity with a more complex plot than her earlier novels, she revels in her native Sardinian landscape and folklore as the servant Efix strives to atone for the involuntary killing of his master, feeling responsible for the ruin of the family (there are three surviving daughters). We give the very opening of the novel.

**55.** Umberto Saba (pseudonym of Umberto Poli, 1883–1957) was one of the major Italian poets of the early twentieth century; he ran a second-hand bookstore in his native Trieste, where he was a friend of

Svevo (No. 50); he also wrote stories and other prose. Of the four poems reprinted here in their entirety, the first two are from the collection *Cose leggere e vaganti* (Light, Wandering Things; published 1920) and the other two are from the collection *L'amorosa spina* (The Loving Thorn; published 1921). Saba is a lucid poet of honest self-analysis.

# First Italian Reader

# 1. *Novellino* (ca 1300): 3 novelle

(A) Uno re fu nelle parti di Egitto, lo quale avea uno suo figliuolo primogenito, lo quale dovea portare la corona del reame dopo lui. Questo suo padre dalla fantilitade sì cominciò e fecelo nodrire intra savi uomini di tempo, sì che, anni avea quindici, giamai non avea veduto niuna fanciullezza. Un giorno avenne che lo padre li comise una risposta ad ambasciadori di Grecia. Il giovane stando in su la ringhiera per rispondere alli ambasciadori, il tempo era turbato, e piovea; volse li occhi per una finestra del palagio, e vide altri giovani che accoglievano l'acqua piovana, e facevano pescaie e mulina di paglia. Il giovane vedendo ciò, lasciò stare la ringhiera e gittossi subitamente giù per le scale del palagio, e andò alli altri giovani che stavano a ricevere l'acqua piovana; e cominciò a fare le mulina e le bambolitadi. Baroni e cavalieri lo seguirono assai, e rimenârlo al palazzo; chiusero la finestra, e 'l giovane diede sufficiente risposta. Dopo il consiglio si partio la gente. Lo padre adunò filosofi e maestri di grande scienzia; propuose il presente fatto. Alcuno de' savi riputava movimento d'omori, alcuno fievolezza d'animo; chi dicea infermità di celabro, chi dicea una e chi un'altra, secondo le diversità di loro scienzie. Uno filosofo disse: «Ditemi come lo giovane è stato nodrito». Fuli contato come nudrito era stato con savi e con uomini di tempo, lungi da ogni fanciullezza. Allora lo savio rispuose: «Non vi maravigliate se la natura domanda ciò ch'ella ha perduto; ragionevole cosa è bamboleggiare in giovinezza, e in vecchiezza pensare».

(B) Federigo imperadore fece impendere un giorno un grande gentile uomo per certo misfatto. E per fare rilucere la giustizia, sì 'l faceva guardare ad un grande cavaliere con comandamento di gran pena, che nol lasciasse spiccare. Sì che questi non guardando bene, lo 'mpiccato fu portato via. Sì che quando quelli se n'avide, prese consiglio da se medesimo per paura di perdere la testa. E istando così pensoso in quella notte, sì prese ad andare ad una badia ch'era ivi presso, per sapere se potesse trovare alcuno corpo che fosse novellamente morto,

# 1. *Storybook* (ca. 1300): 3 stories

(A) There was a king in the area of Egypt who had a firstborn son that was to bear the crown of the kingdom after him. Beginning with his childhood, this father of his had him raised among wise, elderly men, so that when he was fifteen he had never known any childish ways. It came about one day that his father entrusted him with a reply to ambassadors from Greece. As the youth stood on a platform to reply to the ambassadors, the sky clouded over and it began to rain; looking out through a palace window, he saw other youths welcoming the rainwater and damming up pools and making straw mills. Seeing this, the youth left the platform, suddenly raced down the palace stairs, and joined the other youths who were receiving the rainwater; and he began to make mills and play games. Many barons and knights followed him and brought him back to the palace; they shuttered the window, and the youth made the proper reply. After the council the people departed. His father assembled philosophers and teachers of great wisdom, and expounded that event to them. One of the sages thought the boy's bodily humors were out of kilter; another, that his mind had become weak; one said he was brainsick; they said this and that, depending on their various store of knowledge. One philosopher said: "Tell me how the boy was brought up." He was told how he had been raised among sages and old men, far from any childish matters. Then the sage replied: "Don't be surprised that nature claims what it has lost; it's a reasonable thing to play games in youth and to be a thinker in old age."

(B) One day the Emperor Frederick had a great nobleman hanged for a certain crime. And to make his justice conspicuous, he had him guarded by a high-ranking knight, setting a severe penalty if the body were taken down. This knight guarding the body inadequately, the hanged man was carried away. When the knight became aware of this, he took counsel with himself in fear of losing his head. Thinking and thinking all that night, he decided to go to a nearby abbey to see if he could find some corpse recently dead, so that he could hang it on the gallows in place of that other

3

acciò che 'l pottesse mettere alle forche in colui scambio. Giunto alla badia la notte medesima, sì vi trovò una donna in pianto, scapigliata e scinta, forte lamentando; ed era molto sconsolata, e piangea uno suo caro marito lo quale era morto lo giorno. El cavaliere la domandò dolcemente: «Madonna, che modo è questo?». E la donna rispuose: «Io l'amava tanto, che mai non voglio essere più consolata, ma in pianto voglio finire li miei dì». Allora il cavaliere le disse: «Madonna, che savere è questo? Volete voi morire qui di dolore? Ché per pianto né per lagrime non si può recare a vita il corpo morto. Onde che mattezza è quella che voi fate? Ma fate così: prendete me a marito, che non ho donna, e campatemi la persona, perch'io ne sono in periglio, e non so là dov'io mi nasconda: che io per comandamento del mio signore guardava un cavaliere impenduto per la gola; li uomini del suo legnaggio il m'hanno tolto. Insegnatemi campare, che potete, e io sarò vostro marito, e terròvi onorevolmente». Allora la donna, udendo questo, si innamorò di questo cavaliere e disse: «Io farò ciò che tu mi comanderai, tant'è l'amore ch'io vi porto. Prendiamo questo mio marito, e traiallo fuori della sepultura, e impicchiallo in luogo di quello che v'è tolto». E lasciò suo pianto; e atò trarre il marito del sepulcro, e atollo impendere per la gola così morto. El cavaliere disse: «Madonna, elli avea meno un dente della bocca, e ho paura che, se fosse rivenuto a rivedere, ch'io non avesse disinore». Ed ella, udendo questo, li ruppe un dente di bocca; e s'altro vi fosse bisognato a quel fatto, sì l'avrebbe fatto. Allora il cavaliere, vedendo quello ch'ella avea fatto di suo marito, disse: «Madonna, siccome poco v'è caluto di costui che tanto mostravate d'amarlo, così vi carebbe vie meno di me». Allora si partì da lei e andossi per li fatti suoi, ed ella rimase con grande vergogna.

(C) La volpe andando per un bosco, si trovò un mulo, che mai non n'avea più veduti. Ebbe gran paura, e fuggì; e così fuggendo trovò il lupo. E disse come avea trovata una novissima bestia, e non sapeva suo nome. Il lupo disse: «Andianvi». Furono giunti a lui; al lupo parve via più nuova. La volpe il domandò di suo nome. Il mulo rispuose: «Certo io non l'ho ben a mente; ma se tu sai leggere, io l'ho scritto nel piè diritto di dietro». La volpe rispuose: «Lassa! ch'io non so leggere: che molto lo saprei voluntieri». Rispuose il lupo: «Lascia fare a me, che molto lo so ben fare». Il mulo sì li mostrò il piede dritto, sì che li chiovi pareano lettere. Disse il lupo: «Io non le veggio bene». Rispuose il mulo: «Fatti più presso, però che sono minute». Il lupo si fece sotto, e guardava fiso. Il mulo trasse, e dielli un calcio tale che

one. Reaching the abbey that same night, he found there a woman in mourning, her hair disheveled, her clothes in disarray, lamenting loudly; quite disconsolate, she was weeping for her dear husband, who had died that day. The knight asked her gently: "Madam, why are you carrying on so?" And the lady replied: "I loved him so much that I never want to be consoled anymore; I want to end my days in weeping." Then the knight said to her: "Madam, is this wise? Do you wish to die of grief here? Because neither lamenting nor tears can bring a dead man back to life. And so, what is this folly you are committing? Rather, do this: take me for a husband, for I have no wife, and save my life because it's in danger and I don't know where to hide: because by my master's orders I was guarding a knight who had been hanged by the neck, and men of his family have taken him from me. Show me how to stay alive, for you can do it, and I shall be your husband and shall keep you honorably." Hearing this, the woman then fell in love with this knight and said: "I'll do whatever you order me to, so great is the love I bear toward you. Let us take this husband of mine, let us draw him out of his grave, and let us hang him in place of the man taken away from you." And she left off her weeping, and helped draw her husband out of the grave, and helped hang him by the neck, dead as he was. The knight said: "Madam, the other man was missing a tooth from his mouth, and I fear being dishonored if the body were inspected again." Hearing this, she broke a tooth out of the dead man's mouth; and if anything else had been necessary in that matter, she would have done it. Then the knight, seeing what she had done to her husband, said: "Madam, just as you have cared so little about the man you gave signs of loving so much, so you would care even less about me." Then he left her and returned to his business, while she was left there covered with shame.

(C) The fox, walking through the woods, found a mule; she had never seen one before. She was very frightened and ran away; as she ran, she met the wolf. She told him she had come across a very strange animal, and didn't know its name. The wolf said: "Let's go there." They came up with him; the wolf found it even odder. The fox asked it its name. The mule replied: "I can't exactly recall it, but if you know how to read, I have it written on my right hind foot." The fox replied: "Alas, I don't know how to read, and I'd be very glad to learn this." The wolf replied: "Leave it to me, because I know how to read very well." The mule showed him its right foot, on which the horseshoe nails looked like letters. The wolf said: "I don't see them very well." The mule replied: "Come closer, because they're tiny." The wolf placed himself below and looked hard. The mule

l'uccise. Allora la volpe se n'andò, e disse: «Ogni uomo che sa lettera, non è savio».

## 2. Dante (1265–1321): *La divina commedia*

Nel mezzo del cammin di nostra vita
mi ritrovai per una selva oscura,
ché la diritta via era smarrita.
Ahi quanto a dir qual era è cosa dura,
esta selva selvaggia e aspra e forte
che nel pensier rinova la paura!
Tant'è amara che poco è più morte;
ma per trattar del ben ch'i' vi trovai,
dirò de l'altre cose ch'i' v'ho scorte.
Io non so ben ridir com'i' v'entrai:
tant'era pien di sonno a quel punto
che la verace via abbandonai.
Ma poi ch'i' fui al piè d'un colle giunto,
là dove terminava quella valle,
che m'avea di paura il cor compunto,
  guardai in alto, e vidi le sue spalle
vestite già de' raggi del pianeta
che mena dritto altrui per ogne calle.
  Allor fu la paura un poco queta,
che nel lago del cor m'era durata
la notte ch'i' passai con tanta pieta.
  E come quei che con lena affannata,
uscito fuor del pelago a la riva,
si volge a l'acqua perigliosa e guata,
  così l'animo mio, ch'ancor fuggiva,
si volse a retro a rimirar lo passo
che non lasciò già mai persona viva.
  Poi ch'èi posato un poco il corpo lasso,
ripresi via per la piaggia diserta,
sì che 'l piè fermo sempre era 'l più basso.
  Ed ecco, quasi al cominciar de l'erta,
una lonza leggera e presta molto,
che di pel macolato era coverta;
  e non mi si partia dinanzi al volto,
anzi 'mpediva tanto il mio cammino,

recoiled and gave him such a hard kick that it killed him. Then the fox departed, saying: "Not every man who knows his letters is wise."

## 2. Dante (1265–1321): *The Divine Comedy*

Halfway through our allotted span of life
I found myself in a dark forest,
for I had strayed from the straight-and-narrow path.
   Ah! What a hard thing it is to tell what it was like,
that wild, rough, dense forest,
the very thought of which renews my fear!
   It's so bitter that death is not much more so;
but to discuss the benefit I found there,
I shall tell of the other things I observed in it.
   I can't readily recall how I entered it:
I was so full of slumber at the moment
when I deserted the true way.
   But after I had reached the foot of a hill
which was the termination of that valley
which had afflicted my heart with fear,
   I looked upward and saw its sides
already clad in the beams from that planet
which guides men straight, whatever their road.
   Then my fear was somewhat calmed,
that fear which had remained in the lake of my heart
all that night I spent in such a pitiful state.
   And like a man who, with panting breath,
having emerged from the sea onto the shore,
turns back to the perilous waters and stares at them,
   thus my thoughts, which were still in flight,
turned back to gaze again at the passage
that had never admitted a living person.
   After I had rested my weary body a while,
I resumed my journey up the deserted slope,
so that the foot that supported me was always the lower one.
   And behold, almost at the outset of the ascent:
a very slender and swift leopard,
covered with spotted skin,
   which wouldn't depart from its place before my eyes,
but hindered my ascent so much

ch'i' fui per ritornar più volte vòlto.

Temp'era dal principio del mattino,
e 'l sol montava 'n sù con quelle stelle
ch'eran con lui quando l'amor divino
   mosse di prima quelle cose belle;
sì ch'a bene sperar m'era cagione
di quella fera a la gaetta pelle
   l'ora del tempo e la dolce stagione;
ma non sì che paura non mi desse
la vista che m'apparve d'un leone.

Questi parea che contra me venisse
con la test'alta e con rabbiosa fame,
sì che parea che l'aere ne tremesse.

Ed una lupa, che di tutte brame
sembiava carca ne la sua magrezza,
e molte genti fé già viver grame,
   questa mi porse tanto di gravezza
con la paura ch'uscia di sua vista,
ch'io perdei la speranza de l'altezza.

E qual è quei che volentieri acquista,
e giugne 'l tempo che perder lo face,
che 'n tutti suoi pensier piange e s'attrista;
   tal mi fece la bestia sanza pace,
che, venendomi 'ncontro, a poco a poco
mi ripigneva là dove 'l sol tace.

Mentre ch'i' rovinava in basso loco,
dinanzi a li occhi mi si fu offerto
chi per lungo silenzio parea fioco.

Quando vidi costui nel gran diserto,
«*Miserere* di me», gridai a lui,
«qual che tu sii od ombra od omo certo!»

Rispuosemi: «Non omo, omo già fui,
e li parenti miei furon lombardi,
mantoani per patrïa ambedui.

Nacqui *sub Julio*, ancor che fosse tardi,
e vissi a Roma sotto 'l buono Augusto
al tempo de li dei falsi e bugiardi.

Poeta fui, e cantai di quel giusto
figliuol d'Anchise che venne di Troia,
poi che 'l superbo Ilïòn fu combusto.

Ma tu perché ritorni a tanta noia?

that I turned to go back several times.
   It was early in the morning
and the sun was rising in that constellation
it had been in when divine love
   first set those lovely things in motion;
so that I was given cause for hope
of protection from that beast with the variegated hide
   by the hour of the day and the sweet spring season;
but not so much so that I failed to be frightened
by the sudden appearance of a lion.
   It seemed to be coming toward me
with head held high and a ravenous hunger,
so that the air seemed to tremble at it.
   And a she-wolf, which seemed to be laden
with all longings, skinny as it was,
and which has already made many nations live in sadness,
   instilled such great oppression in me
through the fear that emanated from the sight of it
that I lost all hope of reaching the summit.
   And like a man who loves to acquire wealth
and, when the time comes that makes him lose it,
weeps and is saddened in all his thoughts,
   thus I felt when faced by that insatiable beast,
which, coming toward me, was gradually
driving me back to the place where the sunshine can't enter.
   While I was plunging back to the plain,
there was presented to my eyes
one who seemed to have a faint voice because of long silence.
   When I saw him in the great wilderness,
I shouted to him: "Take pity on me,
whoever you are, whether ghost or living man!"
   He replied: "I'm not living, though I once was,
and my parents were Lombards,
both natives of Mantua.
   I was born at the time of Julius Caesar, though late in his life,
and I lived in Rome under good Augustus
in the days of the false, lying gods.
   I was a poet, and I sang of that just
son of Anchises who came from Troy
after proud Ilium was burned.
   But why are you returning to such distress?

Perché non sali il dilettoso monte
ch'è principio e cagion di tutta gioia?»
«Or se' tu quel Virgilio e quella fonte
che spandi di parlar sì largo fiume?»
rispuos'io lui con vergognosa fronte. [. . .]

## 3. Petrarca (1304–1374): 5 sonetti

(A) Voi ch'ascoltate in rime sparse il suono
di quei sospiri ond'io nudriva 'l core
in sul mio primo giovenile errore
quand'era in parte altr'uom da quel ch' i' sono,

del vario stile in ch'io piango e ragiono
fra le vane speranze e 'l van dolore,
ove sia chi per prova intenda amore,
spero trovar pietà, non che perdono.

Ma ben veggio or sì come al popol tutto
favola fui gran tempo, onde sovente
di me medesmo meco mi vergogno;

e del mio vaneggiar vergogna è 'l frutto,
e 'l pentersi, e 'l conoscer chiaramente
che quanto piace al mondo è breve sogno.

(B) Movesi il vecchierel canuto e bianco
del dolce loco ov'ha sua età fornita
e da la famigliuola sbigottita
che vede il caro padre venir manco;

indi traendo poi l'antiquo fianco
per l'extreme giornate di sua vita,
quanto più pò, col buon voler s'aita,
rotto dagli anni, e dal camino stanco;

e viene a Roma, seguendo 'l desio,
per mirar la sembianza di colui
ch'ancor lassù nel ciel vedere spera:

così, lasso, talor vo cercand' io,
donna, quanto è possibile, in altrui
la disiata vostra forma vera.

Why don't you climb the delightful mountain
which is the source and cause of all joy?"
    "Now, are you that Vergil and that fountain
which pours forth so rich a river of eloquence?"
I replied to him with a shame-covered brow. [. . .]

## 3. Petrarca (1304–1374): 5 sonnets

(A) All you who listen, in my scattered rhymes, to the sound
of those sighs with which I nourished my heart
in my early, youthful distraction
when I was partly a different man from the one I am:

for the varied manner in which I weep and discourse
amid my futile hopes and futile pain,
if there is any of you who understands love through experience,
I hope to find compassion, if not forgiveness.

But I now see that for all the people
I have long been a subject of talk, so that often
I'm ashamed of myself in my mind;

and shame is the fruit of my idle thoughts,
and regret, and the clear knowledge
that everything which delights the world is only a brief dream.

(B) The hoary, white-haired old man departs
from the beloved place where he spent his life
and from his little family, who are dismayed
to see their dear father lost to them;

then, from there, dragging his aged body
through the last days of his life,
to the best of his ability, he relies on his willpower,
broken by the years, weary from the pilgrimage;

and he comes to Rome in pursuit of his desire,
to gaze on the image of Him
whom he hopes to see again up in heaven:

in the same way, alas, I sometimes seek,
my lady, to the extent possible, in other women
that true form of yours which I desire.

(C)  Solo e pensoso i più deserti campi
vo mesurando a passi tardi e lenti,
e gli occhi porto per fuggire intenti
ove vestigio uman l'arena stampi.

Altro schermo non trovo che mi scampi
dal manifesto accorger de le genti,
perchè negli atti d'alegrezza spenti
di fuor si legge com'io dentro avampi:

sì ch'io mi credo omai che monti e piagge
e fiumi e selve sappian di che tempre
sia la mia vita, ch'è celata altrui.

Ma pur sì aspre vie nè sì selvagge
cercar non so ch'Amor non venga sempre
ragionando con meco, ed io co·llui.

(D)  Padre del ciel, dopo i perduti giorni,
dopo le notti vaneggiando spese,
con quel fero desio ch'al cor s'accese,
mirando gli atti per mio mal sì adorni,

piacciati omai col tuo lume ch'io torni
ad altra vita ed a più belle imprese,
sì ch'avendo le reti indarno tese,
il mio duro adversario se ne scorni.

Or volge, signor mio, l'undecimo anno
ch'i' fui sommesso al dispietato giogo
che sopra i più soggetti è più feroce.

Miserere del mio non degno affanno;
reduci i pensier' vaghi a miglior luogo;
ramenta lor come oggi fusti in croce.

(E)  Passa la nave mia colma d'oblio
per aspro mare, a mezza notte il verno,
enfra Scilla e Caribdi; ed al governo
siede 'l signore, anzi 'l nimico mio.

A ciascun remo un penser pronto e rio
che la tempesta e 'l fin par ch'abbi a scherno;
la vela rompe un vento umido eterno
di sospir', di speranze e di desio.

(C) Alone and pensive, I measure
the most deserted fields with slow, sluggish steps,
and I keep my eyes alert and ready to flee
wherever a human foot has imprinted the sand.

I find no other protection to save me
from clear observation by other people,
because in my features devoid of happiness
it can be read outwardly how I blaze within:

so that by now I believe that mountains and slopes
and rivers and forests know of what nature
my life is, though it's hidden from others.

And yet I'm unable to seek out ways so rough
or so wild that Love doesn't always come
to converse with me, and I with him.

(D) Father in heaven, after the wasted days,
after the nights consumed in vain thoughts,
with that fierce desire ignited in my heart,
gazing on the features so beautiful to my detriment,

deign now to let me return by Your light
to a different life and more noble enterprises,
so that, having spread his nets in vain,
my harsh enemy may be mocked.

This, my Lord, is the eleventh year
since I was subjected to the pitiless yoke
that is most severe to those who are most submissive.

Take pity on my unworthy anguish;
lead my straying thoughts back to a better place;
remind them that today You were nailed to the cross.

(E) My ship, laden with oblivion, is sailing
through a rough sea, at midnight in winter,
between Scylla and Charybdis; and at the helm
sits my master—no, my enemy.

At every oar, a ready, evil thought
that seems to scorn the tempest and destruction;
the sail is torn by a perpetual wet wind
of sighs, hopes, and desire.

Pioggia di lagrimar, nebbia di sdegni
bagna e rallenta le già stanche sarte,
che son d'error con ignorantia attorto.

Celansi i duo mei dolci usati segni;
morta fra l'onde è la ragion e l'arte,
tal ch'incomincio a desperar del porto.

## 4. Boccaccio (1313–1375): *Decameron*

Maravigliosamente era piaciuta a tutti la novella della Fiammetta, affermando ciascuno ottimamente la donna aver fatto, e quel che si convenia al bestiale uomo. Ma poi che finita fu, il re a Pampinea impose che seguitasse; la quale incominciò a dire:

Molti sono li quali, semplicemente parlando, dicono che Amore trae altrui del senno e quasi chi ama fa divenire smemorato. Sciocca oppinione mi pare: e assai le già dette cose l'hanno mostrato, e io ancora intendo di dimostrarlo.

Nella nostra città, copiosa di tutti i beni, fu già una giovane donna e gentile e assai bella, la qual fu moglie d'un cavaliere assai valoroso e da bene. E come spesso avviene che sempre non può l'uomo usare un cibo, ma talvolta disidera di variare, non soddisfaccendo a questa donna molto il suo marito, s'innamorò d'un giovane il quale Leonetto era chiamato, assai piacevole e costumato, come che di gran nazion non fosse, ed egli similmente s'innamorò di lei; e come voi sapete che rade volte è senza effetto quello che vuole ciascuna delle parti, a dare al loro amor compimento molto tempo non si interpose. Ora avvenne che, essendo costei bella donna e avvenevole, di lei un cavalier chiamato messer Lambertuccio s'innamorò forte, il quale ella, per ciò che spiacevole uomo e sazievole le parea, per cosa del mondo ad amar lui disporre non si potea; ma costui con ambasciate sollicitandola molto e non valendogli, essendo possente uomo la mandò minacciando di vituperarla se non facesse il piacer suo; per la qual cosa la donna, temendo e conoscendo come fatto era, si condusse a fare il voler suo.

Ed essendosene la donna, che madonna Isabella avea nome, andata, come nostro costume è di state, a stare ad una sua bellissima possessione in contado, avvenne, essendo una mattina il marito di lei cavalcato in alcun luogo per dovere stare alcun giorno, che ella mandò per Leonetto che si venisse a star con lei; il quale lietissimo incontanente v'andò. Messer Lambertuccio, sentendo il marito della donna

A rain of tears, a mist of disdain
moistens and slackens the already weary rigging,
which is composed of error intertwined with ignorance.

Hidden are my two sweet customary beacons;
dead in the billows are reason and craft,
so that I begin to despair of making port.

## 4. Boccaccio (1313–1375): *Decameron*

Fiammetta's story had pleased everyone tremendously, each one asserting
that the lady in it had behaved very well, doing what suited that bestial
man. But after it was over, the master of ceremonies ordered Pampinea
to speak next, and she began as follows:

"'There are many who, speaking foolishly, say that Love drives people
out of their senses and almost makes lovers become scatterbrained. This
seems like a silly opinion to me, and the stories already told have shown
this; I intend to demonstrate it, too.

"In our city, rich in all good things, there once was a young woman
who was noble and extremely beautiful; she was the wife of a very brave
and worthy knight. And as it often happens that a man can't always eat
the same dish, but sometimes wants a change, this lady, being rather
dissatisfied with her husband, fell in love with a young man who was
called Leonetto, very pleasant and good-mannered, though not of lofty
birth, and he likewise fell in love with her; and as you know, something
desired by both partners is seldom without its effect, and it wasn't long
before their love was consummated. Now, it came about that, she being
a lovely and attractive woman, a knight called Lord Lambertuccio fell
deeply in love with her but, because she found him an unpleasant, tiresome man, she couldn't bring herself to love him for all the world; yet
after courting her in vain with many messages, he, being a powerful
man, wrote her, threatening to disgrace her if she didn't do as he
wished; therefore, afraid and knowing what he was like, she brought
herself to do his will.

"And the woman, who was called Lady Isabella, having gone, as is our
custom in the summer, to stay in a very lovely country house of hers, it
came about that, one morning when her husband had ridden off somewhere where he was to stay a few days, she sent word to Leonetto to
come and be with her; he went there at once, as happy as can be. Lord
Lambertuccio, hearing that the lady's husband was away from home,

essere andato altrove, tutto solo montato a cavallo, a lei se n'andò e picchiò alla porta. La fante della donna, vedutolo, n'andò incontanente a lei, che in camera era con Leonetto, e chiamatala le disse: — Madonna, messer Lambertuccio è qua giù tutto solo.— La donna, udendo questo, fu la piú dolente femina del mondo; ma, temendol forte, pregò Leonetto che grave non gli fosse il nascondersi alquanto dietro alla cortina del letto infino a tanto che messer Lambertuccio se n'andasse. Leonetto, che non minor paura di lui avea che avesse la donna, vi si nascose; ed ella comandò alla fante che andasse ad aprire a messer Lambertuccio; la quale apertogli, ed egli nella corte smontato d'un suo pallafreno e quello appiccato ivi ad uno arpione, se ne salí suso. La donna, fatto buon viso e venuta infino in capo della scala, quanto piú poté in parole lietamente il ricevette e domandollo quello che egli andasse faccendo. Il cavaliere, abbracciatala e basciatala, disse: —Anima mia, io intesi che vostro marito non c'era, sí ch'io mi son venuto a stare alquanto con essovoi.— E dopo queste parole, entratisene in camera e serratisi dentro, cominciò messer Lambertuccio a prender diletto di lei.

E cosí con lei standosi, tutto fuori della credenza della donna, avvenne che il marito di lei tornò: il quale quando la fante alquanto vicino al palagio vide, cosí subitamente corse alla camera della donna e disse: —Madonna, ecco messer che torna: io credo che egli sia già giú nella corte.

La donna, udendo questo e sentendosi aver due uomini in casa, e conosceva che il cavaliere non si poteva nascondere per lo suo pallafreno che nella corte era, si tenne morta; nondimeno, subitamente gittatasi del letto in terra, prese partito, e disse a messer Lambertuccio: —Messere, se voi mi volete punto di bene e voletemi da morte campare, farete quello che io vi dirò. Voi vi recherete in mano il vostro coltello ignudo, e con un mal viso e tutto turbato ve n'andrete giú per le scale, e andrete dicendo: «Io fo boto a Dio che io il coglierò altrove»; e se mio marito vi volesse ritenere o di niente vi domandasse, non dite altro che quello che detto v'ho, e montato a cavallo, per niuna cagione seco ristate.

Messer Lambertuccio disse che volentieri; e tirato fuori il coltello, tutto infocato nel viso tra per la fatica durata e per l'ira avuta della tornata del cavaliere, come la donna gl'impose cosí fece. Il marito della donna, già nella corte smontato, maravigliandosi del pallafreno e volendo su salire, vide messer Lambertuccio scendere, e maravigliossi e delle parole e del viso di lui, e disse: —Che è questo, messere?

mounted a horse and, unaccompanied, went to her place and knocked at the door. The lady's maid, seeing him, went straight to her (she was in her bedroom with Leonetto) and called to her, saying: 'Madam, Lord Lambertuccio is downstairs all by himself.' Hearing this, the lady was the saddest woman in the world; but, very much afraid of him, she asked Leonetto if he wouldn't mind hiding for a while behind the bed curtains until Lord Lambertuccio went away. Leonetto, who was no less afraid of him than the lady was, hid there; and she ordered her maid to go and let Lord Lambertuccio in; she did so, and in the courtyard he alighted from his palfrey and tied it to a hook, then went upstairs. The lady, putting a good face on things and venturing as far as the head of the stairs, welcomed him with the most cheerful words she could muster up and asked him what his business was. The knight, having hugged and kissed her, said: 'My darling, I heard your husband was out, so I came to be with you a while.' After saying this, he entered the bedroom with her, they locked themselves in, and Lord Lambertuccio began to have his way with her.

"And while he was with her that way, quite contrary to the lady's expectations her husband happened to return; when the maid saw him somewhat close to the house, she immediately ran to the lady's room and said: 'Madam, the master is returning; I think he's already down in the courtyard.'

"The lady, hearing this, realizing she had two men in the house, and knowing that the knight couldn't hide because his palfrey was in the yard, thought she was a dead woman; all the same, suddenly leaping out of bed onto the floor, she made a decision and said to Lord Lambertuccio: 'My lord, if you care for me the least little bit and if you want to save my life, you'll do what I tell you. You must hold your drawn dagger in your hand and, with a vicious, very angry look on your face, you must go downstairs, saying as you go: "I swear to God that I'll catch him somewhere else!" And if my husband tries to hold you back or ask you anything, say no more than I've told you; get on your horse, and don't remain with him for any reason.'

"Lord Lambertuccio said he'd gladly comply; drawing his dagger, all red in the face, what with the fatigue he had undergone and his anger at the knight's return, he did as the lady had commanded. The lady's husband, who had already dismounted in the yard, surprised to see the palfrey and wishing to go upstairs, saw Lord Lambertuccio coming down; marveling at his words and his expression, he said: 'What's all this, my lord?'

Messer Lambertuccio, messo il piè nella staffa e montato su, non disse altro, se non: —Al corpo di Dio, io il giugnerò altrove;— e andò via.

Il gentile uomo montato su trovò la donna sua in capo della scala tutta sgomentata e piena di paura; alla quale egli disse: —Che cosa è questa? Cui va messer Lambertuccio cosí adirato minacciando?

La donna, tiratasi verso la camera acciò che Leonetto l'udisse, rispose: —Messere, io non ebbi mai simil paura a questa. Qua entro si fuggí un giovane, il quale io non conosco e che messer Lambertuccio col coltello in man seguitava, e trovò per ventura questa camera aperta, e tutto tremante disse: «Madonna, per Dio aiutatemi, ché io non sia nelle braccia vostre morto». Io mi levai diritta, e come io il voleva domandare chi fosse e che avesse, ed ecco messer Lambertuccio venir su dicendo: «Dove se', traditore?». Io mi parai in su l'uscio della camera, e volendo egli entrar dentro, il ritenni; ed egli in tanto fu cortese che, come vide che non mi piaceva che egli qua entro entrasse, dette molte parole, se ne venne giú come voi vedeste.

Disse allora il marito: —Donna, ben facesti: troppo ne sarebbe stato gran biasimo se persona fosse stata qua entro uccisa; e messer Lambertuccio fece gran villania a seguitar persona che qua entro fuggita fosse.— Poi domandò dove fosse quel giovane.

La donna rispose: —Messere, io non so dove egli si sia nascoso.

Il cavaliere allora disse: —Ove se' tu? Esci fuori sicuramente.

Leonetto, che ogni cosa udita avea, tutto pauroso, come colui che paura aveva avuta da vero, uscí fuori del luogo dove nascoso s'era.

Disse allora il cavaliere: —Che hai tu a fare con messer Lambertuccio?

Il giovane rispose: —Messer, niuna cosa che sia in questo mondo, e per ciò io credo fermamente che egli non sia in buon senno, o che egli m'abbia colto in iscambio: per ciò che, come poco lontano da questo palagio nella strada mi vide, cosí mise mano al coltello e disse: «Traditor, tu se' morto!». Io non mi posi a domandare per che cagione, ma quanto potei cominciai a fuggire e qui me ne venni, dove, mercé di Dio e di questa gentil donna, scampato sono.

Disse allora il cavaliere: —Or via, non aver paura alcuna; io ti porrò a casa tua sano e salvo, e tu poi sappi far cercar quello che con lui hai a fare.

E, come cenato ebbero, fattol montare a cavallo, a Firenze il ne menò, e lasciollo a casa sua; il quale, secondo l'ammaestramento della donna avuto, quella sera medesima parlò con messer Lambertuccio occultamente, e sí con lui ordinò, che, quantunque poi molte parole ne fossero, mai per ciò il cavalier non s'accorse della beffa fattagli dalla moglie.

"Lord Lambertuccio, setting his foot on the stirrup and mounting, said nothing but: 'By God's body, I'll overtake him elsewhere!' And he left.

"Going upstairs, the nobleman found his wife at the head of the flight completely alarmed and filled with fright; he said to her: 'What's this all about? Whom is Lord Lambertuccio threatening so angrily?'

"The lady, drawing near her room so Leonetto could hear her, answered: 'My lord, I've never been as frightened as this. A young man whom I don't know ran in here, followed by Lord Lambertuccio with a dagger in his hand, and luckily found this room open; trembling all over, he said: "Madam, for God's sake help me, or else I'll be dead in your arms!" I got up and when I tried to ask him who he was and what was the matter, there was Lord Lambertuccio coming up, saying: "Where are you, villain?" I took a stand on the threshold of the room and when he tried to come in, I stopped him; and he was polite to the extent that, when he saw I didn't like his coming in here, he said many things and went downstairs as you saw.'

"Then her husband said: 'My lady, you did the right thing: it would have been a great reproach if anyone had been killed in here; and Lord Lambertuccio was very rude to pursue anyone who had taken refuge in here.' Then he asked where that young man was.

"The lady replied: 'My lord, I don't know where he hid.'

"Then the knight called: 'Where are you? It's safe for you to come out.'

"Leonetto (who had heard everything), very timidly, because he really had been frightened, emerged from the place where he had hidden.

"Then the knight said: 'What business do you have with Lord Lambertuccio?'

"The young man replied: 'My lord, absolutely none! That's why I firmly believe that he's not in his right mind, or else that he mistook me for somebody else; because when he saw me on the road not far from this house, he grasped his dagger and said: "Villain, you're a dead man!" I didn't stop to ask the reason, but began to run as fast as I could, and I arrived here, where, thanks to God and this noble lady, I was saved.'

"Then the knight said: 'Come now, have no more fear; I'll take you home safe and sound, and then make it your business to find out what you must do with him.'

"And after they had had supper, he furnished him with a horse, led him to Florence, and left him at his home; that very evening, following the lady's instructions, Leonetto spoke privately with Lord Lambertuccio and arranged matters with him in such a way that, however much talk there later was about it, the knight never found out about the trick his wife had played on him."

## 5. Sacchetti (ca 1330–1400): *Trecentonovelle*

Tanto avea voglia questa contata donna d'andar drieto al morto marito quanto ebbe voglia di coricarsi allato a un morto in questa novella
Lapaccio di Geri da Montelupo nel contado di Firenze. Fu a' miei dì,
e io il conobbi, e spesso mi trovava con lui, però che era piacevole e
assai semplice uomo. Quando uno gli avesse detto: «Il tale è morto» e
avesselo ritocco con la mano, subito volea ritoccare lui; e se colui si
fuggìa, e non lo potea ritoccare, andava a ritoccare un altro che pas-
sasse per la via, e se non avesse potuto ritoccare qualche persona,
avrebbe ritocco o un cane, o una gatta; e se ciò non avesse trovato, nel-
l'ultimo ritoccava il ferro del coltellino; e tanto ubbioso vivea, che se
subito, essendo stato tocco, per la maniera detta non avesse ritocco altrui, avea per certo di far quella morte che colui per cui era stato
tocco, e tostamente. E per questa cagione, se un malfattore era
menato alla justizia, o se una bara o una croce fosse passata, tanto avea
preso forma la cosa che ciascuno correa a ritoccarlo; ed elli correndo
or drieto all'uno or drieto all'altro, come uno che uscisse di sé; e per
questo quelli che lo ritoccavano, ne pigliavono grandissimo diletto.

Avvenne per caso che, essendo costui per lo comune di Firenze
mandato ad eleggere uno podestà ed essendo di quaresima, uscì di
Firenze, e tenne verso Bologna e poi a Ferrara, e passando più oltre,
pervenne una sera al tardi in un luogo assai ostico e pantanoso che si
chiama la Ca' Salvadega. E disceso all'albergo, trovato modo d'ac-
conciare i cavalli e male, però che vi erano Ungheri e romei assai, che
erano già andati a letto; e trovato modo di cenare, cenato che ebbe,
disse all'oste dove dovea dormire. Rispose l'oste:

«Tu starai come tu potrai; entra qui che ci sono quelle letta che io
ho, e hacci molti romei; guarda se c'è qualche proda, fa' e acconciati
il meglio che puoi, ché altre letta o altra camera non ho».

Lapaccio n'andò nel detto luogo, e guardando di letto in letto così
al barlume, tutti li trovò pieni salvo che uno, là dove da l'una proda era
un Unghero, il quale il dì dinanzi s'era morto. Lapaccio, non sapiendo
questo (che prima si sarebbe coricato in un fuoco che essersi coricato
in quel letto), vedendo che dall'altra proda non era persona, entrò a
dormire in quella. E come spesso interviene che volgendosi l'uomo
per acconciarsi, gli pare che il compagno occupi troppo del suo terreno, disse:

«Fatti un poco in là, buon uomo.»

## 5. Franco Sacchetti (ca. 1330–1400): *The Three Hundred Tales*

The above-mentioned lady had just as much desire to follow her dead husband as, in this story, Lapaccio di Geri from Montelupo in the Florence countryside had to lie down beside a corpse. It was in my day, and I knew him, and often found myself in his company, because he was a pleasant, though very simple fellow. Whenever someone told him, "So-and-so has died," and touched him with his hand, he immediately wanted to touch him back; and if the man ran away and he couldn't touch him, he went and touched someone else who was passing by in the street; and if he hadn't been able to touch some person, he'd touch a dog or a cat; and if he hadn't found even that, as a last resort he'd touch the blade of his knife; and he was so superstitious that, having been touched and not having immediately touched someone else in the way I described, he was sure he'd die the same death as the person because of whom he'd been touched—and before very long. And for that reason, if a criminal was being led to execution, or if a coffin or a cross had passed by, his habit was so well known that everyone ran up to touch him; and he would run after now this person, now that, like a man beside himself; therefore those who touched him were highly amused.

It came about by chance that, being sent by the Florence council to choose a chief magistrate (it was during Lent), he left Florence and headed for Bologna and then for Ferrara; passing beyond that, late one evening he arrived at a very boggy and marshy spot called Ca' Salvadega. Alighting at the inn; having managed to stable his horses, but badly because the place was full of Hungarians and pilgrims bound for Rome, who had already gone to bed; and having wangled a supper, he afterwards asked the innkeeper where he was to sleep. The innkeeper replied:

"You'll sleep as best you can; go in there, where there are whatever beds I have, though there are a lot of pilgrims there; see if one side of any bed is unoccupied, and arrange yourself the best you can, because I have no other beds or rooms."

Lapaccio went to the place indicated and, looking from one bed to another in the dim light, he found them all full except one where there was a Hungarian on one side; he had died the previous day. Lapaccio, not knowing this (because he would sooner have lain on a fire than on that bed) and seeing there was no one on the other side, got in it in order to sleep. And as it often occurs that when a man turns around to get comfortable, he thinks his companion is taking up too much of the space, he said:

"Move over a little, my good man."

L'amico stava cheto e fermo, ché era nell'altro mondo. Stando un poco, e Lapaccio il tocca, e dice:

«O tu dormi fiso, fammi un poco di luogo, te ne priego».

E 'l buon uomo cheto.

Lapaccio, veggendo che non si movea, il tocca forte:

«Deh, fatti in là con la mala pasqua».

Al muro: ché non era per muoversi. Di che Lapaccio si comincia a versare, dicendo:

«Deh, morto sia tu a ghiado, che tu déi essere uno rubaldo».

E recandosi alla traversa con le gambe verso costui, e poggiate le mani alla lettiera, trae a costui un gran paio di calci, e colselo sì di netto che 'l corpo morto cadde in terra dallo letto tanto grave, e con sì gran busso, che Lapaccio cominciò fra sé stesso a dire: «Oimé! che ho io fatto?» e palpando il copertoio si fece alla sponda, appié della quale l'amico era ito in terra: e comincia a dire pianamente:

«Sta' su; ha'ti fatto male? Torna nel letto».

E colui cheto com'olio, e lascia dire Lapaccio quantunche vuole, ché non era né per rispondere, né per tornare nel letto. Avendo sentito Lapaccio la soda caduta di costui, e veggendo che non si dolea, e di terra non si levava, comincia a dire in sé: «Oimè sventurato! che io l'avrò morto». E guata e riguata, quanto più mirava, più gli parea averlo morto: e dice: «O Lapaccio doloroso! che farò? dove n'andrò? che almeno me ne potess'io andare! ma io non so donde, ché qui non fu'io mai più. Così foss'io innanzi morto a Firenze che trovarmi qui ancora! E se io sto, serò mandato a Ferrara, o in altro luogo, e serammi tagliato il capo. Se io il dico all'oste, elli vorrà che io moia in prima ch'elli n'abbia danno». E stando tutta notte in questo affanno e in pena, come colui che ha ricevuto il comandamento dell'anima, la mattina vegnente aspetta la morte.

Apparendo l'alba del dì, li romei si cominciano a levare e uscir fuori. Lapaccio, che parea più morto che 'l morto, si comincia a levare anco elli, e studiossi d'uscir fuori più tosto che poteo per due cagioni che non so quale gli desse maggior tormento: la prima era per fuggire il pericolo e andarsene anzi che l'oste se ne avvedesse; la seconda per dilungarsi dal morto, e fuggire l'ubbìa che sempre si recava de' morti.

Uscito fuori Lapaccio, studia il fante che selli le bestie; e truova l'oste, e fatta ragione con lui, il pagava e annoverando li danari, le mane gli tremavono come verga. Dice l'oste:

His friend remained quiet and still, because he was in the next world. After a while Lapaccio touched him and said:

"My, you're a solid sleeper! Make a little room for me, please!"

But the good fellow was quiet.

Lapaccio, seeing that he wasn't moving, poked him harder:

"Hey, move over, damn you!"

Like talking to the wall: he wasn't about to move. So that Lapaccio began to get angry, shouting:

"Say, I wish you were stabbed to death, because you must be a scoundrel!"

And placing himself crosswise with his legs toward the other man, and supporting his hands on the bedstead, he gave the man a couple of hard kicks, hitting him so accurately that the dead body fell out of the bed onto the floor so heavily and with such a loud thud that Lapaccio began to say to himself: "My goodness! What have I done?" And gripping the blanket, he made his way to the other side, at the foot of which his friend had hit the floor. And he began to say softly:

"Get up! Did you hurt yourself? Come back to bed."

But the man was cool and collected, and allowed Lapaccio to say whatever he wanted, because he was in no condition either to reply or to get back in bed. Having heard the man's heavy fall and noticing that he was neither complaining nor getting up from the floor, Lapaccio began to say to himself: "Oh, how unlucky I am! I must have killed him! And he kept on staring at him; the more he looked, the more he thought he had killed him. And he said: "Oh, unhappy Lapaccio! What shall I do? Where shall I go? If, at least, I were able to go away! But I don't know where, because I've never been here before. I should have died earlier in Florence rather than being here now! If I remain, I'll be sent to Ferrara or elsewhere and I'll be beheaded. If I tell the innkeeper about it, he'll want me to die rather than suffer for it himself!" Remaining all night in that anguish and pain, like a man who has received a death sentence, on the following morning he awaited his death.

When dawn appeared, the pilgrims began to get up and go out. Lapaccio, who looked more dead than the corpse, began to get up also and strove to go out as soon as he could, for two reasons (I don't know which one tormented him more): the first was to escape from his danger and leave before the innkeeper noticed anything; the second, to get far away from the corpse and escape the superstitious dread which dead people always inspired in him.

Going out, Lapaccio ordered the groom to saddle his horses; he found the innkeeper, received his bill, and paid him. While counting out the coins, his hands were trembling like twigs. The innkeeper said:

«O fatti freddo?».
Lapaccio appena poté dire che credea che fosse per la nebbia che
era levata in quel padule. [. . .]

## 6. *I fioretti di San Francesco* (ca 1390)

Al tempo, che santo Francesco dimorava nella città d'Agobio, nel contado d'Agobio apparì uno lupo grandissimo, terribile e feroce, il quale
non solamente divorava gli animali ma eziandio gli uomini; intantoché
tutti i cittadini istavano in grande paura, perocché spesse volte s'ap-
pressava alla città; e tutti andavano armati quando uscivano della
terra, come se eglino andassono a combattere: e contuttociò non si
poteano difendere da lui, chi in lui si scontrava solo. E per paura di
questo lupo e' vennono a tanto, che niuno era ardito d'uscire della
terra. Per la qual cosa, santo Francesco avendo compassione agli uomini della terra, sì volle uscire fuori a questo lupo, benché i cittadini
al tutto ne lo isconsigliavano: e facendosi il segno della santa croce,
uscì fuori della terra egli co' suoi compagni, tutta la sua fidanza po-
nendo in Dio. E dubitando gli altri d'andare più oltre, santo
Francesco prese il cammino inverso il luogo ov'era il lupo. Et ecco
che, veggendo molti cittadini, i quali erano venuti a vedere cotesto
miracolo, il detto lupo si fa incontro a santo Francesco colla bocca
aperta; et appressandosi a lui, santo Francesco gli fa il segno della
croce e chiamalo a sé, e dicegli così: «Vieni qua, frate lupo, io ti comando dalla parte di Cristo che tu non facci male né a me né a persona». Mirabile a dire! immantinente che santo Francesco ebbe fatta
la croce, il lupo terribile chiuse la bocca e ristette di correre; e fatto il
comandamento, venne mansuetamente come uno agnello, e gittossi a'
piedi di santo Francesco a giacere. Allora santo Francesco gli parla
cosi: «Frate lupo, tu fai molti danni in queste parti, et hai fatti grandi
malifici, guastando et uccidendo le creature di Dio sanza sua licenza:
e non solamente uccise e divorate le bestie, ma hai avuto ardimento
d'uccidere gli uomini fatti alla immagine di Dio; per la qual cosa tu se'
degno delle forche come ladro et omicida pessimo; et ogni gente grida
e mormora di te, e tutta questa terra t'è nemica. Ma io voglio, frate
lupo, fare pace fra te e costoro; sicché tu non gli offenda più et eglino
ti perdonino ogni offesa passata, e né uomini né cani ti perseguitino
più». Dette queste parole, il lupo con atti di corpo e di coda e di orecchi e con inchinare di capo mostrava d'accettare ciò che santo
Francesco dicea, e di volerlo osservare. Allora santo Francesco disse:

"Are you cold, then?"
Lapaccio could scarcely reply that he thought it was on account of the
fog that had risen in that swamp. [. . .]

## 6. *The Little Flowers of Saint Francis* (ca. 1390)

At the time when Saint Francis was living in the town of Gubbio, a
huge wolf appeared in the Gubbio countryside, terrible and ferocious,
devouring not only animals but even people; so that all the townspeople were in great fear, because he often came near the town, and everyone carried arms when leaving town as if on the way to battle.
Nevertheless they couldn't defend themselves against him if alone
when they ran into him. And their fear of the wolf reached such proportions that no one dared to leave town. Therefore Saint Francis, having compassion for the townspeople, decided to go out to that wolf,
even though the citizens all advised him not to; making the sign of the
holy cross, he left town with his companions, placing all his trust in
God. Though the others feared to proceed farther, Saint Francis took
the path leading to the wolf's quarters. And behold: in the sight of
many townspeople who had come to view so great a miracle, the aforesaid wolf came toward Saint Francis with his mouth open; and, nearing
him, Saint Francis made the sign of the cross over him, summoned him
to his side, and said: "Come here, Brother Wolf; I order you on behalf
of Christ to do no harm to me or anyone else." Wondrous to tell! As
soon as Saint Francis had made the cross, the terrible wolf shut his
mouth and stopped running; at the command he came up as meekly as
a lamb and threw himself at Saint Francis's feet, where he lay down.
Then Saint Francis spoke to him as follows: "Brother Wolf, you do
much damage around here, and you've committed great crimes, destroying and killing God's creatures without His permission; and not
only have you slain and devoured animals, you've been bold enough to
kill men made in the image of God; for this you deserve the gallows as
a vile robber and assassin; and everyone yells and grumbles at you, and
this whole town is your enemy. But, Brother Wolf, I wish to make
peace between you and them, so that you no longer harm them and
they forgive you for every past misdeed and neither men nor dogs pursue you anymore." After those words were spoken, the wolf showed
with gestures of his body, tail, and ears, and by nodding his head, that
he accepted Saint Francis's terms and was willing to abide by them.
Then Saint Francis said: "Brother Wolf, since you are pleased to con-

«Frate lupo, dappoiché ti piace di fare e di tenere questa pace, io ti prometto ch'io ti farò dare le spese continuamente, mentre che tu viverai, dagli uomini di questa terra, sicché tu non patirai fame; imperocché io so bene che per la fame tu hai fatto ogni male. Ma poich'io t'accatterò questa grazia, io voglio, frate lupo, che tu mi prometta che tu non nocerai mai a niuno uomo, né a niuno animale: promettimi tu questo?» Et il lupo con inchinare di capo fece evidente segnale che prometteva. E santo Francesco dice: «Frate lupo, io voglio che tu mi faccia fede di questa promessa, acciocch'io me ne possa bene fidare»; e distendendo santo Francesco la mano per ricevere fede, il lupo levò il piè dinanzi, e dimesticamente lo puose sopra la mano di santo Francesco, dandogli quello segnale di fede ch'elli potea. Et allora disse santo Francesco: «Frate lupo, io ti comando nel nome di Gesù Cristo, che tu venga ora meco senza dubitare di nulla, et andiamo a fermare questa pace al nome di Dio». Et il lupo ubbidiente se ne va con lui, come uno agnello mansueto; di che i cittadini, vedendo questo, forte si maravigliarono. E subitamente questa novità si seppe per tutta la città: di che ogni gente, grandi e piccoli, maschi e femmine, giovani e vecchi traggono alla piazza a vedere il lupo con santo Francesco. Et essendo bene ragunato tutto il popolo, levasi sù santo Francesco e predica loro, dicendo, tra l'altre cose, come per li peccati Iddio permette cotali pestilenzie; e troppo è più pericolosa la fiamma dello inferno, la quale ha a durare eternalmente a' dannati, che non è la rabbia del lupo il quale non può uccidere se non il corpo: quanto dunque è da temere la bocca dello inferno, quando tanta moltitudine tiene in paura et in tremore la bocca d'uno piccolo animale? Tornate dunque, carissimi, a Dio e fate degna penitenzia de' vostri peccati, e Dio vi libererà dal lupo nel presente tempo, e nel futuro dal fuoco infernale. —E fatta la predica, disse santo Francesco: «Udite, fratelli miei: frate lupo, che è qui dinanzi da voi, m'ha promesso e fattomene fede, di fare pace con voi e di non vi offendere mai in cosa niuna, se voi gli promettete di dargli ognidì le spese necessarie; et io v'entro mallevadore per lui che 'l patto della pace egli osserverà fermamente». Allora tutto il popolo a una boce promise di nutricarlo continuamente. E santo Francesco inanzi a tutti disse al lupo: «E tu, frate lupo, prometti d'osservare a costoro il patto della pace, che tu non offenderai né gli uomini né gli animali né niuna creatura?» Et il lupo s'inginocchiò, e china il capo, e con atti mansueti di corpo e di coda e d'orecchi dimostra, quanto è possibile, di volere osservare loro ogni patto. Dice santo Francesco: «Frate lupo, io voglio che come tu mi desti fede di questa promessa fuori della porta, così dinanzi a tutto il

clude and observe this peace, I promise you that I'll have you fed regularly, as long as you live, by the men of this town, so that you won't suffer hunger; because I'm well aware that you have done every misdeed because of hunger. But since I shall beg this favor for you, Brother Wolf, I want you to promise me that you'll no longer harm any man or any animal; do you promise me this?" And by nodding his head the wolf gave a clear indication that he promised. And Saint Francis said: "Brother Wolf, I want you to give me a pledge for this promise, so that I can trust in it firmly." And when Saint Francis held out his hand to receive the pledge, the wolf raised his forepaw and tamely placed it on Saint Francis's hand, giving him that token of compliance which was within his power. Then Saint Francis said: "Brother Wolf, I order you in the name of Jesus Christ to come with me now, having no fear; let us go and sign this peace treaty in God's name." And the obedient wolf went with him like a meek lamb; at which the townspeople, seeing it, marveled greatly. And this strange news was known at once throughout the town, so that everyone, adults and children, men and women, young and old, entered the square to see the wolf with Saint Francis. And when the people were all assembled, Saint Francis arose and preached to them, saying among other things that God permits such calamities because of sins: "The flames of hell, which the damned are to suffer eternally, are much more dangerous than the fury of the wolf, who can kill only the body; thus, how greatly is the mouth of hell to be feared when such a multitude is held in fear and trembling by the mouth of a small animal? And so, dear children, return to God and do proper penance for your sins, and God will free you from the wolf in this life, and from the fires of hell in the future life." After the sermon Saint Francis said: "Listen, my brothers: Brother Wolf, who is here before you, has promised me and given me a pledge to make peace with you and no longer harm you in any way, if you promise to give him the necessary food every day; and I am here as a guarantor for him that he will faithfully observe the peace treaty." Then all the people with one voice promised to feed him regularly. And in front of everyone Saint Francis said to the wolf: "And you, Brother Wolf, do you promise to abide by the peace treaty with them, and never again harm either people or animals, or any creature?" And the wolf knelt and nodded his head and, as best he could, showed with meek gestures of his body, tail, and ears that he was willing to abide by every agreement with them. Saint Francis said: "Brother Wolf, I wish that, just as you gave me a pledge for this promise outside the gate, you will give me a pledge for your promise in front of all the people, and that you won't disappoint

popolo mi dia fede della tua promessa, e che tu non mi ingannerai della mia malleveria ch'io ho fatta per te». Allora il lupo, levando il piè ritto, sì lo puose in mano di santo Francesco. Onde tra di questo atto e degli altri detti di sopra fu tanta ammirazione et allegrezza in tutto il popolo, sì per la divozione del santo e sì per la novità del miracolo e sì per la pace del lupo; che tutti cominciarono a gridare a cielo, lodando e benedicendo Iddio il quale aveva mandato loro santo Francesco, che per li suoi meriti gli avea liberati dalla bocca della crudele bestia. E poi il detto lupo vivette due anni in Agobio; et entravasi dimesticamente per le case a uscio a uscio, sanza fare male a persona e sanza esserne fatto a lui; e fu notricato cortesemente dalle genti; et andandosi così per la terra e per le case, giammai niuno cane gli abbaiava. Finalmente dopo due anni frate lupo si morì di vecchiaia; di che i cittadini forte si dolsono, imperocché, veggendolo andare così mansueto per la città, si ricordavano meglio della virtù e santità di santo Francesco. A laude di Cristo. Amen.

## 7. Ser Giovanni Fiorentino: *Pecorone* (ca 1400)

Egli ebbe in Firenze in casa gli Scali un mercatante, il quale ebbe nome Bindo, il quale era stato più volte alla Tana e in Alessandria, e in tutti que' gran viaggi che si fanno con le mercatanzie. Era questo Bindo assai ricco, e aveva tre figliuoli maschi grandi; e venendo a morte, chiamò il maggiore e 'l mezzano, e fece in loro presenza testamento, e lasciò lor due eredi di ciò ch'egli aveva al mondo, e al minore non lasciò niente. E fatto ch'egli ebbe testamento, il figliuolo minore che aveva nome Giannetto, sentendo questo, andò a lui al letto e gli disse: «Padre mio, io mi maraviglio forte di quello che voi avete fatto, a non esservi ricordato di me in su 'l testamento». Rispose il padre: «Giannetto mio, e' non è creatura a cui voglia meglio che a te; e però io non voglio che dopo la morte mia tu stia qui, anzi voglio, come io son morto, che tu te ne vada a Vinegia a un tuo santolo che ha nome messer Ansaldo, il quale non ha figliuolo nessuno, e hammi scritto più volte ch'io te gli mandi. E sotti dire ch'egli è il più ricco mercatante che sia oggi tra' Cristiani. E però voglio che, come io son morto, tu te ne vada a lui, e portagli questa lettera; e se tu saprai fare, tu rimarrai ricco uomo». Disse il filiuolo: «Padre mio, io sono apparecchiato a fare ciò che voi mi comandate». Di che il padre gli dié la sua benedizione: e ivi a pochi dì si morì, e tutti i figliuoli ne fecero grandissimo lamento, e fecero al corpo quello onore che gli si conveniva. E poi ivi a pochi

me for giving the guarantee for you that I have given." Then the wolf, raising his right paw, placed it in Saint Francis's hand. At which, what with this action and the others mentioned above, there was so much amazement and joy among all the people, because of the saint's devotion, the unusualness of the miracle, and the peacefulness of the wolf, that everyone began to call to heaven, praising and blessing God for having sent them Saint Francis, who by his merit had freed them from the mouth of the cruel beast. And then the aforesaid wolf lived in Gubbio for two years, and used to enter the houses tamely from door to door, without harming anyone or having harm done to him; and he was courteously fed by the people; and as he roamed in that way through the town and the houses, never did any dog bark at him. Finally, after two years Brother Wolf died of old age; whereupon the townspeople grieved mightily, because, having seen him roam through the town so meekly, they remembered all the more the virtue and sanctity of Saint Francis. Christ be praised. Amen.

## 7. Ser Giovanni Fiorentino: *Pecorone* (ca. 1400)

There was in Florence in the house of the Scali a merchant named Bindo who had often been in Tánais and Alexandria and on all those great voyages which are made with merchandise. This Bindo was extremely wealthy, and had three grown sons; when near death, he summoned the eldest and the middle one, and made his will in their presence, leaving the two of them heirs to all he had in the world; to the youngest he left nothing. And after he had made his will, his youngest son, named Giannetto, hearing of it, approached his bed and said: "Father, I'm greatly surprised at what you've done, not having remembered me in your will." His father replied: "My Giannetto, there's no living being I love more dearly than you, and thus I don't want you to remain here after my death; rather, I want you, as soon as I die, to go to Venice to a godfather of yours named Master Ansaldo, who has no son and who has written to me several times to send you to him. And I can tell you that he's the richest merchant in Christendom today. Therefore I want you to go to him after I die and take this letter to him; and if you manage things properly, you'll become a rich man." His son said: "Father, I'm prepared to do as you order me." Whereupon his father gave him his blessing; and a few days later he died, and all his sons lamented greatly and paid his body the suitable respects. A few days after that, the two older brothers called for Giannetto and said to him:

dì, questi due fratelli chiamarono Giannetto, e sì gli dissero: «Fratello nostro, egli è vero che nostro padre fece testamento, e lasciò eredi noi, e di te non fe' veruna menzione, nondimeno tu se' pure nostro fratello, e per tanto a quell'ora manchi a te, che a noi, quello che c'è». Rispose Giannetto: «Fratelli miei, io vi ringrazio della vostra profferta; ma, quanto a me, l'animo mio è d'andare a procacciare mia ventura in qualche parte; e così son fermo di fare, e voi v'abbiate l'eredità segnata e benedetta». Onde i fratelli veggendo la volontà sua, dierongli un cavallo e danari per le spese. Giannetto prese commiato da loro e andòssene a Vinegia, e giunse al fondaco di messere Ansaldo, e diégli la lettera che 'l padre gli aveva data innanzi che morisse. Per che messere Ansaldo leggendo questa lettera, conobbe che costui era il figliuolo del suo carissimo Bindo, e come l'ebbe letta, di subito l'abbracciò, dicendo: «Ben venga il figliuolo mio, il quale io ho tanto desiderato». E subito lo domandò di Bindo, dove Giannetto gli rispose ch'egli era morto; per ch'egli con molte lagrime l'abbracciò e baciò, e disse: «Or ecco, ben mi duole la morte di Bindo, perch'egli m'aiutò a guadagnare gran parte di quel ch'io ho; ma egli è tanta l'allegrezza ch'io ho ora di te, che mitiga quel dolore». E fecelo menare a casa, e comandò a' fattori suoi e a' compagni e agli scudieri e a' fanti, e quanti n'erano in casa, che Giannetto fosse ubidito e servito più che la sua persona. E prima a lui consegnò le chiavi di tutti i suoi contanti e disse: «Figliuolo mio, ciò che c'è è tuo: e vesti e calza oggimai come ti piace, e metti tavola a' cittadini, e fatti conoscere; però ch'io lascio a te questo pensiero, e tanto meglio ti vorrò, quanto più ti farai valere». Per che Giannetto cominciò a usare co' gentiluomini di Vinegia, cominciò a fare cene e desinari, cominciò a donare, e vestir famigli, e a comperare di buoni corsieri, e a giostrare e bagordare, come quel ch'era esperto e pratico e magnanimo e cortese in ogni cosa; e ben sapeva fare onore e cortesia dove si conveniva, e sempre rendeva onore a messere Ansaldo, più che se fosse stato cento volte suo padre. E seppesi sì saviamente mantenere con ogni maniera di gente, che quasi tutto il comune di Vinegia gli voleva bene, veggendolo tanto savio e con tanta piacevolezza, e cortese oltre a misura. Di che le donne e gli uomini ne erano innamorati, e messere Ansaldo non vedeva più oltre che lui, tanto gli piacevano i modi e le maniere che tenea. E quasi non si facea niuna festa in Vinegia, che il detto Giannetto non vi fosse invitato, tanto gli era voluto bene da ogni persona.

　　Ora avvenne che due suoi cari compagni volsero andare in Alessandria con loro mercatanzie e con loro due navi, com'erano usati di fare ogni anno. Di che eglino il dissero a Giannetto s'egli volea

"Brother, it's true that our father made a will and left us heirs, making no mention of you; all the same, you're still our brother, and so let whatever we have fail us whenever it fails you." Giannetto replied: "Brothers, I thank you for your offer, but, as for me, it's my intention to go and seek my fortune elsewhere; and thus I'm determined to do; you hold on to the blessed inheritance that was meant for you." Whereupon his brothers, seeing that his mind was made up, gave him a horse and money for expenses. Giannetto took leave of them and went to Venice; arriving at Master Ansaldo's warehouse, he handed him the letter his father had given him before dying. And so, reading this letter, Master Ansaldo learned that this was the son of his beloved Bindo; after finishing the letter, he embraced him at once, saying: "Welcome, my son, whom I have so longed for!" And at once he asked for news of Bindo, whereupon Giannetto replied that he was dead; then with many tears the older man hugged and kissed him, saying: "See now, I'm very sorry about Bindo's death because he helped me acquire much of what I own; but the joy I now have in you is so great that it soothes that grief." And he had him brought to his house, and he ordered his stewards, companions, grooms, and servants, and everyone in the house, to obey Giannetto and serve him even better than himself. And first he handed over to him the keys to all his valuables, saying: "My son, all that's here is yours: from now on, buy whatever clothing and footwear you like, invite the citizens to meals, and make yourself known; because I leave such matters to you, and I'll like you all the better, the more you make a name for yourself." And so Giannetto began to rub elbows with the noblemen of Venice, he began to give suppers and dinners, he began to make presents and keep liveried servants, and to buy fine horses and to joust and carouse, like a man experienced, knowledgeable, generous, and courteous in all matters; he knew just how to pay respects and show courtesy wherever appropriate, and always gave honor to Master Ansaldo, more than if he had been his own father a hundred times over. And he knew how to get along so cleverly with all sorts of people that almost the entire city of Venice wished him well, seeing how wise he was, how affable, how exceedingly polite. And so both women and men loved him, and he was Master Ansaldo's all in all, so greatly did the older man like his ways and manners. And there was practically no festivity in Venice to which this Giannetto wasn't invited, so greatly was he liked by everybody.

Now, it came about that two dear comrades of his decided to go to Alexandria with their merchandise and their two ships, as they were accustomed to do every year. Thereupon they asked Giannetto

dilettarsi d'andare con loro per vedere del mondo, e massimamente quel Damasco e quel paese di là. Rispose Giannetto: «In buona fe ch'io verrei molto volentieri, se 'l padre mio messere Ansaldo mi desse la parola». Disser costoro: «Noi faremo sì ch'e' te la darà, e ch'e' sarà contento». E subito se n'andarono da messer Ansaldo, e dissero: «Noi vi vogliamo pregare che vi piaccia di dare la parola a Giannetto che ne venga in questa primavera con noi in Alessandria, e che gli forniate qualche legno o nave, acciò ch'egli vegga un poco del mondo». Disse messere Ansaldo: «Io son contento, se piace a lui». Risposero costoro: «Messere, egli è contento». Per che messer Ansaldo subito gli fe' fornire una bellissima nave, e fella caricare di molta mercatanzia, e guernire di bandiere e d'armi quanto fe' mestiere. E di poi ch'ella fu acconcia, messer Ansaldo comandò al padrone e agli altri ch'erano al servizio della nave, che facessero ciò che Giannetto comandasse loro, e che fosse loro raccomandato: «però ch'io non lo mando per guadagno ch'io voglia ch'e' faccia, ma perch'egli vada a suo diletto veggendo il mondo». [. . .]

## 8. Pulci (1432–1484): *Morgante*

Poi si partì, portato dal furore,
e terminò passare in Pagania;
e mentre che cavalca, il traditore,
di Gan sempre ricorda per la via;
e, cavalcando d'uno in altro errore,
in un deserto truova una badia,
in luoghi scuri e paesi lontani,
ch'era a' confin tra cristiani e pagani.

L'abate si chiamava Chiaramonte,
era del sangue disceso d'Angrante.
Di sopra alla badia v'era un gran monte,
dove abitava alcun fiero gigante,
de' quali uno avea nome Passamonte,
l'altro Alabastro e 'l terzo era Morgante;
con certe frombe gittavan da alto,
ed ogni dì facevon qualche assalto.

I monachetti non potieno uscire
del monistero o per legne o per acque.
Orlando picchia e non volieno aprire,

whether he'd enjoy going with them to see some of the world, especially Damascus and the lands yonder. Giannetto replied: "To tell the
truth, I'd love to come if my father Master Ansaldo gave me permission." They said: "We'll see to it that he does, and that he'll be
pleased to do so." And at once they went to Master Ansaldo and said:
"We want to ask you for your permission for Giannetto to come with
us to Alexandria this spring, and for you to supply him with some ves-
sel or ship so he can see a little of the world." Master Ansaldo said:
"I'm willing if he wants to go." They replied: "Master, he does." And
so Master Ansaldo immediately supplied him with a beautiful ship,
which he ordered to be laden with a great deal of trade goods and
furnished with all necessary flags and arms. And after it was ready,
Master Ansaldo ordered the captain and crew of the ship to do whatever Giannetto ordered; he bade them take good care of him:
"Because I'm not sending him to make any kind of profit, but to enjoy
himself seeing the world." [. . .]

## 8. Pulci (1432–1484): *Morgante*

Then he departed, carried away by rage,
and decided to travel into heathen territory;
and while he rode, along the way
he kept recalling the traitor Ganelon;
and riding from one straying path to another,
he found an abbey in a wilderness,
amid dark places and distant lands,
on the border between Christians and heathens.

The abbot was named Chiaramonte,
and was descended from the line of Angrante.
Above the abbey was a high mountain
where several fierce giants lived,
one of whom was named Passamonte;
the second, Alabastro; and the third, Morgante;
with sure slings they hurled stones from the heights,
making some attack every day.

The monks were unable to leave
the monastery for either firewood or water.
Orlando knocked, but they refused to open

fin ch'all'abate alla fine pur piacque.
Entrato drento, cominciava a dire
come Colui che di Maria già nacque
adora, ed era cristian battezzato
e come egli era alla badia arrivato.

Disse l'abate: —Il ben venuto sia;
di quel ch'io ho, volentier ti daremo,
poi che tu credi al Figliuol di Maria;
e la cagion, cavalier, ti diremo,
acciò che non la imputi villania,
perché all'entrar resistenza facemo,
e non ti volle aprir quel monachetto;
così intervien chi vive con sospetto.

Quand'io ci venni al principio abitare
queste montagne, ben che sieno oscure,
come tu vedi, pur si potea stare
sanza sospetto, ché l'eron sicure;
sol dalle fiere t'avevi a guardare;
fernoci spesso di strane paure.
Or ci bisogna, se vogliamo starci,
dalle bestie dimestiche guardarci.

Queste ci fan più tosto stare a segno;
sonci appariti tre fieri giganti,
non so di qual paese o di qual regno;
ma molto son feroci tutti quanti.
La forza e 'l malvoler giunta allo 'ngegno,
sai che può tutto, e noi non siam bastanti;
questi perturban sì l'orazion nostra,
ch'io non so più che far, s'altri nol mostra.

Gli antichi padri nostri nel deserto,
se le loro opre sante erano e giuste,
del ben servir da Dio n'avean buon merto;
né creder sol vivessin di locuste;
piovea dal ciel la manna, questo è certo;
ma qui convien che spesso assaggi e guste
sassi, che piovon di sopra quel monte,
che gettano Alabastro e Passamonte.

Il terzo, che è Morgante, assai più fiero,
isveglie e pini e faggi e cerri e gli oppi,

until the abbot finally consented.
Entering, he began to say
that he worshipped the One born of Mary long ago
and was a baptized Christian,
and he told how he had reached the abbey.

The abbot said: "Welcome!
Of what I possess we shall gladly give to you
because you believe in the Son of Mary;
and we shall tell you, O knight, the reason
(so you don't tax us with rudeness)
why we resist having anyone enter,
and why that monk refused to let you in;
this is what happens to those who live in fear.

"When I first came to live
in these mountains, though they're dark
as you can see, nevertheless it was possible to be here
without fear, because they were safe;
you had to protect yourself from wild animals only,
which often gave us unusual scares.
Now, if we want to remain here, we have to
protect ourselves from the domestic animals.

"It's they, instead, that make us toe the mark;
three fierce giants have appeared,
I don't know from what land or realm,
but they're all very ferocious.
Strength and ill will, combined with intelligence, as you know,
are capable of anything, and there aren't enough of us;
those giants disturb our prayers so badly
that I no longer know what to do, unless someone shows me.

"Our ancient forefathers in the wilderness,
if their actions were holy and just,
had a proper reward from God for serving Him well;
and don't think they lived on locusts only:
manna rained from heaven, it's a certainty;
but here you often have to taste and sample
stones that rain down from high on that mountain,
hurled by Alabastro and Passamonte.

"The third giant, Morgante, much fiercer,
uproots pines, beeches, Turkey oaks, and maples,

e gettagli insin qui, questo è pur vero;
non posso far, che d'ira non iscoppi—.
Mentre che parlan così in cimitero,
un sasso par che Rondel quasi sgroppi,
che da' giganti giù venne da alto,
tanto che e' prese sotto il tetto un salto.

—Tirati drento, cavalier, per Dio,—
disse l'abate —ché la manna casca.—
Rispose Orlando: —Caro abate mio,
costui non vuol che 'l mio caval più pasca;
vego che lo guarrebbe del restio;
quel sasso par che di buon braccio nasca—.
Rispose il santo padre: —Io non t'inganno,
credo che 'l monte un giorno gitteranno—. [. . .]

## 9. Boiardo (1441–1494): *Orlando innamorato*

Signori e cavallier che ve adunati
per odir cose dilettose e nove,
state attenti e quieti, ed ascoltati
la bella istoria che 'l mio canto muove;
e vedereti i gesti smisurati,
l'alta fatica e le mirabil prove
che fece il franco Orlando per amore
nel tempo del re Carlo imperatore.

Non vi par già, signor, meraviglioso
odir cantar de Orlando inamorato,
ché qualunche nel mondo è più orgoglioso,
è da Amor vinto, al tutto subiugato;
né forte braccio, né ardire animoso,
né scudo o maglia, né brando affilato,
né altra possanza può mai far diffesa,
che al fin non sia da Amor battuta e presa.

Questa novella è nota a poca gente,
perché Turpino istesso la nascose,
credendo forse a quel conte valente
esser le sue scritture dispettose,
poi che contra ad Amor pur fu perdente

and hurls them all the way here, that's true, too;
I can't help bursting with anger."
While they were saying this in the graveyard,
there came a stone that nearly shattered Rondel's rump,
thrown down by the giants high above
so hard that it rebounded under the roof.

"Get inside for God's sake, O knight,"
said the abbot, "because the manna is falling!"
Orlando replied: "My dear abbot,
this fellow doesn't want my horse to graze anymore;
I see that he'd cure him of jibbing;
that stone seems to have come from a strong arm."
The holy father replied: "I won't deceive you:
I think they'll hurl the whole mountain some day!" [. . .]

## 9. Boiardo (1441–1494): *Orlando in Love*

Lords and knights assembled here
to listen to delightful and strange matters,
be attentive and still, and hear
the fine story that inspires my song;
and you'll see the titanic exploits,
the enormous labors, and the wondrous deeds
performed by the Frenchman Orlando for the sake of love
in the days of the Emperor Charlemagne.

Let it not seem unusual to you now, my lord,
if you hear a song about Orlando in love,
because the proudest man in the world
is conquered by Love, completely subjugated;
neither strength of arm, nor courageous daring,
neither shield or chainmail, nor sharp sword,
nor any other power can ever afford such protection
that it isn't finally beaten and captured by Love.

This story is known to very few,
because Turpin himself concealed it,
perhaps in the belief that that valiant count
would be angered by his writings,
since that same man lost out to Love

colui che vinse tutte l'altre cose:
dico di Orlando, il cavalliero adatto.
Non più parole ormai, veniamo al fatto.

La vera istoria di Turpin ragiona
che regnava in la terra de Oriente,
di là da l'India, un gran re di corona,
di stato e de ricchezze sì potente
e sì gagliardo de la sua persona,
che tutto il mondo stimava niente:
Gradasso nome avea quello amirante,
che ha cor di drago e membra di gigante.

E sì come egli avviene a' gran signori,
che pur quel voglion che non ponno avere,
e, quanto son difficultà maggiori
la desiata cosa ad ottenere,
pongono il regno spesso in grandi errori,
né posson quel che voglion possedere;
così bramava quel pagan gagliardo
sol Durindana e 'l bon destrier Baiardo.

Unde per tutto il suo gran tenitoro
fece la gente ne l'arme asembrare,
ché ben sapeva lui che per tesoro
né il brando, né il corsier puote acquistare;
duo mercadanti erano coloro
che vendean le sue merce troppo care:
però destina di passare in Franza
ed acquistarle con sua gran possanza.

Cento cinquanta millia cavallieri
elesse di sua gente tutta quanta:
né questi adoperar facea pensieri,
perché lui solo a combatter se avanta
contra al re Carlo ed a tutti guerreri
che son credenti in nostra fede santa;
e lui soletto vincere e disfare
quanto il sol vede e quanto cinge il mare.

Lassiam costor che a vella se ne vano,
che sentirete poi ben la sua gionta;
e ritornamo in Francia a Carlo Mano,

who had conquered all other things:
I mean Orlando, the accomplished knight.
No further words: let's come to deeds.

Turpin's true history relates
that in the lands of the Orient, beyond India,
there reigned a mighty crowned king
so powerful in condition and wealth
and so vigorous in body
that he counted the rest of the world as nought:
that emir was named Gradasso;
he had a dragon's heart and a giant's limbs.

And as is the case with great lords,
who always want what they can't have
and, the greater the difficulties
in acquiring the thing they desire,
the more often they place their realm in great peril
but can't possess what they want,
thus that vigorous heathen longed for
nothing but Durindana and the good steed Baiardo.

Therefore throughout his extensive territory
he had the people assemble in arms,
for he was well aware that he couldn't
gain either the sword or the steed for money;
he'd be dealing with two "merchants"
who'd charge too much for their "goods"!
And so he determined to invade France
and acquire them with his great force.

A hundred fifty thousand horsemen
he chose out of all his people;
but he wasn't planning to use them,
because he boasted of fighting alone
against Charlemagne and every warrior
who believed in our holy religion;
he by himself would conquer and destroy
all that the sun beholds and the sea girds.

Let's now leave them sailing across the sea,
for later on you'll definitely hear of their arrival,
and let's return to Charlemagne in France,

che e soi magni baron provede e conta;
imperò che ogni principe cristiano,
ogni duca e signore a lui se afronta
per una giostra che avea ordinata
allor di maggio, alla pasqua rosata.

Erano in corte tutti i paladini
per onorar quella festa gradita,
e da ogni parte, da tutti i confini
era in Parigi una gente infinita.
Eranvi ancora molti Saracini,
perché corte reale era bandita,
ed era ciascaduno assigurato,
che non sia traditore o rinegato. [. . .]

## 10. Lorenzo de' Medici (1449–1492): 2 liriche

(A) Chi non è innamorato
esca di questo ballo,
ché saria fallo    a stare in sì bel lato.

Se alcuno è qui, che non conosca Amore,
parta di questo loco;
perch'esser non potria mai gentil core
chi non sente quel foco.
Se alcun ne sente poco,
sì le sue fiamme accenda
che ognun lo intenda,    e non sarà scacciato.

Amor in mezzo a questo ballo stia;
e chi gli è servo, intorno.
E, se alcuno ha sospetto o gelosia,
non faccia qui soggiorno;
se non, che avrebbe scorno.
Ognun ci s'innamori,
o esca fuori    del loco tanto ornato.

Se alcuna per vergogna si ritiene
di non s'innamorare,
vergognerassi, s'ella pensa bene,
più tosto a non lo fare:
non è vergogna amare

who was reviewing and counting his chief barons;
because every Christian prince,
every duke and lord was presenting himself to him
at a joust he had ordered held
then in May, at Pentecost.

All the paladins were at his court
to do honor to that delightful festival,
and from everywhere, from every border
an infinite number had assembled in Paris.
Many Saracens were there, too,
because a royal assemblage had been proclaimed,
for which everyone had a safe conduct
except for traitors or renegades. [. . .]

## 10. Lorenzo de' Medici (1449–1492): 2 lyric poems

(A) Let whoever is not in love
leave this dance,
for it would be wrong    for him to be in such a fine place.

If there's anyone here unfamiliar with Love,
let him depart from this spot;
because there could never be a noble heart
that didn't feel that blaze.
If anyone feels too little of it,
let him ignite his flames so brightly
that all will notice,    and he won't be driven away.

Let Love be in the midst of this dance,
with all his servants around him.
And if anyone has suspicions or jealousy,
let him not linger here;
otherwise, he'd be held in scorn.
Let everyone here fall in love,
or depart    from this highly decorated place.

If any lady, because ashamed, is refraining
from falling in love,
if she considers it well, she'll be ashamed,
on the contrary, *not* to do so:
it's no shame to love

chi di servirti agogna;
saria vergogna,    chi gli fusse ingrato.

Se alcuna ce ne fussi tanto vile,
che lasci per paura,
pensi bene che un core alto e gentile
queste cose non cura.
Non ha dato Natura
tanta bellezza a voi,
acciò che poi    sia il tempo male usato.

## (B) Trionfo di Bacco e Arianna

Quant'è bella giovinezza,
che si fugge tuttavia!
Chi vuol esser lieto, sia:
di doman non c'è certezza.

Quest'è Bacco e Arianna,
belli, e l'un dell'altro ardenti:
perché 'l tempo fugge e inganna,
sempre insieme stan contenti.
Queste ninfe ed altre genti
sono allegre tuttavia.
Chi vuol esser lieto, sia:
di doman non c'è certezza.

Questi lieti satiretti,
delle ninfe innamorati,
per caverne e per boschetti
han lor posto cento agguati;
or da Bacco riscaldati,
ballon, salton tuttavia.
Chi vuol esser lieto, sia:
di doman non c'è certezza.

Queste ninfe anche hanno caro
da lor esser ingannate:
non può fare a Amor riparo,
se non gente rozze e ingrate:
ora insieme mescolate
suonon, canton tuttavia.
Chi vuol esser lieto, sia:
di doman non c'è certezza.

a man who yearns to be your humble servant;
it would be a shame   to be ungrateful to him.

If any lady here were so base
as to shun love out of fear,
let her reflect that a lofty, noble heart
pays no heed to such things.
Nature hasn't given
so much beauty to you women
for you to go   and use the time badly.

## (B) Triumph of Bacchus and Ariadne

How beautiful is youth,
which is constantly fleeting!
Let all who wish to be happy, be so:
there's no certainty about tomorrow.

Here come Bacchus and Ariadne,
handsome, yearning for each other:
because time flies and disappoints us,
they're always happy together.
These nymphs and other folk
are constantly cheerful.
Let all who wish to be happy, be so:
there's no certainty about tomorrow.

These merry young satyrs,
in love with the nymphs,
in caves and in groves
have laid a hundred ambushes for them;
now heated by Bacchus,
they constantly dance and leap.
Let all who wish to be happy, be so:
there's no certainty about tomorrow.

These nymphs, too, enjoy
being deceived by them:
only those oppose Love
who are coarse and ungrateful:
now the nymphs mingled together
play music and sing constantly.
Let all who wish to be happy, be so:
there's no certainty about tomorrow.

Questa soma, che vien drieto
sopra l'asino, è Sileno:
così vecchio è ebbro e lieto,
già di carne e d'anni pieno;
se non può star ritto, almeno
ride e gode tuttavia.
Chi vuol esser lieto, sia:
di doman non c'è certezza.

Mida vien drieto a costoro:
ciò che tocca, oro diventa.
E che giova aver tesoro,
s'altri poi non si contenta?
Che dolcezza vuoi che senta
chi ha sete tuttavia?
Chi vuol esser lieto, sia:
di doman non c'è certezza.

Ciascun apra ben gli orecchi:
di doman nessun si paschi;
oggi siàn, giovani e vecchi,
lieti ognun, femmine e maschi;
ogni tristo pensier caschi;
facciam festa tuttavia.
Chi vuol esser lieto, sia:
di doman non c'è certezza.

Donne e giovinetti amanti,
viva Bacco e viva Amore!
Ciascun suoni, balli e canti!
Arda di dolcezza il core!
Non fatica, non dolore!
Quel c'ha a esser, convien sia.
Chi vuol esser lieto, sia:
di doman non c'è certezza.

## 11. Poliziano (1454–1494): 2 liriche

(A) Udite, selve, mie dolce parole,
poi che la ninfa mia udir non vuole.

La bella ninfa è sorda al mio lamento

This bulky fellow, following after
on the donkey, is Silenus:
old as he is, he's drunk and happy,
already full of flesh and years;
if he can't sit straight, at least
he's constantly laughing and having fun
Let all who wish to be happy, be so:
there's no certainty about tomorrow.

Midas is coming behind them:
whatever he touches turns to gold.
And what's the use of gaining a treasure
if you aren't pleased afterward?
What sweetness do you expect a man to taste
if he's constantly thirsty?
Let all who wish to be happy, be so:
there's no certainty about tomorrow.

Let everyone open his ears wide:
let no one be contented with tomorrow;
young and old, women and men,
let's all be happy today;
let every sad thought drop away;
let's celebrate constantly.
Let all who wish to be happy, be so:
there's no certainty about tomorrow.

Ladies and amorous young men,
long live Bacchus, long live Love!
Let everyone play music, dance, and sing!
Let each heart blaze with pleasure!
No weariness, no sorrow!
What must be, let it happen!
Let all who wish to be happy, be so:
there's no certainty about tomorrow.

## 11. Poliziano (1454–1494): 2 lyric poems

(A) Hear, O forests, my sweet words,
since my nymph refuses to hear them!

The lovely nymph is deaf to my lament

e 'l suon di nostra fistula non cura;
di ciò si lagna el mio cornuto armento,
né vuol bagnare il grifo in acqua pura;
non vuol toccar la tenera verdura,
tanto del suo pastor gl'incresce e duole.
   Udite, selve, mie dolce parole,
poi che la ninfa mia udir non vuole.

Ben si cura l'armento del pastore,
la ninfa non si cura dello amante;
la bella ninfa che di sasso ha 'l core,
anzi di ferro, anzi l'ha di diamante:
ella fugge da me sempre davante,
come agnella dal lupo fuggir suole.
   Udite, selve, mie dolce parole,
poi che la ninfa mia udir non vuole.

Digli, zampogna mia, come via fugge
cogli anni insieme suo belleza snella;
e digli come 'l tempo ne distrugge,
né l'età persa mai si rinnovella;
digli che sappi usar sua forma bella,
ché sempre mai non son rose e viole.
   Udite, selve, mie dolce parole,
poi che la ninfa mia udir non vuole.

Portate, venti, questi dolci versi
drento all'orecchie della ninfa mia:
dite quant'io per lei lacrime versi,
e lei pregate che crudel non sia;
dite che la mia vita fugge via
e si consuma come brina al sole.
   Udite, selve, mie dolce parole,
poi che la ninfa mia udir non vuole.

(B) I' mi trovai, fanciulle, un bel mattino
di mezo maggio, in un verde giardino.

Erano intorno violette e gigli
fra l'erba verde e vaghi fior novelli
azurri gialli candidi e vermigli:
ond'io porsi la mano a còr di quelli
per adornar e mie' biondi capelli

and doesn't heed the sound of our panpipes;
my horned flock complains about this,
and they won't moisten their muzzles in the pure water;
they won't touch the tender green grass,
so greatly do they pity and grieve for their shepherd.
    Hear, O forests, my sweet words,
since my nymph refuses to hear them!

The flock is concerned for its shepherd,
but the nymph isn't concerned for her suitor,
that lovely nymph whose heart is of stone—
no, of iron! No, of adamant!
She always flees from my presence,
as a she-lamb is wont to flee the wolf.
    Hear, O forests, my sweet words,
since my nymph refuses to hear them!

Tell her, my panpipes, that her lithe beauty
is fleeting away together with the years;
and tell her that time destroys us,
and that lost youth is never made new again;
tell her to make wise use of her beauty,
because roses and violets don't last forever.
    Hear, O forests, my sweet words,
since my nymph refuses to hear them!

Winds, carry these sweet verses
to my nymph's ears:
tell her how many tears I'm shedding for her,
and beseech her not to be cruel;
say that my life is fleeting away
and being consumed like hoarfrost in the sun.
    Hear, O forests, my sweet words,
since my nymph refuses to hear them!

(B) I found myself, girls, one fine morning
in mid-May in a green garden.

There were violets and lilies round about
amid the green grass, and lovely new flowers:
blue, yellow, white, and red.
So that I extended my hand to pick some of them
to adorn my blonde hair

e cinger di grillanda el vago crino.
   I' mi trovai, fanciulle . . .

Ma poi ch'i' ebbi pien di fiori un lembo,
vidi le rose, e non pur d'un colore;
io corsi allor per empier tutto el grembo,
perch'era sì soave il loro odore,
che tutto mi senti' destar el core
di dolce voglia e d'un piacer divino.
   I' mi trovai, fanciulle . . .

I' posi mente: quelle rose allora
mai non vi potre' dir quant'eran belle:
quale scoppiava della boccia ancora;
qual erano un po' passe e qual novelle.
Amor mi disse allor: —Va, cò' di quelle
che più vedi fiorite in sullo spino—.
   I' mi trovai, fanciulle . . .

Quando la rosa ogni suo foglia spande,
quando è più bella, quando è più gradita,
allora è buona a mettere in ghirlande,
prima che sua belleza sia fuggita:
sicché, fanciulle, mentre è più fiorita,
cogliàn la bella rosa del giardino.
   I' mi trovai, fanciulle . . .


## 12. Sannazaro (1455–1530): *Arcadia*

Sovra una verde riva
di chiare e lucide onde,
in un bel bosco di fioretti adorno,
vidi di bianca oliva
ornato e d'altre fronde
un pastor, che 'n su l'alba appiè d'un orno
cantava il terzo giorno
del mese inanzi aprile;
a cui li vaghi ucelli
di sopra gli arboscelli
con voce rispondean dolce e gentile;
et ei rivolto al sole,
dicea queste parole:

and encircle my lovely hair with a garland.
  I found myself, girls . . .

But after I had filled a hem of my skirt with flowers,
I saw the roses, and not of one color only;
then I ran over to fill my entire lap,
because their fragrance was so sweet
that I felt my whole heart awakening
with sweet desire and a divine pleasure.
  I found myself, girls . . .

I reflected: I could never tell you
how lovely those roses were then;
some were still bursting from their buds;
some were a little withered and some fresh.
Then Love said to me: "Go, pick some of those
which you see blossoming most fully on the thorns."
  I found myself, girls . . .

When the rose opens all its petals wide,
when it's loveliest, when it's most delightful,
then it's fit to be put in garlands,
before its beauty has fled:
and so, girls, while it's at its peak of bloom
let's gather the lovely rose in the garden.
  I found myself, girls . . .


## 12. Sannazaro (1455–1530): *Arcadia*

On a green bank
of bright, transparent waters,
in a lovely grove adorned with young flowers,
I saw, decorated with silvery olive
and other leafy branches,
a shepherd, who at dawn at the foot of an ash
was celebrating the third day
of the month that precedes April;
to him the pretty birds
that perched in the bushes
responded in sweet, gentle tones,
and he, addressing the sun,
spoke as follows:

"Apri l'uscio per tempo,
leggiadro almo pastore,
e fa vermiglio il ciel col chiaro raggio;
mostrane inanzi tempo
con natural colore
un bel fiorito e dilettoso maggio;
tien più alto il viaggio,
acciò che tua sorella
più che l'usato dorma,
e poi per la sua orma
se ne vegna pian pian ciascuna stella;
ché, se ben ti ramenti,
guardasti i bianchi armenti.

Valli vicine e rupi,
cipressi, alni et abeti,
porgete orecchie a le mie basse rime;
e non teman de' lupi
gli agnelli mansueti,
ma torni il mondo a quelle usanze prime.
Fioriscan per le cime
i cerri in bianche rose,
e per le spine dure
pendan l'uve mature;
suden di mèl le querce alte e nodose,
e le fontane intatte
corran di puro latte.

Nascan erbette e fiori,
e li fieri animali
lassen le lor asprezze e i petti crudi;
vegnan li vaghi Amori
senza fiammelle o strali,
scherzando inseme pargoletti e 'gnudi;
poi con tutti lor studi
canten le bianche Ninfe,
e con abiti strani
salten Fauni e Silvani;
ridan li prati e le correnti linfe,
e non si vedan oggi
nuvoli intorno ai poggi.

"Open your gates early,
charming, excellent shepherd,
and redden the sky with your bright beams;
show us ahead of time
with natural color
a lovely, blossoming, delightful spring;
prolong your journey
so that the moon, your sister,
sleeps longer than usual,
and then on her traces
each star comes out very softly;
for, if you remember well,
you once guarded white flocks.

"Nearby valleys and crags,
cypresses, alders, and firs,
lend an ear to my humble rhymes;
and let not the meek lambs
fear the wolves,
but let the world return to its pristine peace.
On the hilltops let the Turkey oaks
bloom with white roses,
and on the harsh brambles
let ripened grapes hang;
let the lofty, knotty oaks sweat honey,
and let the untouched springs
flow with pure milk!

"Let young herbs and flowers shoot,
and let the wild animals
abandon their harshness and cruelty of heart;
let the pretty Cupids come
without tongues of flame or arrows,
sporting together like naked babies;
then with all their diligence
let the white nymphs sing,
and in bizarre attire
let fauns and satyrs leap;
let the meadows and the flowing waters smile,
and let no clouds be seen today
around the hillocks!

In questo dì giocondo
nacque l'alma beltade,
e le virtuti raquistaro albergo;
per questo il cieco mondo
conobbe castitade,
la qual tant'anni avea gittata a tergo;
per questo io scrivo e vergo
i faggi in ogni bosco;
tal che omai non è pianta
che non chiami 'Amaranta',
quella ch'adolcir basta ogni mio tòsco;
quella per cui sospiro,
per cui piango e m'adiro.

Mentre per questi monti
andran le fiere errando,
e gli alti pini aràn pungenti foglie;
mentre li vivi fonti
correran murmurando
ne l'alto mar che con amor li accoglie;
mentre fra speme e doglie
vivran gli amanti in terra;
sempre fia noto il nome,
le man, gli occhi e le chiome
di quella che mi fa sì lunga guerra;
per cui quest'aspra amara
vita m'è dolce e cara.

Per cortesia, canzon, tu pregherai
quel dì fausto et ameno
che sia sempre sereno".

## 13. Machiavelli (1469–1527): *Il principe*

Scendendo appresso alle altre preallegate qualità, dico che ciascuno
principe debbe desiderare di essere tenuto pietoso e non crudele:
nondimanco debbe avvertire di non usare male questa pietà. Era
tenuto Cesare Borgia crudele: nondimanco quella sua crudeltà aveva
racconcia la Romagna, unitola, ridottola in pace e in fede. Il che se si
considerrà bene, si vedrà quello essere stato molto più pietoso che il
populo fiorentino, il quale, per fuggire el nome del crudele, lasciò de-

"On this happy day
that excellent beauty was born
in whom the virtues found lodging;
thereby the blind world
learned the meaning of chastity,
which for so many years it had cast aside;
therefore I inscribe and write on
the beeches in every grove;
so that by now there's no tree
that doesn't proclaim, 'Amaranta,'
the woman able to sweeten every poison for me;
the woman for whom I sigh,
for whom I weep and get enraged.

"As long as through these mountains
the wild beasts will go roaming,
and the lofty pines will have sharp needles;
for as long as the living streams
will flow with a murmur
into the deep sea that welcomes them lovingly;
as long as lovers will live on earth
suspended between hope and grief:
there will always be known the name,
the hands, the eyes, and the tresses
of the woman at war with me for so long;
on whose account this harsh, bitter
life is sweet and dear to me.

"I beg of you, my song, to ask
that auspicious, pleasant day
to be always unclouded."


## 13. Machiavelli (1469–1527): *The Prince*

Turning now to the other above-mentioned qualities, I say that every
prince should wish to be deemed compassionate, not cruel. Nevertheless,
he should take care not to make bad use of this compassion. Cesare
Borgia was deemed cruel, and yet that cruelty of his had restored
Romagna, unified it, and reduced it to peace and loyalty. If this is considered rightly, it will be seen that he was much more compassionate than
the people of Florence, who, to avoid the name of cruelty, allowed Pistoia

struggere Pistoia. Debbe pertanto uno principe non si curare della infamia di crudele, per tenere li sudditi sua uniti e in fede: perché con pochissimi esempli e' sarà più pietoso che quelli e quali per troppa pietà lasciono seguire e disordini, di che ne nasca occisioni o rapine: perché queste sogliano offendere una universalità intera, e quelle esecuzioni che vengano dal principe offendano uno particulare. E intra tutti e principi, al principe nuovo è impossibile fuggire el nome del crudele, per essere li stati nuovi pieni di periculi. E Virgilio nella bocca di Dido dice:

*Res dura, et regni novitas me talia cogunt*
*moliri, et late fines custode tueri.*

Nondimanco debbe essere grave al credere e al muoversi, né si fare paura da se stesso, e procedere in modo temperato con prudenzia e umanità, che la troppa confidenzia non lo facci incauto e la troppa diffidenzia non lo renda intollerabile.

Nasce da questo una disputa: s'elli è meglio essere amato che temuto o e converso. Respondesi che si vorrebbe essere l'uno e l'altro; ma perché gli è difficile accozzarli insieme, è molto più sicuro essere temuto che amato, quando si abbia a mancare dell'uno de' dua. Perché degli uomini si può dire questo generalmente: che sieno ingrati, volubili, simulatori e dissimulatori, fuggitori de' pericoli, cupidi di guadagno; e mentre fai loro bene, sono tutti tua, òfferoni el sangue, la roba, la vita, e figliuoli, come di sopra dissi, quando il bisogno è discosto; ma quando ti si appressa e' si rivoltano. E quel principe che si è tutto fondato in sulle parole loro, trovandosi nudo di altre preparazioni, ruina; perché le amicizie che si acquistano col prezzo e non con grandezza e nobiltà di animo, si meritano, ma non le si hanno, e a' tempi non si possono spendere. E li uomini hanno meno respetto a offendere uno che si facci amare che uno che si facci temere; perché l'amore è tenuto da uno vinculo di obligo, il quale, per essere li uomini tristi, da ogni occasione di propria utilità è rotto; ma il timore è tenuto da una paura di pena che non ti abbandona mai.

Debbe nondimanco el principe farsi temere in modo che, se non acquista lo amore, che fugga l'odio; perché può molto bene stare insieme essere temuto e non odiato: il che farà sempre quando si astenga dalla roba de' sua cittadini e de' sua sudditi e dalle donne loro; e quando pure li bisognassi precedere contro al sangue di alcuno, farlo quando vi sia iustificazione conveniente e causa manifesta; ma sopra tutto astenersi dalla roba d'altri; perché li uomini sdimenticano più presto la morte del padre che la perdita del patrimonio. Dipoi, le ca-

to be destroyed. Thus, a prince should not worry about the bad name of cruelty if he can keep his subjects united and loyal: because by means of a very few exemplary punishments he will be more compassionate than all those who from an excess of compassion allow disorders to occur which give rise to killings or pillage: because these usually harm an entire community, whereas those executions ordered by a prince affect only individuals. And among all princes, it's impossible for a new prince to avoid a reputation for cruelty, because new states are full of dangers. And Vergil, speaking through Dido, says:

*The hard circumstances and the newness of the realm compel me*
*to make such arrangements and guard my borders far and wide.*

All the same, he must be circumspect in beliefs and actions, and mustn't get frightened himself, and must proceed temperately, prudently, and humanely, so that overconfidence doesn't make him incautious and excessive distrust doesn't make him unbearable.

A dispute arises from this: whether it's better to be loved or to be feared, or vice versa. The answer is that one would like to be both; but because it's difficult to combine them, it's much safer to be feared than to be loved, if one of the two must be given up. Because this can be said of men in general: they're ungrateful, fickle, feigners and dissimulators, they shun dangers and are avid for gain; and as long as you benefit them they're all yours; they offer you their blood, property, life, and children, as I said earlier, when the need has been removed; but when it nears you they change tack. And the prince who has completely relied on their word and finds himself devoid of other defenses, is ruined; because friendships acquired by means of money and not through grandeur and nobility of spirit, are purchased but not securely possessed, and at times can't be used. And men have fewer scruples in harming one who makes himself loved than one who makes himself feared; because love is held by a moral bond which, people being scoundrels, is broken on every occasion of personal interest; whereas fear is maintained by a fear of punishment which never deserts you.

All the same, the prince must make himself feared in such a way that, if he doesn't gain his subjects' love, at least he avoids their hatred; because being feared and not being hated can very readily be combined, and they always will be if the prince keeps his hands off his citizens' and subjects' property and their women; and even if he should need to proceed against someone's family, he should do it when there's appropriate justification for it and a clear-cut case for it; but above all he must keep his hands off others' property; because men forget their father's death

gioni del tòrre la roba non mancono mai; e sempre colui che comincia a vivere con rapina truova cagione di occupare quel d'altri; e per adverso, contro al sangue sono più rare e mancono più presto.

Ma quando el principe è con gli eserciti e ha in governo moltitudine di soldati, allora al tutto è necessario non si curare del nome del crudele: perché sanza questo nome non si tenne mai esercito unito né disposto ad alcuna fazione. Intra le mirabili azioni di Annibale si connumera questa, che avendo uno esercito grossissimo, misto di infinite generazioni di uomini, condotto a militare in terre aliene, non vi surgessi mai alcuna dissensione né infra loro né contro al principe, così nella cattiva come nella sua buona fortuna. Il che non poté nascere da altro che da quella sua inumana crudeltà, la quale insieme con infinite sua virtù lo fece sempre nel conspetto de' suoi soldati venerando e terribile; e sanza quella, a fare quello effetto le altre sua virtù non li bastavano. E li scrittori in questo poco considerati, dall'una parte ammirano questa sua azione e dall'altra dannono la principale cagione di essa.

E che sia vero che l'altre sua virtù non sarebbano bastate, si può considerare in Scipione, rarissimo non solamente ne' tempi sua ma in tutta la memoria delle cose che si sanno, dal quale gli eserciti suoi in Ispagna si rebellorono. Il che non nacque da altro che dalla troppa sua pietà, la quale aveva data a' suoi soldati più licenzia che alla disciplina militare non si conveniva. La qual cosa li fu da Fabio Massimo in Senato rimproverata, e chiamato da lui corruttore della romana milizia. E Locrensi, sendo stati da uno legato di Scipione destrutti, non furono da lui vendicati, né la insolenzia di quello legato corretta, nascendo tutto da quella sua natura facile; talmente che volendolo alcuno in Senato escusare disse come egli erano di molti uomini che sapevano meglio non errare che correggere li errori. La qual natura arebbe col tempo violato la fama e la gloria di Scipione se elli avessi con essa perseverato nello imperio, ma vivendo sotto el governo del Senato, questa sua qualità dannosa non solum si nascose ma li fu a gloria.

Concludo adunque, tornando allo essere temuto e amato, che amando li uomini a posta loro e temendo a posta del principe, debbe uno principe savio fondarsi in su quello che è suo, non in su quello che è d'altri: debbe solamente ingegnarsi di fuggire l'odio, come è detto.

sooner than the loss of their inheritance. Next, reasons for taking away property are never lacking; and a man who begins to live by pillaging always finds a reason to seize what belongs to others; while, on the other hand, reasons for attacking family members are rarer and sooner lacking.

But when the prince is with his army and is commanding a large number of soldiers, then it's absolutely necessary not to worry about being called cruel; because without that reputation no army was ever held together or readied for any battle. Among the wonderful accomplishments of Hannibal is counted this one: that, though he had a vast army, composed of an infinite number of races, and brought to fight on foreign soil, there never arose any dissension either among themselves or against their prince, in times of either bad or good fortune. This cannot be ascribed to anything but his inhuman cruelty, which, together with his numerous merits, always made him respected and feared in the sight of his soldiers; without it, his other merits were insufficient to achieve such results. And historians, thoughtless in this respect, admire his accomplishments on the one hand, but, on the other, condemn the chief reason for them.

And the truth of the statement that his other merits wouldn't have sufficed can be seen in the case of Scipio—outstanding not only in his own day but in all recorded history known to us—whose army mutinied in Spain. This was due to nothing but his excessive compassion, which had given his soldiers greater license than was consistent with military discipline. Fabius Maximus reproached him for this in the senate, calling him a corruptor of the Roman army. And the people of Locri, when they were ruined by one of Scipio's commanders, weren't avenged by him, nor was that commander's insolence punished; all this arose from that indulgence of his; so that someone in the senate, wishing to apologize for him, said that many men were better able to avoid mistakes than to correct them. In time this indulgence would have defiled Scipio's fame and glory, had he persisted in it during the empire, but since he lived under the rule of the senate, this damaging trait of his not only was kept under wraps, but even redounded to his credit.

And so, returning to the question of being feared or loved, my conclusion is that, since men love at their own will but fear at the prince's will, a wise prince should base himself on that which belongs to him, not that which belongs to others: he should merely strive to avoid being hated, as I've said.

## 14. Bembo (1470–1547): *Gli Asolani*

"Hanno tra le loro più secrete memorie gli antichi maestri delle sante cose, essere una Reina in quelle isole, che io dico, Fortunate, bellissima e di maraviglioso aspetto e ornata di cari e preziosi vestiri e sempre giovane. La qual marito non vuole già e servasi vergine tutto tempo, ma bene d'essere amata e vagheggiata si contenta. E a quegli, che più l'amano, ella maggior guiderdone dà de' loro amori, e convenevole, secondo la loro affezione, agli altri. Ma ella di tutti in questa guisa ne fa pruova. Perciò che venuto che ciascun l'è davanti, che è secondo che essi sono dallei fatti chiamare or uno or altro, essa, con una verghetta toccatigli, ne gli manda via. E questi, incontanente che del palagio della Reina sono usciti, s'addormentano, e così dormono infin attanto che essa gli fa risvegliare. Ritornano adunque costoro davanti la Reina un'altra volta risvegliati, e i sogni che hanno fatti dormendo porta ciascuno scritti nella fronte tali, quali fatti gli hanno né più né meno, i quali essa legge prestamente. E coloro i cui sogni ella vede essere stati solamente di cacciagioni, di pescagioni, di cavagli, di selve, di fiere, essa da sé gli scaccia e mandagli a stare così vegghiando tra quelle fiere, con le quali essi dormendo si sono di star sognati, perciò che dice che, se essi amata l'avessero, essi almeno di lei si sarebbono sognati qualche volta, il che poscia che essi non hanno fatto giamai, vuole che vadano e sì si vivano con le lor fiere. Quegli altri poi a' quali è paruto ne' loro sogni di mercatantare o di governare le famiglie e le comunanze o di fare somiglianti cose, tuttavia poco della Reina ricordandosi, essa gli fa essere altresì quale mercatante, quale cittadino, quale anziano nelle sue città, di cure e di pensieri gravandogli e poco di loro curandosi parimente. Ma quelli, che si sono sognati con lei, essa gli tiene nella sua corte a stare e a ragionar seco tra suoni e canti e sollazzi d'infinito contento, chi più presso di sé e chi meno, secondo che essi con lei sognando più o meno si sono dimorati ciascuno. Ma io per aventura, Lavinello, oggimai troppo lungamente ti dimoro, il quale più voglia déi avere o forse mestiero di ritornarti alla tua compagnia, che di più udirmi. Senza che oltre acciò a te gravoso potrà essere lo indugiare a più alto sole la partita, che oggimai tutto il cielo ha riscaldato e vassi tuttavia rinforzando". "A me voglia né mestiero fa punto che sia, Padre", diss'io "ancora di ritornarmi, e dove a voi noioso non sia il ragionare, sicuramente niuna cosa mi ricorda che io facessi giamai così volentieri, come ora volentieri v'ascolto. Né di sole che sormonti vi pigliate pensiero, poscia che io altro che a scendere non

## 14. Bembo (1470–1547): *The Asolo Discourses*

"The ancient masters of holy matters preserve among their most secret memories that there is a queen in those isles called Fortunate, as I say, who is very beautiful and of a wonderful appearance and adorned with expensive and precious attire and always young. She wants no husband and keeps herself always a virgin, but she *is* pleased to be loved and admired. And to those men who love her most she gives the greatest reward for their love, and gives the others a suitable reward in proportion to their affection. But she tests them all in the following way. As soon as each one has come before her (in consequence of their having been summoned by her individually), she touches them with a wand and dismisses them. And as soon as they have left the queen's palace, they fall asleep and stay asleep until she makes them wake up. Then they return to the queen's presence again, now awake, and each one has the dreams he dreamed while sleeping written on his forehead, precisely as they occurred, and she reads them promptly. And those whose dreams she sees to have been merely about hunting, fishing, horses, forests, and wild animals she drives away, ordering them to spend their waking hours among the beasts they dreamed they were with while they were sleeping, because, she says, if they had loved her they'd at least have dreamed about her occasionally; and since they never have, she wants them to go and live with their wild animals. Then, those others who seemed in their dreams to be trading with merchandise or governing families and communities or doing similar things, and remembering the queen only slightly, she sends out likewise to be either a merchant or a townsman or a magistrate in her cities, burdening them with cares and worries and caring little about them, either. But those who dreamed about her she keeps at her court to converse with her amid music and song and pleasures that give infinite delight, some nearer to her and some less so, depending on whether they have dreamt about her more or less. But maybe, Lavinello, I have now retained you too long; you must have more desire, or perhaps need, to return to your companions than to listen to me any longer. Not to mention that, in addition, it may be burdensome to you to delay your departure till the sun is higher, because by now it has heated the whole sky and is still getting stronger." "I have no such desire or need whatsoever to return yet, Father," I said, "and if the discourse isn't unpleasant to you, I certainly recall nothing I've ever done so gladly as listening to you now. And don't worry about the sun getting higher, because all I have to do is descend, which can be done easily at any time." "Now, talking isn't usually unpleasant for elderly people," the good old man said; "it's more of a pas-

ho, il che ad ogni ora far si può agevolmente". Noioso agli antichi uomini non suole già essere il ragionare", disse il buon vecchio "che è più
tosto un diporto della vecchiezza che altro. Né a me può noiosa esser
cosa, che di piacere ti sia: perché seguasi". E così seguendo disse:
"Dirai adunque a Perottino e a Gismondo, figliuolo, che se essi non
vogliono essere tra le fiere mandati a vegghiare, quando essi si risve-
glieranno, essi miglior sogno si procaccino di fare, che quello non è,
che essi ora fanno. E tu, Lavinello, credi che non sarai perciò caro alla
Reina, che io dico, poscia che tu poco di lei sognandoti, tra questi tuoi
vaneggiamenti consumi più tosto senza pro, che tu in alcuna vera utilità di te usi e spenda, il dormire che t'è dato. E infine sappi che buono
amore non è il tuo. Il quale, posto che non sia malvagio in ciò, che con
le bestievoli voglie non si mescola, sì è egli non buono in questo, che
egli ad immortale obbietto non ti tira, ma tienti nel mezzo dell'una e
dell'altra qualità di disio, dove il dimorare tuttavia non è sano; con ciò
sia cosa che nel pendente delle rive stando, più agevolmente nel fondo
si sdrucciola, che alla vetta non si sale. E chi è colui che piaceri d'alcun senso dando fede, per molto che egli si proponga di non inchinare
alle ree cose, egli non sia almeno alle volte per inganno preso? considerando che pieno d'inganni è il senso, il quale una medesima cosa
quando ci fa parer buona, quando malvagia, quando bella, quando
sozza, quando piacevole, quando dispettosa. Senza che come può essere alcun disio buono, che ponga ne' diletti delle sentimenta quasi
nell'acqua il suo fondamento, quando si vede che essi avuti invili-
scono, e tormentano non avuti, e tutti sono brevissimi e di fuggitivo
momento? Né fanno le belle e segnate parole, che da cotali amanti
sopra ciò si dicono, che pure così non sia. I qua' diletti tuttavolta, se il
pensiero fa continui, quanto sarebbe men male che noi la mente non
avessimo celeste e immortale, che non è, avendola, di terreno pensiero ingombrarla e quasi sepellirla? Ella data non ci fu, perché noi
l'andassimo di mortal veleno pascendo, ma di quella salutevole ambrosia, il cui sapore mai non tormenta, mai non invilisce, sempre è
piacevole, sempre caro. E questo altramente non si fa, che a quello dio
i nostri animi rivolgendo, che ce gli ha dati. Il che farai tu, figliuolo, se
me udirai; e penserai che esso tutto questo sacro tempio, che noi
mondo chiamiamo, di sé empiendolo, ha fabricato con maraviglioso
consiglio ritondo e in sé stesso ritornante e di sé medesimo bisognoso
e ripieno, e cinselo di molti cieli di purissima sustanza sempre in giro
moventesi e allo 'ncontro del maggiore tutti gli altri, ad uno de' quali
diede le molte stelle, che da ogni parte lucessero, e a quelli, di cui esso
è contenitore, una n'assegnò per ciascuno, e tutte volle che il loro

time in old age than anything else. And nothing can be unpleasant to me that pleases you; and so, let's continue." And he continued as follows:

"And so you'll tell Perottino and Gismondo, my son, that if they don't want to be sent to spend their waking hours among the wild animals when they wake up, they should strive to have a better dream than the one they're now having. And you, Lavinello, trust me: you won't be dear to the queen, I say, since, scarcely dreaming about her, amid your vain thoughts you're using up the sleeping time allotted to you unprofitably instead of using and spending it on anything really useful to you. And, lastly, I'll have you know that your love is not a good one. Though it's not evil, to the extent that it isn't mingled with bestial thoughts, it isn't good because it doesn't draw you to an immortal goal but keeps you betwixt and between the two types of desire, where it's unhealthy to remain constantly; inasmuch as when one stands on a sloping bank one can more easily slip down into the depths than climb to the peak. And what man is there who, trusting in the pleasures of any of the senses, no matter how firmly he's determined not to lean toward evil things, isn't deceived at least at times? Since the senses are full of deceptions, making one and the same thing appear to us to be now good, now evil, now beautiful, now vile, now pleasant, now hateful. Not to mention this: how can any desire be good if it's based on the pleasures of the senses as if on water, when we see that, when those desires are attained, they degrade us, and torment us when they're not, and that all of them are ephemeral and of only temporary importance? Nor do the fine, fancy words spoken by such lovers on this subject make any difference in the true state of things. Yet if our thoughts turn constantly to such pleasures, wouldn't it be much better if our minds weren't divinely given and immortal than if, having such minds, we cluttered them and nearly buried them with earthly thoughts? Our mind wasn't given to us to be constantly fed with deadly poison, but with that salutary ambrosia the flavor of which never torments us, never degrades us, but is always pleasant, always dear. And this isn't done in any other way than by turning our minds toward that god who has given them to us. And you'll do this, my son, if you listen to me; and you'll reflect that this entire holy temple that we call the world, filling it with himself, *he,* with marvelous wisdom, created round in shape, spinning on its own axis, needful and full of him, and that he ringed it around with many heavens of purest substance perpetually turning in a circle, all those but the largest moving in the opposite direction from the largest; to one of them he assigned the vast number of fixed stars so they would shine everywhere, and to each of those that are contained within that largest one he assigned one of the planets; and he decreed that all of them should

lume da quello splendore pigliassero, che è reggitore de' loro corsi,
facitore del dì e della notte, apportatore del tempo, generatore e mo-
deratore di tutte le nascenti cose. [. . .]

## 15. Ariosto (1474–1533): *Orlando furioso*

Le donne, i cavallier, l'arme, gli amori,
le cortesie, l'audaci imprese io canto,
che furo al tempo che passaro i Mori
d'Africa il mare, e in Francia nocquer tanto,
seguendo l'ire e i giovenil furori
d'Agramante lor re, che si diè vanto
di vendicar la morte di Troiano
sopra re Carlo imperator romano.

Dirò d'Orlando in un medesmo tratto
cosa non detta in prosa mai né in rima:
che per amor venne in furore e matto,
d'uom che sì saggio era stimato prima;
se da colei che tal quasi m'ha fatto,
che 'l poco ingegno ad or ad or mi lima,
me ne sarà però tanto concesso,
che mi basti a finir quanto ho promesso.

Piacciavi, generosa Erculea prole,
ornamento e splendor del secol nostro,
Ippolito, aggradir questo che vuole
e darvi sol può l'umil servo vostro.
Quel ch'io vi debbo, posso di parole
pagare in parte e d'opera d'inchiostro;
né che poco io vi dia da imputar sono,
che quanto io posso dar, tutto vi dono.

Voi sentirete fra i più degni eroi,
che nominar con laude m'apparecchio,
ricordar quel Ruggier, che fu di voi
e de' vostri avi illustri il ceppo vecchio.
L'alto valore e' chiari gesti suoi
vi farò udir, se voi mi date orecchio,
e vostri alti pensier cedino un poco,
sì che tra lor miei versi abbiano loco.

receive their light from that glowing body which regulates their orbits,
creates day and night, brings the weather, and generates and moderates
all things that are born. [. . .]

## 15. Ariosto (1474–1533): *The Frenzy of Orlando*

Those ladies, knights, arms, loves,
courteous deeds, and bold exploits I sing
which existed in the days when the Moors crossed
the African sea and did so much damage in France,
following the wrath and youthful frenzies
of their king Agramante, who boasted
that he'd avenge the death of Troiano
on the Holy Roman Emperor Charlemagne.

In the same story I shall tell of Orlando
something never told before in prose or rhyme:
that he became frenzied and mad through love,
having been deemed so wise a man earlier;
that is, if the woman who has almost done the same to me,
she who from time to time polishes my slight talent,
will grant me enough
to complete all that I've promised.

May it please you, noble descendant of Hercules,
ornament and splendor of our age,
Ippolito, to accept this, which your humble servant
wishes and is alone able to give to you.
What I owe to you I can partially
pay in words and inky efforts;
nor am I to blame for giving you little thereby,
because I'm giving you all I can.

You shall hear, among the most meritorious heroes
whom I am preparing to name with praise,
mention of that Ruggiero who was the ancient founder
of your line and your illustrious ancestors'.
His lofty valor and bright deeds
I shall let you hear, if you lend me your ear;
and let your lofty cares relax a bit
so my verses can find a place among them.

Orlando che gran tempo inamorato
fu de la bella Angelica, e per lei
in India, in Media, in Tartaria lasciato
avea infiniti et immortal trofei,
in Ponente con essa era tornato,
dove sotto i gran monti Pirenei
con la gente di Francia e de Lamagna
re Carlo era attendato alla campagna,

per far al re Marsilio e al re Agramante
battersi ancor del folle ardir la guancia,
d'aver condotto, l'un, d'Africa quante
genti erano atte a portar spada e lancia;
l'altro, d'aver spinta la Spagna inante
a destruzion del bel regno di Francia.
E così Orlando arrivò quivi a punto:
ma tosto si pentì d'esservi giunto;

ché vi fu tolta la sua donna poi:
ecco il giudicio uman come spesso erra!
Quella che dagli esperii ai liti eoi
avea difesa con sì lunga guerra,
or tolta gli è fra tanti amici suoi,
senza spada adoprar, ne la sua terra.
Il savio imperator, ch'estinguer volse
un grave incendio, fu che gli la tolse.

Nata pochi dì inanzi era una gara
tra il conte Orlando e il suo cugin Rinaldo,
che ambi avean per la bellezza rara
d'amoroso disio l'animo caldo.
Carlo, che non avea tal lite cara,
che gli rendea l'aiuto lor men saldo,
questa donzella, che la causa n'era,
tolse, e diè in mano al duca di Bavera;

in premio promettendola a quel d'essi
ch'in quel conflitto, in quella gran giornata,
degli infideli più copia uccidessi,
e di sua man prestassi opra più grata.
Contrari ai voti poi furo i successi;
ch'in fuga andò la gente battezzata,
e con molti altri fu 'l duca prigione,
e restò abbandonato il padiglione. [. . .]

Orlando, who had long been in love
with the beautiful Angelica, and for her sake
had left behind in India, Media, and Tartary
infinite, immortal trophies,
had returned with her to the West,
where below the great peaks of the Pyrenees
with the men of France and Germany
Charlemagne was encamped in the open field,

in order to make King Marsilio and King Agramante
repentantly smite their cheeks again for the mad temerity
of having (in the latter case) led from Africa all
the men fit for bearing sword and spear;
and (in the former case) of having urged Spain onward
to the destruction of the beautiful realm of France.
And so Orlando arrived there just in time:
but he soon regretted having come there;

because his lady was then taken from him there:
see how often human judgment errs!
The woman whom, from western to eastern shores,
he had defended in so long a war,
is now taken from him amid so many friends of his,
without swordplay, in his own land.
The wise emperor, who tried to put out
a serious fire, was the one who took her from him.

A few days earlier, a contention had arisen
between Count Orlando and his cousin Rinaldo,
both of whom, because of her amazing beauty,
had minds heated by amorous desire.
Charlemagne, who disliked such a dispute,
which made their assistance less reliable for him,
took away that maiden, who was the cause of it,
and handed her over to the duke of Bavaria,

promising her as a reward to the one of them
who in that conflict, in that great battle,
would slay the greater number of infidels,
doing him a more pleasing service with his hand.
Later the events didn't turn out as desired,
because the baptized army was routed,
and with many others the duke was captured,
his tent remaining deserted. [. . .]

## 16. Michelangelo (1475–1564): 2 sonetti

(A) Veggio co' be' vostr' occhi un dolce lume
che co' mie' ciechi già veder non posso,
porto co' vostri piedi un pondo addosso
che de' miei zoppi non è lor costume.

Volo con le vostr'ale e senza piume.
Col vostro ingegno al ciel sempre son mosso.
Dal vostro arbitrio son pallido e rosso,
freddo al sol, caldo alle più fredde brume.

Nel voler vostro è sol la voglia mia.
I miei pensier' nel vostro cor si fanno.
Nel vostro fiato son le mie parole.

Come luna da sè sol par ch'io sia,
chè gli occhi nostri in ciel veder non sanno
se non quel tanto che n'accende il sole.

(B) I' mi son caro assai più ch'i' non soglio:
poi ch'i' t'ebbi nel cor, più di me vaglio,
come pietra, c'aggiuntovi l'intaglio,
è di più pregio che 'l suo primo scoglio;

o come scritta o pinta carta o foglio
più si riguarda d'ogni straccio o taglio:
tal di me fo, da po' ch'i' fu' berzaglio
segnato dal tuo viso, e non mi doglio.

Sicur con tale stampa in ogni loco
vo, come quel c'ha incanti o arme seco,
c'ogni periglio gli fan venir meno.

I' vaglio contra l'acqua e contra 'l foco,
col segno tuo rallumino ogni cieco
e col mie sputo sano ogni veleno.

## 17. Castiglione (1478–1529): *Il cortegiano*

—Pur sotto la nostra regula si potrà ancor intendere che, ritrovandosi
il cortegiano nella scaramuzza o fatto d'arme o battaglia di terra o in
altre cose tali, dée discretamente procurar d'appartarsi dalla moltitu-

## 16. Michelangelo (1475–1564): 2 sonnets

(A) I see with your lovely eyes a sweet light
that with my blind ones I can no longer see;
with your feet I carry around a weight
to which my lame ones are unaccustomed.

I fly with your wings and without feathers.
With your talent I'm always borne to heaven.
At your will I'm pale or flushed,
cold in the sunshine, hot in the coldest mists.

My wishes reside only in your will.
My thoughts arise in your heart.
My words are carried on your breath.

I seem to be like the moon on its own,
because our eyes can see in the sky only
that which the sun illuminates for us.

(B) I've been much dearer to myself than usual:
ever since I've had you in my heart, I've been worth more,
just as a stone to which carving is added
is more valuable than the unhewn rock;

or as an inscribed or painted sheet or loaf
is more highly regarded than any old scrap or piece:
thus I regard myself since I've been the target
aimed at by your eyes, and I don't regret it.

I go about everywhere safely with such an imprint,
like a man bearing charms or weapons,
which dispel all his dangers.

I'm safe from drowning and from burning,
with your mark I give light to every blind man
and with my saliva I counteract every poison.

## 17. Castiglione (1478–1529): *The Courtier*

"Under our rule it can also be understood that when the courtier finds
himself in a skirmish, combat, land battle or other such fray, he should
discreetly try to separate himself from the throng and perform those

dine e, quelle cose segnalate ed ardite che ha da fare, farle con minor
compagnia che pò, ed al cospetto de tutti i più nobili ed estimati omini
che siano nell'esercito, e massimamente alla presenzia e, se possibil è,
inanzi agli occhi proprii del suo re o di quel signore a cui serve; perché
in vero è ben conveniente valersi delle cose ben fatte. Ed io estimo
che, siccome è male cercar gloria falsa e di quello che non si merita,
così sia ancor male defraudar se stesso del debito onore e non cercarne
quella laude, che sola è vero premio delle virtuose fatiche. Ed io ricor-
domi aver già conosciuti di quelli, che, avvenga che fossero valenti, pur
in questa parte erano grossieri; e così metteano la vita a periculo per
andar a pigliar una mandra di pecore come per esser i primi che mon-
tassero le mura d'una terra combattuta: il che non farà il nostro cortegiano, se terrà a memoria la causa che lo conduce alla guerra, che dée
esser solamente l'onore. E, se poi si ritroverà armeggiare nei spettaculi
pubblici, giostrando, torneando, o giocando a canne o facendo qual-
sivoglia altro esercizio della persona, ricordandosi il loco ove si trova ed
in presenzia di cui, procurerà esser nell'arme non meno attillato e leggiadro che sicuro, e pascer gli occhi dei spettatori di tutte le cose che
gli parrà che possano aggiungergli grazia; e porrà cura d'aver cavallo
con vaghi guarnimenti, abiti ben intesi, motti appropriati ed invenzioni
ingeniose, che a sé tirino gli occhi de' circonstanti come calamita il
ferro. Non sarà mai degli ultimi che compariscano a mostrarsi, sapendo
che i populi, e massimamente le donne, mirano con molto maggior at-
tenzione i primi che gli ultimi; perché gli occhi e gli animi, che nel
principio sono avidi di quella novità, notano ogni minuta cosa e di
quella fanno impressione; poi per la continuazione non solamente si
saziano, ma ancora si stancano. Però fu un nobile istrione antico, il qual
per questo rispetto sempre voleva nelle fabule esser il primo che a
recitare uscisse. Così ancor, parlando pur d'arme, il nostro cortegiano
avrà risguardo alla profession di coloro con chi parla, ed a questo ac-
comodarassi; altramente ancor parlandone con omini, altramente con
donne; e, se vorrà toccar qualche cosa che sia in laude sua propria, lo
farà dissimulatamente, come a caso e per transito e con quella discre-
zione ed avvertenzia, che ieri ci mostrò il conte Ludovico.

"Non vi par ora, signor Morello, che le nostre regule possano insegnar qualche cosa? Non vi par che quello amico nostro, del qual
pochi dì sono vi parlai, s'avesse in tutto scordato con chi parlava e perché, quando, per intertenere una gentildonna, la quale per prima mai
più non aveva veduta, nel principio del ragionar le cominciò a dire che
aveva morti tanti omini e come era fiero e sapea giocar di spada a due
mani? né se le levò da canto che venne a volerle insegnar come

noteworthy and bold feats he is to do with the least company possible, but in view of all the noblest and most highly esteemed men that are in the army, especially in the presence and, if possible, before the very eyes of his king or the lord he serves; because truly it's perfectly proper to be valued for things well done. And I believe that, just as it's wrong to seek false and undeserved glory, it's also wrong to cheat oneself of due honor and fail to seek that praise which is the sole true reward for virtuous labors. And I recall having met some in the past who, though they were brave, yet were vulgar in this respect; and they used to put their life in danger to go and seize a flock of sheep just as readily as if they were the first to scale the walls of a besieged city. This our ideal courtier won't do if he keeps in mind the reason that impels him to war, which should be solely honor. And if later on he finds himself bearing arms in public shows, jousting, tourneying, hurling reeds, or performing any other physical exercise, he should remember what place he's in and in whose presence, and try to be in these shows of weaponry no less elegant and suave than skillful, and to feast the spectators' eyes on everything that he feels can add to his grace; and he'll take care to have a horse with beautiful trappings, well-made garments, and appropriate and clever mottoes and sayings on his equipment which will attract the eyes of the bystanders as a magnet attracts iron. He must never be one of the last to appear, knowing that the audience, and especially the ladies, gaze with much greater attention at the first than at the last; because their eyes and minds, which at the outset are greedy for that novelty, notice each little thing and are impressed thereby; later, because of the passing of time they are not only sated, but even wearied. Thus there was a well-known ancient actor who, for fear of this, always wanted to be the first to enter on stage in a play. Thus also, still speaking of combat, our courtier will have regard for the profession of those he addresses and adapt himself thereto; speaking differently to women than to men; and if he wants to mention anything that redounds to his own praise, he must disguise the matter, touching on it as if by chance and fleetingly, and with that discretion and prudence that Count Ludovico showed us yesterday.

"Don't you now think, Sir Morello, that our rules can teach something? Don't you think that that friend of ours of whom I spoke to you a few days ago, had completely forgotten whom he was addressing, and why, when, conversing with a noblewoman he had never seen before, at the outset of his speech he began to tell her how many men he had killed, how fierce he was, and how he knew how to wield a two-handed sword? And he didn't let her go before trying to teach her how certain battle-axe blows were to be parried when wearing armor, and when without armor, and

s'avessero a riparar alcuni colpi d'accia essendo armato, e come disar-
mato, ed a mostrarle prese di pugnale; di modo che quella meschina
stava in su la croce e parvele un'ora mill'anni levarselo da canto,
temendo quasi che non ammazzasse lei ancora come quegli altri. In
questi errori incorrono coloro che non hanno riguardo alle circon-
stanzie, che voi dite aver intese dai frati.

"Dico adunque che degli esercizii del corpo sono alcuni che quasi
mai non si fanno se non in publico, come il giostrare, il torneare, il giocare a canne e gli altri tutti che dependono dall'arme. Avendosi adunque in questi da adoperar il nostro cortegiano, prima ha da procurar
d'esser tanto bene ad ordine di cavalli, d'arme e d'abbigliamenti che
nulla gli manchi; e, non sentendosi ben assettato del tutto, non vi si
metta per modo alcuno, perché, non facendo bene, non si pò escusare
che questa non sia la profession sua. Appresso dée considerar molto in
presenzia di chi si mostra e quali siano i compagni; perché non saria
conveniente che un gentilom andasse ad onorare con la persona sua una
festa di contado, dove i spettatori ed i compagni fossero gente ignobile".

Disse allor il signor Gasparo Pallavicino: —Nel paese nostro di
Lombardia non s'hanno questi rispetti; anzi molti gentilomini giovani
trovansi, che le feste ballano tutto 'l dì nel sole coi villani, e con essi
giocano a lanciar barra, lottare, correre e saltare: ed io non credo che
sia male, perché ivi non si fa paragone della nobiltà, ma della forza e
destrezza, nelle quali cose spesso gli omini di villa non vaglion meno
che i nobili; e par che quella domestichezza abbia in sé una certa
liberalità amabile—. —Quel ballar nel sole— rispose messer
Federico— a me non piace per modo alcuno, né so che guadagno vi
si trovi. Ma chi vòl pur lottar, correr e saltar coi villani, dée, al parer
mio, farlo in modo di provarsi e, come si sòl dir, per gentilezza, non
per contender con loro; e dée l'omo esser quasi sicuro di vincere;
altramente non vi si metta; perché sta troppo male e troppo è brutta
cosa e fuor della dignità vedere un gentilomo vinto da un villano, e
massimamente alla lotta: però credo io che sia ben astenersene,
almeno in presenzia di molti, perché il guadagno nel vincere è
pochissimo e la perdita nell'esser vinto è grandissima. [. . .]

## 18. Guicciardini (1483–1540): *Storie fiorentine & Storia d'Italia*

(A) Così fu vituperosamente morto fra Girolamo Savonarola; del
quale non sarà fuora di proposito parlare più prolissamente delle qua-

showing her various dagger grips; so that the poor woman was in torment and thought that the hour was a thousand years until she was rid of him, almost in fear lest he kill her, too, like those others. Such errors are incurred by those who pay no heed to circumstances, which you say you've heard from the friars.

"And so I say that among physical exercises some are never performed except in public, like jousting, tourneying, hurling reeds, and all the others connected with weaponry. And so, since our courtier has to take part in these, he must first strive to be so well furnished with regard to horses, weapons, and clothing that nothing is lacking; and, if he feels he's not completely well furnished, he mustn't participate in any way, because, if he doesn't perform well, he can't say to excuse himself that this isn't his profession. Further, he must consider seriously in whose presence he performs and who his companions are; because it wouldn't be proper for a nobleman to go and honor with his person a rural festivity where the spectators and companions are lowborn folk."

Then Lord Gasparo Pallavicino said: "In our region, Lombardy, we don't have those constraints; rather, there are many young noblemen who dance at parties with rustics all day in the open air, and compete with them at hurling the bar, wrestling, running, and jumping; and I don't think it's wrong, because it isn't a contest of high birth that is being made there, but one of strength and skill, at which matters rural men often are just as good as noblemen; and that chumminess seems to have a certain pleasing liberality in it." "Such dancing outdoors," Master Federico rejoined, "I cannot like at all, nor do I know what profit you see in it. But if someone insists on wrestling, running, and jumping with peasants, I think he should do it so as to test himself and, as the expression goes, out of condescendence, and not in order to compete with them; and the fellow ought to be almost sure of winning, or else he shouldn't participate; because it's too improper and ugly a thing, beneath one's dignity, to see a nobleman bested by a peasant, especially at wrestling: and so I believe it's well to refrain from that, at least where there are many onlookers, because the profit in victory is almost nil and the loss in being beaten is tremendous." [. . .]

## 18. Guicciardini (1483–1540): *Florentine Histories & History of Italy*

(A) Thus Brother Girolamo Savonarola was killed with dishonor; with regard to whose merits it won't be irrelevant to speak more at length;

lità sua; perché né l'età nostra né anche e nostri padri, e avoli non viddono mai uno religioso sì bene instructo di molte virtù né con tanto credito e autorità quanto fu in lui. Confessano eziandio gli avversarii suoi lui essere stato dottissimo in molte facultà, massime in filosofia, la quale possedeva sì bene e se ne valeva sì a ogni suo proposito, come se avessi fattala lui; ma sopra tutto nella Scrittura sacra, in che si crede già qualche secolo non essere stato uomo pari a lui. Ebbe uno giudicio grandissimo non solo nelle lettere, ma ancora nelle cose agibili del mondo, negli universali delle quali si intese assai, come a giudicio mio dimostrano le prediche sue; nella quale arte trapassò con queste virtù di gran lunga gli altri della età sua, aggiugnendosigli una eloquenzia non artificiosa e sforzata, ma naturale e facile; e vi ebbe drento tanta audienzia e credito che fu cosa mirabile, avendo predicato tanti anni continuamente, non solo le quaresime, ma molti dì festivi dello anno, in una città piena di ingegni sottilissimi e anche fastidiosi, e dove e predicatori, benché eccellenti, sogliono, al più lungo termine da una quaresima o due in là, rincrescere. E furono in lui sì chiare e manifeste queste virtù che vi concordano drento così gli avversarii suoi come e fautori e seguaci. [. . .]

(B) Ma più maravigliosa ancora è stata la navigazione degli Spagnuoli, cominciata l'anno mille quattrocento novanta . . . per invenzione di Cristoforo Colombo genovese. Il quale, avendo molte volte navigato per il mare Oceano, e congetturando, per l'osservazione di certi venti, quel che poi veramente gli succedette, impetrati dai re di Spagna certi legni, e navigando verso l'occidente, scoperse, in capo di trentatré dì, nell'ultime estremità del nostro emisperio, alcune isole, delle quali prima niuna notizia s'aveva; felici per il sito del cielo, per la fertilità della terra, e perché, da certe popolazioni fierissime in fuora che si cibano de' corpi umani, quasi tutti gli abitatori, semplicissimi di costumi e contenti di quel che produce la benignità della natura, non sono tormentati né da avarizia né da ambizione; ma infelicissime, perché, non avendo gli uomini né certa religione né notizia di lettere, non perizia di artificii, non armi, non arte di guerra, non scienza, non esperienza alcuna delle cose, sono, quasi non altrimenti che animali mansueti, facilissima preda di chiunque gli assalta. Onde allettati gli Spagnuoli dalla facilità dell'occuparle e dalla ricchezza della preda, perché in esse sono state trovate vene abbondantissime d'oro, cominciorno molti di loro come in domicilio proprio ad abitarvi: e penetrato Cristoforo Colombo più oltre, e doppo lui Amerigo Vespucci fiorentino, e successivamente molti altri, hanno scoperte altre isole e

because neither our generation nor even our fathers' and grandfathers' has ever seen a friar so well endowed with many virtues, nor enjoying such repute and authority as were his. Even his adversaries admit that he was very learned in many disciplines, especially in philosophy, which he knew as well, and made as good use of whenever it was relevant, as if he had invented it himself; but above all in Holy Scripture, in which it's believed that for some centuries now he has had no equal. His judgment was wonderful not only in literature, but also in practical worldly matters, all of which he understood perfectly, as his sermons show, in my opinion. In that art, with such merits, he far surpassed the others of his generation, because to those other merits he added an eloquence that was not artificial and forced, but natural and easy-flowing; and his sermons were attended by such great crowds, and were so highly regarded, that it was a marvel, since he had preached continually for so many years not only Lenten sermons, but those for many holy days during the year, in a city filled with extremely subtle and even pretentious intellects, where preachers, excellent as they may be, usually become tiresome beyond one or two Lenten sermons. And these merits were so clear and manifest in him that his enemies as well as his partisans and followers are in agreement about them. [. . .]

(B) But even more wonderful was the navigation of the Spaniards, begun in the year fourteen hundred and ninety . . . with the discoveries of Christopher Columbus of Genoa. He, having sailed the Atlantic many times, and conjecturing through the observation of certain winds that which later actually befell him, requested and received certain vessels from the king of Spain and, sailing westward, discovered, after thirty-three days, at the farthest reaches of our globe, some islands that had been completely unknown before; islands fortunate in their climatic location, in the fertility of their soil, and because, except for some very fierce tribes that feed on human bodies, nearly all the inhabitants, very simple in their ways and contented with that which a benign nature produces, are tormented neither by avarice nor by ambition; but islands most unfortunate because, the people having no firm religion and no knowledge of letters, no skill in machinery, no weapons, no art of war, no science, no experience of worldly matters, are, almost the same as meek animals, a most easy prey to anyone attacking them. Therefore, many of the Spaniards, lured by the ease of occupying those islands and by the richness of the booty (because extremely abundant seams of gold have been found in them), began to dwell there as if at home. Exploring further, Christopher Columbus, and after him, Amerigo Vespucci of Florence, and many others in succession discovered other islands and

grandissimi paesi di terraferma; e in alcuni di essi (benché in quasi tutti il contrario e nell'edificare pubblicamente e privatamente e nel vestire e nel conversare) costumi e pulitezza civile; ma tutte genti imbelli e facili a essere predate; ma tanto spazio di paesi nuovi che sono, senza comparazione, maggiore spazio che l'abitato che prima era notizia nostra. Ne' quali distendendosi con nuove genti e con nuove navigazioni gli Spagnuoli, e ora cavando oro e argento delle vene che sono in molti luoghi e dell'arene de' fiumi, ora comperandone per prezzo di cose vilissime dagli abitanti, ora rubando il già accumulato, n'hanno condotto nella Spagna infinita quantità; navigandovi privatamente, benché con licenza del re e a spese proprie, molti, ma dandone ciascuno al re la quinta parte di tutto quello che o cavava o altrimenti gli perveniva nelle mani.

Anzi è proceduto tanto oltre l'ardire degli Spagnuoli che alcune navi, essendosi distese verso mezzodì cinquantatré gradi, sempre lungo la costa di terraferma, e di poi entrate in uno stretto mare, e da quello per amplissimo pelago navigando nello oriente, e poi ritornando per la navigazione che fanno i Portogallesi, hanno, come apparisce manifestissimamente, circuito tutta la terra. Degni, e i Portoghesi e gli Spagnuoli, e precipuamente Colombo inventore di questa più maravigliosa e più pericolosa navigazione, che con eterne laudi sia celebrata la perizia, la industria, l'ardire, la vigilanza e le fatiche loro, per le quali è venuta al secolo nostro notizia di cose tanto grandi e tanto inopinate; ma più degno di essere celebrato il proposito loro, se a tanti pericoli e fatiche gli avesse indotti non la sete immoderata dell'oro e delle ricchezze, ma la cupidità di dare a sé stessi e agli altri questa notizia o di propagare la fede cristiana; benché questo sia in qualche parte proceduto per conoscenza, perché in molti luoghi sono stati convertiti alla nostra religione gli abitatori.

Per queste navigazioni si è manifestato essersi nella cognizione della terra ingannati in molte cose gli antichi: passarsi oltre alla linea equinoziale; abitarsi sotto la torrida zona; come medesimamente, contro all'opinione loro, si è per navigazione di altri compreso abitarsi sotto le zone propinque a' poli, sotto le quali affermavano non potersi abitare per i freddi immoderati rispetto al sito del cielo tanto remoto dal corso del sole; èssi manifestato quel che alcuni degli antichi credevano, altri riprendevano, che sotto i nostri piedi sono altri abitatori detti da loro gli antipodi. Né solo ha questa navigazione confuso molte cose affermate dagli scrittori delle cose terrene, ma dato, oltre a ciò, qualche ansietà agli interpreti della Scrittura sacra, soliti a interpretare che quel versicolo del salmo che contiene che "in tutta la terra

very extensive countries on the mainland; and in some of them (though in almost all of them the opposite was true with regard to public and private buildings, clothing, and human interactions) they found cultivated manners and political customs; but all those populations were unwarlike and easily despoiled; there's such an extent of new lands that, without comparison, they cover more ground than the inhabited world we knew before. Spreading out in them with new adventurers and further navigations, the Spaniards, now extracting gold and silver from the seams occurring in many places, and from river sands, now buying them from the natives in exchange for very cheap goods, now stealing what had already been amassed, brought a huge amount of them to Spain; many sailed there privately, though with the king's leave, and at their own expense, but each of them giving the king a fifth of everything that he had extracted or that had fallen into his hands in other ways.

In fact, the boldness of the Spaniards proceeded so far that some ships, having reached fifty-three degrees south, always hugging the coast, and having then entered a strait and having sailed to the Orient from there across a very wide sea, then having come home by the route that the Portuguese follow, have circled the whole world, as it manifestly appears. The Portuguese and Spaniards, and above all Columbus, who initiated that most wonderful and dangerous navigation, deserve to have their skill, diligence, daring, vigilance, and labors celebrated with eternal praise, because through those labors our era has received word of such great and unexpected things; but their intentions would be worthier of celebration if they had been induced into such great dangers and labors not by an immoderate thirst for gold and riches, but by the longing to give this news to themselves and others or to propagate the Christian faith (though this has occurred in some places thanks to the new knowledge; because the natives of many areas have been converted to our religion).

It has become clear through these navigations that the ancients erred in many ways in their knowledge of the world: people have passed beyond the Equator; they can live in the Torrid Zone; just as, similarly, contrary to the opinion of the ancients, thanks to the navigation of others, it has been learned that one can live in the zones near the poles, in which they affirmed it was impossible to live because of the extreme cold caused by their being located so far from the sun's course. That which some ancients believed and others denied has been clarified: that beneath our feet there are other inhabitants, whom they called the Antipodeans. Not only have these navigations refuted many things asserted by the old geographers, but they have also given some alarm to the interpreters of Holy Scripture, who usually state that the Psalm verse [19:4] reading, "Their line is gone

uscì il suono loro e ne' confini del mondo le parole loro", significasse
che la fede di Cristo fusse per la bocca degli apostoli penetrata per
tutto il mondo.

## 19. Bandello (1484–1561): *Novelle*

Voi, signori miei, devete sapere che questa signora Bianca Maria de la
quale s'è parlato —dico signora per rispetto ai dui mariti che ha avuti—
fu di basso sangue e di legnaggio non molto stimato, il cui padre fu
Giacomo Scappardone, uomo plebeo in Casal di Monferrato. Questo
Giacomo, tutto quello che aveva ridotto in danari, si diede a prestar ad
usura publicamente con sì larghi interessi, che avendo da giovine cominciato a far questo mestieri, ci divenne tanto ricco che comperò pos-
sessioni assai, e tuttavia prestando e poco spendendo acquistò grandis-
sime facultà. Ebbe per moglie una giovane greca, venuta di Grecia con
la madre del marchese Guglielmo, che fu padre de la duchessa di
Mantova. Era la moglie di Giacomo donna bellissima e piacevol molto,
ma dal marito assai differente d'età, perciò che egli era già vecchio ed
ella non passava venti anni. Ebbero una figliuola senza più, che fu
questa Bianca Maria, per la quale ho cominciato a parlare. Morì il
padre e restò questa figliuola molto picciola sotto il governo de la
madre greca, con facultà di beni stabili al sole per più assai di cento
mila ducati. Era la figliuola assai bella, ma tanto viva e aggraziata che
non poteva esser più. Come ella fu di quindeci in sedeci anni, il signor
Ermes Vesconte, figliuolo di quel venerando patrizio il signor Battista,
la prese per moglie, e con solennissima pompa e trionfi grandissimi e
feste la condusse in Milano. A la quale, prima ch'ella v'entrasse, il
signor Francesco, fratel maggiore del signor Ermes, mandò a donar
una superbissima carretta tutta intagliata e messa ad oro, con una coperta di broccato riccio sovra riccio tutto frastagliato e sparso di bellis-
simi ricami e fregi. Conducevano quattro corsieri bianchi come uno
armellino essa carretta, e i corsieri medesimamente erano di grandissimo prezzo. Su questa carretta entrò la signora Bianca Maria trion-
fantemente in Milano, e visse col signor Ermes circa sei anni. Morto
che fu il signor Ermes, ella si ridusse in Monferrato a Casale, e quivi
trovandosi ricca e libera cominciò a viver molto allegramente e fare a
l'amor con questo e con quello. Ella era da molti vagheggiata e do-
mandata per moglie, fra i quali erano principali il signor Gismondo
Gonzaga figliuolo del signor Giovanni e il conte di Cellant barone di
Savoia, che ha il suo stato ne la valle d'Agosta, e v'ha molte castella con

out through all the earth, and their words to the end of the world," means that the Christian faith spread throughout the world through the lips of the Apostles. [. . .]

## 19. Bandello (1484–1561): *Stories*

You, my lords, must know that this Madam Bianca Maria, who has been mentioned—I say "madam" because of the two husbands she had—was of lowly birth and of a quite undistinguished family. Her father was Giacomo Scappardone, a plebeian in Casal di Monferrato. Having turned all his possessions into ready money, this Giacomo began to lend money publicly at such high interest that, having started to ply that trade as a young man, he became so rich at it that he bought many estates, and constantly lending, and spending little, he acquired enormous resources. His wife was a young Greek woman who had come from Greece with the mother of Marquis Guglielmo, who was father of the duchess of Mantua. Giacomo's wife was a very beautiful woman and very charming, but much younger than her husband, because he was already elderly and she wasn't over twenty. They had one daughter, their only child, who was this Bianca Maria I began to speak about. The father died and this daughter, very small, remained in the care of her Greek mother, who possessed real estate worth much more than a hundred thousand ducats. The daughter was very beautiful, and as lively and graceful as it's possible to be. When she was between fifteen and sixteen, Lord Ermes Visconti, son of that venerable patrician Lord Battista, married her and with the most solemn pomp and very great processions and festivities took her to Milan. Before she entered the city Lord Francesco, elder brother of Lord Ermes, sent her as a gift a most superb carriage, all carved and gilded, with a traveling rug of curled and rippled brocade all notched and covered with very beautiful embroideries and ornaments. Four steeds white as ermine drew that carriage, and the steeds, too, were extremely valuable. In this carriage Lady Bianca Maria made a triumphal entry into Milan, where she lived with Lord Ermes about six years. After Lord Ermes died, she returned to Casal di Monferrato, where, finding herself rich and free, she began to lead a very merry life and dally with this man and that. She was courted, and her hand was sought, by many, the chief among them being Lord Gismondo Gonzaga, son of Lord Giovanni, and the count of Cellant, a baron of Savoy, whose residence is in the Val d'Aosta, where he has many castles yielding a very good income. The mar-

bonissima rendita. La marchesana di Monferrato per compiacer al genero signor di Mantova faceva ogni cosa per darla al signor Gismondo, e quasi il matrimonio era per conchiuso. Ma il conte di Cellant seppe sì ben vagheggiarla e dirle sì fattamente i casi suoi, che celatamente insieme si sposaron e consumaron anco il matrimonio. La marchesana di Casale, ancor che questo sommamente le dispiacesse e fosse per farne qualche mal scherzo a la signora Bianca Maria, nondimeno dissimulando lo sdegno, per rispetto del conte non fece altro movimento. Si publicò adunque il matrimonio e si fecero le nozze con tristo augurio, per quello che seguì. E parve bene esser vero il proverbio che volgarmente fra noi si dice, che «chi si piglia d'amore, di rabbia si lascia», perciò che non stettero molto insieme che nacque una discordia tra loro la più fiera del mondo, di modo, che che se ne fosse cagione, ella se ne fuggì dal marito furtivamente e in Pavia si ridusse, ove condusse una buona ed agiata casa, menando una vita troppo libera e poco onesta. Era in quei giorni al servigio de l'imperadore Ardizzino Valperga conte di Masino, col signor Carlo suo fratello. E per sorte trovandosi Ardizzino in Pavia e veggendo costei, se ne innamorò e tutto il dì le stava in casa, facendole il servidore e usando ogni arte per venir a l'intento suo. E quantunque fosse un poco zoppo d'un piede, era nondimeno giovine assai bello e molto gentile, di modo che in pochi giorni venne de la donna possessore, e più d'un anno si diede il meglior tempo del mondo seco, così manifestamente, che non solamente ne la città di Pavia, ma per tutta la contrada se ne tenevano canzoni. Avvenne che il signor Roberto Sanseverino conte di Gaiazzo, giovine de la persona valente e gentilissimo, capitò a Pavia, al quale la signora Bianca Maria gettati gli occhi a dosso, e giudicatolo meglior e più gagliardo macinatore che non era il suo amante, del quale forse ella si trovava sazia, deliberò procacciarselo per nuovo amante. Onde cominciando a far mal viso al signor Ardizzino e non le volendo dar più adito di ritrovarsi seco, vennero insieme a qualche triste parole. La giovane, più baldanzosa che non si conveniva e non pensando ciò che seco aveva fatto, cominciò a dirgli villania, non solamente chiamandolo zoppo sciancato, ma dicendogli molte altre vituperose parole. Egli, che mal volentieri portava in groppa, allargato il freno a la sua còlera, le diede più volte de la putta sfacciata per la testa e de la bagascia e de la villana, di modo che dove era stato grandissimo amore vi nacque ne l'una parte e ne l'altra un fierissimo odio. Partì da Pavia il signor Ardizzino, e in ogni luogo ove accadeva che de la signora Bianca Maria si ragionasse, ne diceva tutti quei vituperosi mali che d'una femina di chiazzo si potessero dire. [. . .]

chioness of Monferrato, in order to please her son-in-law the lord of Mantua, made every effort to bestow her on Lord Gismondo, and the marriage was all but arranged. But the count of Cellant was so good at his wooing and at presenting his case persuasively that they married in secret and also consummated the marriage. The marchioness of Casale, though highly displeased by this and on the verge of doing some bad turn to Madam Bianca Maria, nonetheless concealed her anger and, out of regard for the count, took no other action. And so the marriage was made public and the wedding was celebrated—with evil omens, as things turned out. The saying current among us seemed to be quite true, "Those who take each other in love, leave each other in rage," because they weren't together long before the fiercest possible discord arose between them, so that, whatever the reason for it was, she secretly ran away from her husband and took refuge in Pavia, where she rented a good, comfortable house, leading a life that was too free and not very respectable. In those days Ardizzino Valperga, count of Masino, along with Lord Carlo his brother, were in the service of the emperor. Ardizzino, finding himself in Pavia by chance and seeing her, fell in love with her and remained in her house all day long, playing the wooer and using every wile to obtain his desires. And though he was a little lame in one foot, nevertheless he was a very handsome and very nice young man, so that in a few days he became the possessor of the lady, and for over a year had the best time in the world with her, so openly that people gossiped about it not only in the city of Pavia, but throughout the region. It came about that Lord Roberto Sanseverino, the count of Gaiazzo, a young man of valiant and most noble aspect, chanced to come to Pavia. Madam Bianca Maria, casting her eyes on him and judging him to be better and more vigorous in bed than her lover was (maybe she was tired of him), determined to acquire him as a new lover. And so, beginning to look unkindly on Lord Ardizzino and refusing him further access to trysts with her, she and he came to exchange some bitter words. The young woman, bolder than was proper and not thinking of what they had done together, began to speak to him rudely, not only calling him a miserable cripple, but also addressing many other insulting words to him. He, who took offenses very badly, giving free rein to his anger, several times hurled at her the epithets whore, strumpet, and peasant, so that where there had been very great love there arose very fierce hatred on both sides. Lord Ardizzino left Pavia and wherever Madam Bianca Maria happened to be mentioned, he said all the insulting things about her that can be said about a prostitute in a brothel. [. . .]

## 20. Da Porto (1485–1529): "Istoria . . . di due nobili amanti"

Furono adunque, come dico, in Verona sotto il già detto signor le sopradette nobilissime famiglie, di valorosi omini e di richezza ugualmente dal cielo, da la natura e dalla fortuna dottate; tra le quali, come il più delle volte tra le gran case si vede, che che la cagion si fosse, crudelissima nimistà regnava, per la qual già più omini erano così dall'una come dall'altra parte morti, in guisa che sì per stanchezza, come spesso per questi casi adiviene, come anco per le minacie del signore, che con spiacere grandissimo le vedea nemiche, s'eran ritratte di più farsi dispiacere e senza altra pace col tempo in modo dimesticate, che gran parte degli loro uomini insieme parlavano. Essendo così costoro pacificati, adviene, uno carnevale, ch'in casa di messer Antonio Capelletti, uomo festoso e iocondissimo, il qual primo de la famiglia era, molte feste si fecero e di giorno e di notte, ove quasi tutta la città concorreva. Ad una de le quali una notte (come è degli amanti costume, che le lor donne sì come col cuore così anco col corpo, purché possano, ovunque vanno, seguono), uno giovane delli Montecchi, la sua donna seguendo, si condusse. Era costui giovane molto bellissimo, grande della persona, leggiadro e accostumato assai; per che, trattasi la maschera, come ogni altro facea, e in abito di ninfa trovandosi, non fu occhio, ch'a rimirarlo non volgesse, sì per la sua bellezza, che quella d'ogni donna avanzava che ivi fosse, come per maraviglia ch'in quella casa, massimamente la notte, fosse venuto. Ma con più efficacia che ad alcun altro ad una figliola del detto messer Antonio venne veduto, che egli sola avea, la quale di sopranaturale bellezza e baldanzosa e legiadrissima era. Questa, veduto il giovane, con tanta forza nell'animo la sua bellezza ricevette, che al primo incontro de' loro occhi di più non essere di lei stessa le parve. Stavasi costui in riposta parte della festa con poca baldanza, tutto solo, e rade volte in ballo o in parlamento alcuno si tramettea, come quegli che, d'Amore ivi guidato, con molto sospetto vi stava; il che alla giovane forte dolea, perciochè piacevolissimo udiva che egli era e giocoso. E passando la mezza notte e il fine del festegiare venendo, il ballo del torchio o del cappello, come dire lo vogliamo e che ancora nel fine delle feste veggiamo usarsi, s'incominciò; nel quale, in cerchio standosi, l'omo la donna e la donna l'uomo, a sua voglia permutandosi, piglia. In questa danza d'alcuna donna fu il giovane levato e a caso appresso la già innamorata fanciulla posto. Era dall'altro canto di lei un nobile giovane, Marcuccio guercio nominato, il quale per natura, così il luglio come il genaio, le mani sem-

## 20. Da Porto (1485–1529): "History . . . of Two Noble Sweethearts"

And so, as I say, there lived in Verona under the aforesaid lord the above-mentioned very noble families, comprised of brave men and endowed with wealth by heaven, nature, and fortune combined; between them (as one sees most often between great houses), whatever the cause was, there prevailed a most cruel enmity, through which several men had already been killed on either side, so that both from weariness, as often occurs in such cases, and because of the threats from the lord of the city, who was highly displeased to see them in enmity, they had refrained from anger-ing each other any longer, and with time (no other pact being made) had become so calmed that many of their men spoke to one another. They being thus pacified, it came about, one Carnival time, that at the home of Lord Antonio Capelletti, a merry and very jolly man who was head of his family, many parties were held day and night, in which nearly the whole town participated. One night, to one of these (in accordance with the way of lovers, who follow their sweethearts wherever they go, as much as pos-sible, with their bodies as well as their hearts) there came a young man of the Montecchi clan, following his sweetheart. He was a very handsome young man, tall, comely, and very well-mannered; so that, wearing a mask, like everyone else, and dressed in nymph's costume as he was, there was no eye that didn't turn to gaze at him, both because of his good looks, which surpassed those of every woman there, and because of the oddity of his having come to that house, especially at night. But he was seen to greater effect than by anyone else by a daughter of the aforesaid Lord Antonio, his only one, who was of superhuman beauty and was lively and most comely. Seeing the young man, she was so greatly struck by his good looks that when their eyes first met, she thought she was no longer mistress of herself. He was standing in a remote corner of the party with little self-confidence, all alone, seldom joining in in a dance or any con-versation, like a man who, guided there by Love, was there with much ap-prehension; this grieved the young woman greatly, because she heard he was very charming and playful. After midnight, when the ball was nearly over, there began the taper or hat dance, whichever we call it, and which we still see danced at the end of parties; in this dance people form a circle, and the man takes hold of the woman, and the woman the man, changing around at their will. In this dance the young man was led along by some lady and brought by chance next to the girl who had already fallen in love. On the other side of her was a noble youth dubbed cross-eyed Marcuccio, who by nature, in July as in January, always had very cold

pre fredissime avea. Perché giunto Romeo Montecchi, che così era il
giovane chiamato, al manco lato della donna, e, come in tal ballo se
usa, la bella sua mano in mano presa, disse a lui quasi subito la giovane,
forse vaga d'udirlo favellare: «Benedetta sia la vostra venuta qui presso
me, messer Romeo». Alla quale il giovane, che già del suo mirare ac-
corto s'era, maravigliato del parlar di costei, disse: «Come benedetta la
mia venuta?». Ed ella rispose: «Sì, benedetto il vostro venire qui appo
me, percioché voi almanco questa stanca mano calda mi terrete, onde
Marcuccio la destra mi agghiaccia». Costui, preso alquanto d'ardire,
seguì: «Se io a voi con la mia mano la vostra riscaldo, voi co' begli occhi
il mio core accendete». La donna dopo un breve sorriso, schifando
d'essere con lui veduta o udita ragionare, ancora gli disse: «Io vi giuro,
Romeo, per mia fé, che non è qui donna, la quale, come voi siete, agli
occhi mei bella paia». A la quale il giovane, già tutto di lei acceso,
rispose: «Qual'io mi sia, sarò alla vostra beltade, s'a quella non spia-
cerà, fedel servo». Lassato poco dopo il festeggiare e tornato Romeo
alla sua casa, considerata la crudeltà della prima sua donna, che di
molto languire poca mercede gli dava, diliberò, quando a lei fosse ag-
grado, a costei, quantunque de' soi nemici fosse, tutto donarsi.
Dall'altro canto la giovane, poco ad altro ch'a lui solo pensando, dopo
molti sospiri tra sé istimò lei dovere sempre felice essere, se costui per
sposo avere potesse. Ma per la nimistà, che tra l'una e l'altra casa era,
con molto timore poca speme di giugnere a sì lieto grado tenea; onde,
fra due pensieri di continuo vivendo, a sé stessa più volte disse: «O
sciocca me, a qual vaghezza mi lascio io in così strano labirinto
guidare? Ove, senza scorta restando, uscire a mia posta non ne potrò,
già che Romeo Montecchi non m'ama, percioché per la nimistà, che
ha co' miei, altro che la mia vergogna non può cercare; e posto che per
sposa egli mi volesse, il mio padre di darmegli non consentirebbe giamai». Dapoi, nell'altro pensiero venendo, dicea: «Chi sa, forse, che,
per meglio paceficarsi insieme queste due case, che già stanche e sazie
sono di far tra lor guerra, mi porria ancor venir fatto d'averlo in quella
guisa che io lo disio!» E in questo fermatasi, cominciò esserli d'alcun
sguardo cortese.

　　Accesi dunque gli due amanti di ugual fuoco, l'uno dell'altro il bel
nome e l'effigie nel petto scolpita portando, dier principio quando in
chiesa, quando a qualche fenestra a vagheggiarsi, in tanto che mai
bene né l'uno né l'altro aveva, se non quanto si vedeano. Ed egli massimamente sì di vaghi costumi di lei acceso si trovava, che quasi tutta
la notte, con grandissimo periculo della sua vita, dinanci alla casa de
l'amata donna solo si stava; e ora sopra la fenestra della sua camera per

hands. Because Romeo Montecchi (that was the young man's name) had reached the lady's left side and, as occurs in that dance, had taken her lovely hand in his, the young woman said to him nearly at once, perhaps desirous of hearing him speak: "Blessed be your arrival here next to me, Lord Romeo!" To which the youth, who had already noticed her staring, surprised at her words, replied: "How so is my arrival blessed?" And she replied: "Yes, a blessing on your coming here next to me, because you'll at least keep my left hand warm while Marcuccio freezes my right hand." Romeo, taking heart to some extent, continued: "If I'm warming your hand with mine, you're setting my heart on fire with your beautiful eyes." After a brief smile the lady, avoiding being seen or heard speaking with him, added: "I swear to you, Romeo, on my faith, that there isn't a woman here who seems as good-looking to my eyes as you are." To which the youth, by now completely inflamed with her, replied: "However I may look, I'll be a faithful servant to your beauty if you don't mind." Leaving the ball shortly afterward and returning home, Romeo, reflecting on his first sweetheart's cruelty, which gave him little reward for much languishing, decided to devote himself entirely to this other girl, though she belonged to his enemies. On her part, the young woman, thinking of little else but him alone, after many sighs deemed in her mind that she'd always be happy if she could have him for a husband. But because of the enmity between one house and the other, she had great fear and little hope of attaining such a happy status; so that, constantly torn between two ideas, she often said to herself: "Fool that I am, by what desire am I letting myself be led into so strange a labyrinth? Remaining without an escort, I won't be able to find my way out of it at my own will, since Romeo Montecchi doesn't love me, because on account of his enmity for my family he can't be after anything but my dishonor; and even if he wanted me for a wife, my father would never consent to give me to him." Then, turning to the other idea, she'd say: "Who knows? Perhaps to make a firmer peace between these two houses, which are already sick and tired of warring with each other, I might still succeed in having him the way I wish to!" And making that conclusion, she began to give him some friendly glances.

And so, both lovers being ignited with the same fire, each one bearing the other's dear name and image engraved on his heart, they began to woo, now in church, now at some window, so that neither one was ever happy unless they saw each other. And he especially found himself inspired by her to such pleasant habits that almost all night long, at very great risk to his life, he'd remain alone in front of his beloved's house; now, he'd climb up to her bedroom window by main strength and sit

forza tiratosi, ivi, sanza ch'ella od altri lo sapesse, ad udire lo suo bel parlare si sedea, e ora sopra la strada giacea. [. . .]

## 21. Straparola (ca 1490–ca 1557): *Le piacevoli notti*

In Boemia, piacevoli donne, non è gran tempo che si trovò una vecchiarella, Bagolana Savonese per nome chiamata. Costei, essendo poverella e avendo due figliuole, l'una de' quai Cassandra, l'altra Adamantina si addimandava, volse di quella poca povertà, che ella si trovava avere, ordinare i fatti suoi e contenta morire. E non avendo in casa né fuori cosa alcuna di cui testare potesse, eccetto che una cassettina piena di stoppa, fece testamento; e la cassettina con la stoppa lasciò alle figliuole, pregandole che dopo la morte sua pacificamente insieme vivessero. Le due sorelle, quantunque fussino povere de' beni della fortuna, nondimeno erano ricche de' beni dell'animo, e in costumi non erano inferiori all'altre donne. Morta adunque la vecchiarella e parimenti sepolta, Cassandra, la qual era la sorella maggiore, prese una libra di quella stoppa e con molta sollecitudine si puose a filare; e filata che fu, diede il filo ad Adamantina sua sorella minore, imponendole che lo portasse in piazza e lo vendesse, e del tratto di quello comprasse tanto pane, acciochè ambedue potessero delle sue fatiche la loro vita sostentare. Adamantina, tolto il filo e postolo sotto le braccia, se n'andò in piazza per venderlo secondo il comandamento di Cassandra; ma venuta la cagione e la opportunità, fece il contrario di quello era il voler suo e della sorella: perciochè s'abbatté in piazza in una vecchiarella che aveva in grembo una poavola, la più bella e la più ben formata che mai per l'adietro veduta si avesse. Laonde Adamantina, avendola veduta e considerata, di lei tanto se n'invaghì, che più di averla che di vendere il filo pensava. Considerando adunque Adamantina sopra di ciò, e non sapendo che fare né che dire per averla pur deliberò di tentare sua fortuna, si a baratto la potesse avere. E accostatasi alla vecchia, disse: «Madre mia, quando vi fusse in piacere, io baratterei volentieri con la poavola vostra il filo mio». La vecchiarella, vedendo la fanciulla bella, piacevole e tanto desiderosa della poavola, non volse contradirle; ma preso il filo, la poavola le apprensentò. Adamantina, avuta la poavola, non si vide mai la più contenta; e tutta lieta e gioconda a casa se ne tornò. A cui la sorella Cassandra disse: «Hai tu venduto il filo?». «Sì» rispose Adamantina. «E dov'è il pane che hai comperato?» disse Cassandra. A cui Adamantina, aperto il grembiale di bucato che dinanzi teneva sempre, dimostrò la poavola che barattata

there listening to her lovely voice, without her knowledge or anyone else's; now, he'd lie in the street. [. . .]

## 21. Straparola (ca. 1490–ca. 1557): *The Pleasant Nights*

In Bohemia, charming ladies, not long ago, there was an old woman called Bagolana Savonese. Being poor and having two daughters, one of whom was named Cassandra and the other Adamantina, she decided to settle the affairs of that miserable pittance she possessed and to die contentedly. Having nothing either in the house or out of it that she could leave in a will, except for a little chest full of tow, she made her testament; the chest of tow she left to her daughters, begging them to live peacefully together after her death. Though the two sisters were poor in worldly goods, yet they were rich in spiritual goods, and their manners weren't inferior to those of other women. And so, after the old woman had died and been duly buried, Cassandra, who was the elder sister, took a pound of that tow and with great care began to spin it; after it was spun, she gave the thread to Adamantina, her younger sister, ordering her to take it to the town square and sell it, and from the proceeds buy a lot of bread, so that they could both earn their keep by their labors. Adamantina, taking the thread and putting it under her arms, went to the square to sell it in accordance with Cassandra's orders; but when a reason and opportunity arose, her actions were contrary to her own wishes and her sister's; because in the square she came across an old woman who had a doll in her lap, the most beautiful and well-modeled that had ever been seen. And so Adamantina, seeing and observing it, conceived such a yearning for it that she thought more about acquiring it than about selling the thread. And so, reflecting on this, and not knowing what to do or say, if only she could have the doll, Adamantina decided to try her luck and see if she could get it by barter. And approaching the old woman, she said: "Mother, if you liked, I'd gladly exchange my thread for your doll." The old woman, seeing that the girl was pretty, charming, and so eager for the doll, couldn't refuse her; taking the thread, she offered her the doll. Receiving the doll, Adamantina was more pleased than she had ever been; joyfully and merrily she returned home. Her sister Cassandra asked: "Have you sold the thread?" "Yes," Adamantina replied. "Then where's the bread that you bought?" asked Cassandra. Adamantina, spreading out the laundered pinafore she always wore, showed her the doll she had bartered

aveva. Cassandra, che di fame si sentiva morire, veduta la poavola, di sì fatta ira e sdegno s'accese, che, presa Adamantina per le treccie, le diede tante busse, che appena la meschina si poteva movere. Adamantina, pazientemente ricevute le busse, senza far difesa alcuna, meglio che seppe e puoté con la sua poavola in una camera se n'andò. Venuta la sera, Adamantina, come le fanciullette fanno, tolse la poavola in braccio, e andossene al fuoco; e preso de l'oglio della lucerna, le unse lo stomaco e le rene; indi, rivolta in certi stracci che ella aveva, in letto la mise, e indi a poco, andatasene a letto, appresso la poavola si coricò. Né appena Adamantina aveva fatto il primo sonno, che la poavola cominciò chiamare: «Mamma, mamma, caca». E Adamantina destata, disse: «Che hai, figliuola mia?» A cui rispose la poavola: «Io vorrei far caca, mamma mia». E Adamantina: «Aspetta, figliuola mia» disse. E levatasi di letto, prese il grembiale, che 'l giorno dinanzi portava, e glielo pose sotto dicendo: «Fa' caca, figliuola»; e la poavola, tuttavia premendo, empì il grembiale di gran quantità di danari. Il che vedendo, Adamantina destò la sorella Cassandra, e le mostrò i danari che aveva cacati la poavola. Cassandra, vedendo il gran numero de' danari, stupefatta rimase, Iddio ringraziando che per sua bontà nelle lor miserie abbandonate non aveva; e voltatasi alla sorella, le chiese perdono delle busse che da lei a gran torto ricevute aveva, e fece molte carezze alla poavola, dolcemente basciandola e nelle braccia strettamente tenendola. Venuto il chiaro giorno, le sorelle fornirono la casa di pane, di vino, di oglio, di legna, e di tutte quelle cose che appartengono ad una ben accomodata famiglia. E ogni sera ungevano lo stomaco e le rene alla poavola, e in sottilissimi pannicelli la rivoglievano, e sovente se la voleva far caca le domandavano. Ed ella rispondeva che sì, e molti danari cacava. Avenne che una sua vicina, essendo andata in casa delle due sorelle, e avendo veduta la loro casa in ordine di ciò che le faceva mestieri, molto si maravigliò; né si poteva persuadere che sì tosto fussero venute sì ricche, essendo già state sì poverissime, e tanto più conoscendole di buona vita e sì oneste del corpo loro, che opposizione alcuna non pativano. Laonde la vicina, dimorando in tal pensiero, determinò di operare sì che la potesse intendere dove procedesse la causa di cotanta grandezza. E andatasene alla casa delle due sorelle, disse: «Figliuole mie, come avete fatto voi a fornire sì pienamente la casa vostra, conciosiacosaché per lo adietro voi eravate sì poverelle?». A cui Cassandra, che era la maggior sorella, rispose: «Una libra di filo di stoppa con una poavola barattata abbiamo, la quale senza misura alcuna danari ci rende». Il che la vicina intendendo, nell'animo fieramente si turbò; e tanta invidia le crebbe, che di furargliela al tutto determinò. [. . .]

for. Cassandra, who felt as if she were dying of hunger, flared up so angrily and wrathfully on seeing the doll that she seized Adamantina by her braids and gave her so many blows that the poor girl could hardly move. Adamantina, receiving the blows patiently, without defending herself at all, went off into a room as best she could, taking her doll. When evening came, Adamantina, as little girls do, took the doll in her arms and went over to the hearth; taking oil from the lamp, she smeared it on its stomach and back; then, wrapping it in some rags she had, she put it to bed; shortly thereafter, going to bed herself, she lay down beside the doll. Scarcely had Adamantina fallen asleep when the doll began to call out: "Mama, mama, number two!" And Adamantina, awakening, asked: "What's wrong, daughter?" The doll replied: "I need to make number two, mama!" And Adamantina said: "Wait, daughter." Getting out of bed, she took the pinafore she had worn the day before, and put it under the doll, saying: "Make number two, daughter"; and the doll, constantly squeezing, filled the pinafore with a large number of coins. Seeing this, Adamantina awakened her sister Cassandra and showed her the money that the doll had excreted. Cassandra, seeing the great quantity of coins, was dumbfounded, thanking God for His kindness in not abandoning them in their poverty; turning to her sister, she begged her forgiveness for the blows she had received from her most undeservedly, and gave the doll many caresses, kissing it gently and holding it tightly in her arms. When daylight came, the sisters supplied the house with bread, wine, oil, firewood, and all those things that are wanted in a well-ordered household. And every evening they anointed the doll's stomach and back and wrapped it in very fine cloths, asking it frequently whether it didn't want to make number two. It answered yes and excreted many coins. It came about that a lady neighbor, having gone to the two sisters' house and having found it well supplied with all necessities, was very surprised; she couldn't be convinced that they had so quickly become rich, having been so destitute before; all the more, because she knew they led an honest life and were so chaste that no one could suspect them of misbehaving. And so the neighbor, reflecting on this, decided to take steps to investigate the cause of such grandeur. Going to the two sisters' house, she asked: "Daughters, how have you managed to fill your house with goods this way, seeing that you were so poor in the past?" Cassandra, the elder sister, replied: "We exchanged a pound of thread spun from tow for a doll that brings us huge amounts of money." Hearing this, the neighbor was drastically disturbed in mind; and she became so envious that she absolutely decided to steal the doll from them. [. . .]

## 22. Cellini (1500–1571): *La vita*

(A) In tanto che queste cose seguivano, noi eramo tutti a tavola perché
la mattina s'era desinato più d'un'ora più tardi che 'l solito nostro.
Sentendo questi romori, un di quei figliuoli, il maggiore, si rizzò da
tavola per andare a vedere questa mistia. Questo si domandava
Giovanni, al quale io dissi: —Di grazia non andare, perché a simili cose
sempre si vede la perdita sicura sanza nulla di guadagno.— Il simile gli
diceva suo padre: —Deh, figliuol mio, non andare.— Questo giovane
senza udir persona, corse giù pella scala. Giunto in Banchi, dove era la
gran mistia, veduto Bertino levar di terra, correndo, tornando a drieto,
si riscontrò in Cecchino mio fratello, il quali lo domandò che cosa
quella era. Essendo Giovanni da alcuni accennato che tal cosa non di-
cessi al ditto Cecchino, disse a la 'npazzata come gli era che Bertino
Aldobrandi era stato ammazzato dalla corte. Il mio povero fratello
misse sì grande il mugghio, che dieci miglia si sarebbe sentito; di poi
disse a Giovanni: —Oimè, saprestimi tu dire chi di quelli me l'ha
morto?— Il ditto Giovanni disse che sì e che gli era un di quelli che
aveva uno spadone a dua mane, con una penna azzurra nella berretta.
Fattosi innanzi il mio povero fratello e conosciuto per quel con-
trassegno lo omicida, gittatosi con quella sua maravigliosa prestezza e
bravuria in mezzo a tutta quella corte, e sanza potervi rimediare punto,
messo una stoccata nella trippa, e passato dall'altra banda il detto, cogli
elsi della spada lo spinse in terra, voltosi agli altri con tanta virtù e ardire
che tutti lui solo gli metteva in fuga: se non che, giratosi per dare a uno
archibusiere, il quale per propia necessità sparato l'archibuso, colse il
valoroso sventurato giovane sopra il ginocchio della gamba dritta; e
posto in terra, la ditta corte mezza in fuga sollecitava a 'ndarsene, acciò
che un altro simile a questo sopraggiunto non fussi. [. . .]

(B) In termine d'un mese e mezzo il re ritornò a Parigi; e io, che avevo
lavorato giorno e notte, l'andai a trovare, e portai meco il mio modello,
di tanta bella bozza che chiaramente s'intendeva. Di già era cominciato
a rinnovare le diavolerie della guerra in fra lo imperadore e lui, di modo
che io lo trovai molto confuso; pure parlai col cardinale di Ferrara, dicendogli che io avevo meco certi modelli, i quali m'aveva commesso sua
maestà: così lo pregai che se e' vedeva tempo da commettere qualche
parola per causa che questi modegli si potessin mostrare, —io credo
che il re ne piglierebbe molto piacere.— Tanto fece il cardinale: pro-
pose al re detti modelli; subito il re venne dove io avevo i modelli. [. . .]
    Veduto il re questo modello, subito lo fece rallegrare e lo divertì da

## 22. Cellini (1500–1571): *Autobiography*

(A) While these things were occurring, we were all at table because that morning we had eaten over an hour later than usual. Hearing that racket, one of those sons, the eldest, got up from the table to go and see that brawl. His name was Giovanni. I said to him: "Please don't go, because, in such matters, loss is certain with no prospect of gain." His father said the same: "Come, son, don't go!" Heeding no one, this young man ran downstairs. Reaching Banchi Street, where the great brawl was, and seeing Bertino lifted from the ground, he ran, turning right, and met my brother Cecchino, who asked him what was wrong. Though Giovanni had been tipped off by someone not to tell Cecchino about it, he thoughtlessly told him that Bertino Aldobrandi had been killed by a squad of police. My poor brother emitted such a moan that it could be heard ten miles around; then he asked Giovanni: "Woe is me! Can you tell me which one of them killed him?" This Giovanni said he could do: it was one of those wearing a two-handed sword and a blue feather in his cap. My poor brother, having proceeded onward and recognizing the killer by those signs, hurled himself with his amazing speed and courage into the midst of that whole squad, they being altogether unable to defend themselves; he gave the fellow a thrust in the guts that came out the other side; with the hilt of the sword he pushed him to the ground. Then he faced the others so skillfully and boldly that he, being one man, was putting them all to flight: only, as he turned to strike a harquebusier, that man fired his harquebus to defend himself and hit the unfortunate brave young man in the knee of his right leg. Having thrown him to the ground, he urged that squad, which was in mid-flight, to depart so that another man like this one wouldn't show up. [. . .]

(B) After a month and a half the king returned to Paris; and I, who had labored day and night, went to see him, taking with me my model, which had been so finely crafted that it could be understood clearly. The devilry of the war between him and the emperor had begun again, so that I found him very preoccupied; so I spoke with the cardinal of Ferrara, telling him I had some models with me that His Majesty had commissioned: thus I begged him, if he saw the opportunity, to put in a word so that those models could be shown. "I think the king would derive much pleasure from them." The cardinal did this: he mentioned those models to the king, and at once the king came to the place where I had the models. [. . .]

When the king saw this model, it immediately cheered him up, dis-

quei ragionamenti fastidiosi in che gli era stato più di dua ore. Vedutolo io lieto a mio modo, gli scopersi l'altro modello, quale lui punto non a-spettava, parendogli d'aver veduto assai opera in quello. Questo modello era grande più di due braccia, nel quale avevo fatto una fontana in forma d'un quadro perfetto, con bellissime iscalee intorno, quale s'intrasega-vano l'una nell'altra: cosa che mai più s'era vista in quelle parti, e raris-sima in queste. In mezzo a detta fontana avevo fatto un sodo, il quale si dimostrava un poco più alto che 'l ditto vaso della fontana: sopra questo sodo avevo fatto, a conrispondenza, una figura igniuda di molta bella grazia. Questa teneva una lancia rotta nella man destra elevata in alto, e la sinistra teneva in sul manico d'una sua storta fatta di bellissima forma: posava in sul piè manco e il ritto teneva in su un cimiere tanto riccamente lavorato, quanto inmaginar si possa; e in su e' quattro canti della fontana avevo fatto, in su ciascuno, una figura a sedere elevata, con molte sue vaghe inprese per ciascuna. Comincionmi a dimandare il re che io gli di-cessi che bella fantasia era quella che io avevo fatta, dicendomi che tutto quello che io avevo fatto alla porta, sanza dimandarmi di nulla lui l'aveva inteso, ma che questo della fonte, sebbene gli pareva bellissimo, nulla non n'intendeva; e ben sapeva che io non avevo fatto come gli altri scioc-chi, che se bene e' facevano cose con qualche poco di grazia, le facevano senza significato nissuno. A questo io mi messi in ordine: ché essendo piaciuto col fare, volevo bene che altrentanto piacessi il mio dire. — Sappiate, sacra maestà, che tutta quest'opera piccola è benissimo misu-rata a piedi piccoli, qual mettendola poi in opera, verrà di questa medesi-ma grazia che voi vedete. Quella figura di mezzo si è cinquantaquattro piedi— (questa parola il re fé grandissimo segnio di maravigliarsi); —ap-presso, è fatta figurando lo idio Marte. Quest'altre quattro figure son fatte per le Virtù, di che si diletta e favorisce tanto vostra maestà: questa a man destra è figurata per la scienza di tutte le Lettere: vedete che l'ha i sua contra segni, qual dimostra la Filosofia con tutte le sue vertù compagnie. Quest'altra dimostra essere tutta l'Arte del disegnio, cioè Scultura, Pittura e Architettura. Quest'altra è figurata per la Musica, qual si con-viene per compagnia a tutte queste iscienzie. Quest'altra, che si dimostra tanto grata e benigna, è figurata per la Liberalità: ché sanza lei non si può dimostrare nessuna di queste mirabil Virtù che Idio ci mostra. Questa i-statua di mezzo, grande, è figurata per vostra maestà istessa, quale è un dio Marte, che voi siete sol bravo al mondo; e questa bravuria voi l'adope-rate iustamente e santamente in difensione della gloria vostra.— Appena che gli ebbe tanta pazienza che mi lasciassi finir di dire, che levato gran voce, disse: —Veramente io ho trovato uno uomo sicondo il cuor mio—; e chiamò li tesaurieri ordinatimi, e disse che mi provvedessino tutto quel

tracting him from those tiresome discussions he had attended for over two hours. Seeing him as happy as I wished, I uncovered the second model, which he wasn't at all expecting; he thought he had seen enough in the first one. This second model was over two yards high; in it I had made a fountain in the shape of a perfect square, with very beautiful staircases around it that intersected one another—something that had never been seen before in those parts, and only rarely here in Italy. In the middle of that fountain I had made a pedestal that was a little higher than the basin of the fountain: on this pedestal I had made, in proportion, a nude figure of extremely elegant grace. The figure held a broken lance in its raised right hand, while its left hand held the handle of a beautifully shaped scimitar. It was supported on its left foot and rested its right foot on a helmet that was as richly adorned as can be imagined; at each of the four corners of the fountain I had made an elevated seated figure, with many pretty devices on each one. The king began to ask me to tell him what this lovely imaginative thing was that I had made, saying that he had understood, without asking anything, all that I had done on the portal [the first model], but that this one of the fountain, though he thought it was very beautiful, he couldn't understand at all; he was well aware that I hadn't acted like those fools who, even if they fashioned things with a bit of grace to them, made them with no meaning whatsoever. Thereupon I put my thoughts in order: having pleased him visually, I certainly wanted to please him just as much with my words. "I'll have Your Sacred Majesty know that this entire little work is perfectly constructed to a smaller scale; when it's carried out, it will be just as graceful as you see. That central figure will be fifty-four feet high." (At those words the king gave a conspicuous sign of surprise.) "Next, it depicts the god Mars. These other four figures represent the Virtues which Your Majesty favors and takes such delight in. The one on the right represents the entire art of Literature: you see that it bears emblems betokening Philosophy and all its companion virtues. This second one is meant to be the whole art of design; that is, Sculpture, Painting, and Architecture. This next one is meant to be Music, an appropriate companion for all those other arts. This one, which looks so pleasing and benign, is meant to be Generosity, without which none of those admirable virtues which God shows us can be made manifest. The central statue, the tall one, is meant to be Your Majesty himself, in the form of the god Mars, for you are the only brave man in the world; and you use this bravery justly and sacredly in defense of your fame." No sooner had he been patient enough to let me finish speaking than he said very loudly: "Truly I've found a man after my own heart!" And he called for the treasurers

che mi faceva di bisognio, e fussi grande ispesa quanto si volessi: poi a me
dette in su la spalla con la mana, dicendomi: —*Mon ami* (che vuol dire
"amico mio"), io non so qual s'è maggior piacere, o quello d'un principe
l'aver trovato un uomo sicondo il suo cuore, o quello di quel virtuoso
l'aver trovato un principe che gli dia tanta comodità, che lui possa
esprimere i sua gran virtuosi concetti.— Io risposi che se io ero quello
che diceva sua maestà, gli era stato molto maggior ventura la mia.
Rispose ridendo: —Diciamo che la sia eguale.— Partimmi con grande
allegrezza, e tornai alle mie opere. [. . .]

## 23. Della Casa (1503–1556): *Galateo*

E sappi che in Verona ebbe già un vescovo molto savio di scrittura e di
senno naturale, il cui nome fu messer Giovanni Matteo Giberti; il quale
fra gli altri suoi laudevoli costumi si fu cortese e liberale assai a' nobili gentiluomini che andavano e venivano a lui, onorandogli in casa sua con ma-
gnificenza non soprabbondante, ma mezzana, quale conviene a cherico.
Avvenne che, passando in quel tempo di là un nobile uomo nomato conte
Ricciardo, egli si dimorò più giorni col vescovo e con la famiglia di lui, la
quale era per lo più di costumati uomini e scienziati; e, perciocché gentilissimo cavaliere parea loro e di bellissime maniere, molto lo commen-
darono e apprezzarono; se non che un picciolo difetto avea ne' suoi modi;
del quale essendosi il vescovo, che intendente signore era, avveduto e
avutone consiglio con alcuno de' suoi più domestichi, proposero che
fosse da farne avveduto il conte, comeché temessero di fargliene noia. Per
la qual cosa, avendo già il conte preso commiato e dovendosi partir la
mattina vegnente, il vescovo, chiamato un suo discreto famigliare, gli impose che, montato a cavallo col conte per modo di accompagnarlo, se ne
andasse con esso lui alquanto di via e, quando tempo gli paresse, per
dolce modo gli venisse dicendo quello che essi aveano proposto tra loro.
Era il detto famigliare uomo già pieno d'anni, molto scienziato e oltre ad
ogni credenza piacevole e ben parlante e di grazioso aspetto, e molto avea
de' suoi dì usato alle corti de' gran signori; il quale fu e forse ancora è
chiamato messer Galateo, a petizion del quale e per suo consiglio presi io
da prima a dettar questo presente trattato. Costui, cavalcando col conte,
lo ebbe assai tosto messo in piacevoli ragionamenti, e, di uno in altro passando, quando tempo gli parve di dover verso Verona tornarsi, pregan-
donelo il conte ed accomiatandolo, con lieto viso gli venne dolcemente
così dicendo: —Signor mio, il vescovo mio signore rende a Vostra
Signoria infinite grazie dell'onore che egli ha da voi ricevuto, il quale de-

assigned to me, ordering them to provide me with everything I needed, no matter how great the expense; then he clapped me on the shoulder, saying: *"Mon ami"* (this means, "my friend"), "I don't know which one has the greater pleasure, a ruler who has found a man after his own heart, or an artist who has found a prince that will give him the wherewithal to express his great artistic conceptions." I replied that, if I were the man His Majesty alluded to, *my* good fortune had been by far the greater. Laughing, he replied: "Let's say they're equal!" I departed most joyfully and returned to my work. [. . .]

## 23. Della Casa (1503–1556): *Galateo*

And hear this: In the past there was in Verona a bishop very wise in learning and in common sense, whose name was Giovanni Matteo Giberti; among his other praiseworthy traits he was very courteous and generous to the noble gentlemen who came to see him, honoring them in his house with a munificence that wasn't excessive, but moderate, as befits a priest. It came about that a nobleman called Count Ricciardo passed that way at that time and stayed for a few days with the bishop and his household, comprised for the most part of well-bred and learned men; and because he struck them as being a very elegant knight with beautiful manners, they praised and admired him, except for one little defect in etiquette. The bishop, who was an observant gentleman, having noticed this and discussed it with one of his closest friends, they decided that the count should be made aware of it, though they feared to give him displeasure. Therefore, when the count had already taken leave, being due to depart the next morning, the bishop summoned a discreet member of his staff and ordered him to mount a horse along with the count, as if intending to accompany him, and to travel a good distance with him; then, when it seemed opportune, to tell him gently what they had decided on together. This staff member was a man already full of years, very learned, and amazingly charming, well-spoken, and gracious-looking, and for much of his life he had frequented the courts of grandees; he was, and perhaps still is, called Lord Galateo, and it was at his request and advice that I first began to indite the present treatise. He, riding with the count, had very soon engaged him in pleasant conversations, and moving from one topic to another, when he thought it was time to return to Verona, the count urging him to do so and saying good-bye, he spoke to him as follows with a cheerful expression: "My lord, my master the bishop thanks

gnato vi siete di entrare e di soggiornar nella sua picciola casa; ed oltre a ciò, in riconoscimento di tanta cortesia da voi usata verso di lui, mi ha imposto che io vi faccia un dono per sua parte, e caramente vi manda pregando che vi piaccia di riceverlo con lieto animo: e il dono è questo. Voi siete il più leggiadro e il più costumato gentiluomo che mai paresse al vescovo di vedere. Per la qual cosa avendo egli attentamente risguardato alle vostre maniere ed essaminatole partitamente, niuna ne ha tra loro trovata che non sia sommamente piacevole e commendabile, fuori solamente un atto difforme che voi fate con le labbra e con la bocca masticando alla mensa con un nuovo strepito molto spiacevole ad udire: questo vi manda significando il vescovo e pregandovi che voi v'ingegnate del tutto di rimanervene e che voi prendiate in luogo di caro dono la sua amorevole riprensione ed avvertimento; perciocché egli si rende certo, niuno altro al mondo essere che tale presente vi facesse. —Il conte, che del suo difetto non si era ancora mai avveduto, udendoselo rimproverare arrossò così un poco; ma, come valente uomo, assai tosto ripreso cuore, disse: —Direte al vescovo che, se tali fossero tutti i doni che gli uomini si fanno infra di loro, quale il suo è, eglino troppo più ricchi sarebbono che essi non sono; e di tanta sua cortesia e liberalità verso di me ringraziatelo senza fine, assicurandolo che io del mio difetto senza dubbio, per innanzi bene e diligentemente mi guarderò; e andatevi con Dio.

Ora che crediamo noi che avesse il vescovo e la sua nobil brigata detto a coloro che noi veggiamo talora, a guisa di porci col grifo nella broda tutti abbandonati, non levar mai alto il viso e mai non rimuover gli occhi e molto meno le mani dalle vivande e con ambedue le gote gonfiate, come se essi sonassero la tromba o soffiassero nel fuoco, non mangiare ma trangugiare? i quali, imbrattandosi le mani poco meno che fino al gomito, conciano in guisa le tovagliuole che le pezze degli agiamenti sono più nette? Con le quai tovagliuole anco molto spesso non si vergognano di rasciugare il sudore che per lo affrettarsi e per lo soverchio mangiare gocciola e cade loro dalla fronte e dal viso e d'intorno al collo, e anco di nettarsi con esse il naso quando voglia loro ne viene. Veramente questi così fatti non meriterebbono di essere ricevuti non pure nella purissima casa di quel nobile vescovo, ma doverebbono essere scacciati per tutto là dove costumati uomini fossero. Dée adunque l'uomo costumato guardarsi di non ugnersi le dita sì che la tovagliuola ne rimanga imbrattata: perciocché ella è stomachevole a vedere. Ed anco il fregarle al pane che egli dée mangiare non pare polito costume. I nobili servidori, i quali si essercitano nel servigio della tavola, non si deono per alcuna condizione grattare il capo né altrove dinanzi al loro signore quando e' mangia, né porsi le mani in alcuna di quelle parti del

Your Lordship no end for the honor he has received from you for having deigned to enter and sojourn in his little house; furthermore, in gratitude for the great courtesy you showed him, he ordered me to give you a gift from him, and he begs you sincerely, through me, to deign to receive it cheerfully; and the gift is this: You are the most comely and mannerly gentleman the bishop thinks he's ever seen. Therefore, having attentively observed your manners and examined them minutely, he has found none among them that isn't extremely pleasant and commendable, except a vulgar action you perform with your lips and mouth, chewing at table with an odd noise most unpleasant to hear; the bishop sends me to point this out to you and to urge you to do your best to drop that habit; he wishes you to accept in lieu of an expensive gift his loving reproach and admonition; because he's sure that no one else in the world would make you such a present." The count, who had never been aware of his failing, blushed a little when he heard himself reproached for it; but, like a brave man, he took heart again very quickly and said: "Tell the bishop that if all the gifts people exchange were like his, they'd be much richer than they are; and give him no end of thanks for his great courtesy and generosity to me, assuring him that without any doubt I shall guard myself against my failing in the future very diligently. Farewell!"

Now, what do you think the bishop and his noble followers would have said to those we sometimes see letting themselves go completely, like pigs with their snout in the swill, never raising their face and never ungluing their eyes, let alone their hands, from their food, with both their cheeks swollen as if they were playing the trumpet or blowing up a fire, not eating but gulping down? Dirtying their arms almost up to the elbow, they soil their napkins so badly that latrine rags are cleaner. In fact, very often they aren't ashamed to use those napkins to wipe away the sweat that their haste and their gorging causes to drip and fall from their forehead and face and around their neck, and they even blow their nose into them whenever they feel like it. Truly, people of that sort not only wouldn't deserve to be received in the very pure house of that noble bishop, but should be chased out wherever there are well-mannered men. So a well-bred man should refrain from soiling his fingers so badly that his napkin is dirtied by them: because it's a disgusting sight. And also, wiping them on the bread he is to eat doesn't seem like a polite habit. The noble servants who are employed in waiting on the table should by no means scratch themselves on the head or elsewhere in front of their master while he's eating, or place their hands on any of those parts of the body that are covered up, or even call attention to them, as

corpo che si cuoprono; né pure farne sembiante, sì come alcuni trascu-
rati famigliari fanno, tenendosele in seno o di dietro nascoste sotto a'
panni; ma le deono tenere in palese e fuori d'ogni sospetto, ed averle
con ogni diligenzia lavate e nette senza avervi sù pure un segnuzzo di
bruttura in alcuna parte. E quelli, che arrecano i piattelli o porgono la
coppa, diligentemente si astenghino in quell'ora da sputare, da tossire e
più da starnutire, perciocché in simili atti tanto vale e così noia i signori
la sospezione quanto la certezza: e perciò procurino i famigliari di non
dar cagione a' padroni di sospicare, perciocché quello che poteva addi-
venire così noia come se egli fosse avvenuto. [. . .]

## 24. Cinzio (1504–1573): *Hecatommiti*

Fu già in Venezia un Moro molto valoroso, il quale, per essere
pro'della persona, e per aver dato segno, nelle cose della guerra, di
gran prudenza e di vivace ingegno, era molto caro a que' signori, i
quali, nel dar premio agli atti vertuosi, avanzano quante republiche
fur mai. Avenne che una virtuosa donna, di maravigliosa bellezza,
Disdemona chiamata, tratta non da appetito donnesco, ma dalla virtù
del Moro, s'innamorò di lui, ed egli, vinto dalla bellezza e dal nobile
pensiero della donna, similmente di lei si accese, ed ebbero tanto fa-
vorevole Amore, che si congiunsero insieme per matrimonio, ancora
che i parenti della donna facessero ciò che poterono, perché ella altro
marito si prendesse, che lui; e vissero insieme di sì concorde volere,
ed in tanta tranquillità, mentre furono in Venezia, che mai tra loro non
fu, non dirò cosa, ma parola men che amorevole.

Occorse che i signori Veneziani fecero mutazione delle genti d'arme,
ch'essi sogliono tenere in Cipri, ed elesseno per capitano de' soldati che
là mandavano, il Moro; il quale, ancora che molto lieto fosse dell'onore
che gli era offerto (però che tal grado di degnità non si suol dare, se non
ad uomini e nobili e forti e fedeli, e che abbiano mostrato avere in sé
molto valore), si scemava nondimeno la sua allegrezza, qualora egli si
poneva innanzi la lunghezza e la malagevolezza del viaggio, pensandosi
che Disdemona ne devesse rimanere offesa. La donna, che altro bene
non aveva al mondo che il Moro, ed era molto contenta del testimonio
ch'aveva avuto il marito della sua virtù da così possente e nobile repu-
blica, non vedea l'ora che il marito colle sue genti si mettesse in camino,
ed ella andasse seco in compagnia in così onorato luogo; ma le dava gran
noia il vedere il Moro turbato. E non ne sapendo la cagione, un giorno,
mangiando, gli disse: «Che vuol egli dir, Moro, che poi che vi è stato dato

some careless servants do, keeping them inside their shirts or hidden under their clothes behind them; they ought to keep them out in the open, avoiding all suspicion, having very carefully washed and cleaned them so that there isn't even a trace of dirt anywhere on them. And those who serve dishes or hand out goblets must carefully refrain at such moments from spitting, coughing, and especially sneezing, because in such actions suspicion vexes their masters just as much as certainty would: therefore, let the servants not give their masters cause for suspicion, since a thing that might have occurred is as vexatious as if it had really occurred. [. . .]

## 24. Cinzio (1504–1573): *The Hundred Tales*

There was once in Venice a very brave Moor who, because he was physi cally courageous and had shown tokens in martial affairs of great prudence and lively talent, was very dear to those lords who, in rewarding virtuous actions, surpass all republics that have ever existed. It came about that a virtuous lady of extreme beauty, named Desdemona, attracted not by female lust but by the Moor's excellence, fell in love with him, and that he, vanquished by the lady's beauty and loftiness of mind, was also smitten with her, and that Love was so favorable to them that they joined together in matrimony, though the lady's relatives did all they could to make her take a different husband, not him. And they lived together in such harmony of wills, and so peacefully, while they were in Venice, that there was never anything between them, not even a word, that was less than loving.

It came about that the Venetian lords relieved the troops they customarily maintain on Cyprus and chose the Moor as general of the new soldiers they were sending there; though he was very pleased with the honor shown him (because such a high rank is usually reserved for noble, brave, and loyal men who have shown they have great courage), nonetheless his joy was diminished whenever he thought about the length and discomfort of the voyage, since he believed that it would do harm to Desdemona. The lady, whose only joy in the world was the Moor, and who was very pleased with the tribute to his talent her husband had received from such a mighty and noble republic, couldn't wait for the day when her husband and his men would set out and she would accompany him to such an honored place; but she was very vexed to see the Moor upset. Not knowing the reason for this, one day, while they were eating, she asked him: "What does it mean, Moor, that after being

dalla Signoria così onorato grado, ve ne state tanto maninconico?» A Disdemona disse il Moro: «Turba la contentezza del ricevuto onore l'amore che io ti porto, perché io veggo di necessità delle due cose deverne avenir l'una, overo che io ti meni con esso meco a' pericoli del mare, overo che, per non ti dar questo disagio, ti lasci in Venezia. La prima non mi potrebbe essere se non grave, perché ogni fatica che tu ne sostenessi, ed ogni pericolo che ci sopravenisse, mi recherebbe estrema molestia; la seconda, devendoti lasciare, mi sarebbe odioso a me medesimo, perché, partendomi da te, mi partirei dalla mia vita». Disdemona, ciò inteso: «Deh» disse «marito mio, che pensieri son questi che vi vanno per l'animo? a che lasciate che cosa tal vi turbi? Voglio io venire con voi, ovunque anderete, sebene così devessi passare in camicia per lo fuoco, come son per venire per acqua con voi, in sicura e ben guarnita nave. E se pure vi saranno pericoli e fatiche, io con voi ne voglio essere a parte, e mi terrei d'essere poco amata da voi, quando, per non mi avere in compagnia nel mare, pensaste di lasciarmi in Venezia, o vi persuadeste che più tosto mi volessi star qui sicura, ch'essere con voi in uno istesso pericolo. Però voglio che vi apparecchiate al viaggio, con tutta quella allegrezza che merita la qualità del grado che tenete». Gittò allora le braccia al collo, tutto lieto, il Moro alla mogliera, e, con uno affettuoso bacio, le disse: «Iddio ci conservi lungamente in questa amorevolezza, moglie mia cara». E indi a poco pigliati gli suoi arnesi, e messossi ad ordine per lo camino, entrò colla sua donna e con tutta la compagnia, nella galea, e date le vele al vento, si mise in camino, e con somma tranquillità del mare se n'andò in Cipri. Aveva costui nella compagnia un alfiero di bellissima presenza, ma della più scelerata natura, che mai fosse uomo del mondo. Era questi molto caro al Moro, non avendo egli delle sue cattività notizia alcuna; perché quantunque egli fosse di vilissimo animo, copriva nondimeno coll'alte e superbe parole e colla sua presenza, di modo la viltà ch'egli chiudea nel cuore, che si scopriva nella sembianza un Ettore, od uno Achille. Avea similmente menata questo malvagio la sua moglie in Cipri, la quale era bella ed onesta giovane, e per essere Italiana, era molto amata dalla moglie del Moro, e si stava la maggior parte del giorno con lei. Nella medesima compagnia era anco un capo di squadra, carissimo al Moro. Andava spessissime volte questi a casa del Moro, e spesso mangiava con lui e con la moglie. Laonde la donna, che lo conosceva così grato al suo marito, gli dava segni di grandissima benivolenza; la qual cosa era molto cara al Moro. Lo scelerato alfiero, non curando punto la fede data alla sua moglie, né amicizia, né fede, né obligo ch'egli avesse al Moro, s'innamorò di Disdemona ardentissimamente, e voltò tutto il suo pensiero a vedere se gli poteva venir fatto di godersi di

given such a high rank by the Signoria, you're so melancholy about it?"
The Moor said to Desdemona: "My pleasure in the honor I've received
is clouded by the love I bear you, because I see that one of two things
must necessarily happen, either that I expose you with myself to the
perils of the sea, or that, to avoid giving you that discomfort, I leave you
in Venice. The first case could only be grievous to me, because any fatigue you suffered and any emergency that occurred would give me extreme displeasure; the second case, having to leave you behind, would
be personally hateful to me, because, parting from you, I'd be parting
with my life." Hearing this, Desdemona said: "Ah, husband, what
thoughts are these that are passing through your mind? Why do you let
such things upset you? I want to come with you wherever you go, even
if it meant walking through fire in my shift instead of sailing with you
in a safe, well-furnished ship. And even if there are dangers and fa-
tigues, I want to share them with you, and I'd consider myself not truly
loved by you if, to avoid having my company at sea, you thought of leaving me in Venice or persuaded yourself that I'd rather remain in safety
here than be in the same danger you were in. And so I want you to pre-
pare for the voyage with all the joy that the high rank you have de-
serves." Then the Moor, overjoyed, threw his arms around his wife's
neck and, with a loving kiss, said: "May God long keep us in this state
of love, my dear wife!" Shortly thereafter, taking his equipment, having
made all arrangements for the journey, he boarded the galley with his
wife and all his troops, and, with sails spread, set out and, enjoying a
completely calm sea, arrived in Cyprus. He had in his company an ensign of very fine presence but of the most evil nature that anyone ever
had. He was greatly liked by the Moor, who had no idea of his wicked
ways, because, though his mind was of the basest, nevertheless he so
concealed beneath his lofty, proud words and his good looks the vile-
ness he had locked in his heart that he appeared outwardly like a
Hector or an Achilles. This evil man had also brought his wife to
Cyprus; a beautiful and respectable young woman, because she was
Italian she was greatly loved by the Moor's wife and spent most of every
day with her. In the same company was also a captain much liked by the
Moor. This man would visit the Moor's house very often, frequently
dining with him and his wife. And so the lady, who knew he was so
pleasing to her husband, showed him signs of very great good will; the
Moor was very contented with this. The evil ensign, paying no heed to
the troth he had pledged to his wife, nor to friendship, loyalty, or his
obligation to the Moor, fell passionately in love with Desdemona, and
turned all his thoughts to see whether he could succeed in enjoying

lei; ma non ardiva di dimostrarsi, temendo che se il Moro se ne avedesse, non gli desse subito morte. Cercò egli con varii modi, quanto più occultamente poteva, di fare accorta la donna ch'egli l'amava; ma ella, ch'avea nel Moro ogni suo pensiero, non pensava punto né allo alfiero, né ad altri. E tutte le cose ch'egli facea per accenderla di lui, non più operavano, che se fatte non le avesse. Onde s'imaginò costui che ciò avenisse, perché ella fosse accesa del capo di squadra, e pensò volerlosi levar dinanzi agli occhi. [. . .]

## 25. Vasari (1511–1574): *Le vite*

(A) Ma quello che sopra tutte le cose dette fu di perdita e danno infinitamente alle predette professioni, fu il fervente zelo della nuova religione cristiana; la quale dopo lungo e sanguinoso combattimento, avendo finalmente con la copia de' miracoli e con la sincerità delle operazioni abbattuta e annullata la vecchia fede de' gentili; mentre che ardentissimamente attendeva con ogni diligenza a levar via ed a stirpare in tutto ogni minima occasione, donde poteva nascere errore; non guastò solamente o gettò per terra tutte le statue maravigliose, e le sculture e pitture, musaici ed ornamenti de' fallaci Dii de' gentili; ma le memorie ancora e gli onori d'infinite persone egregie, alle quali per gli eccellenti meriti loro dalla virtuosissima antichità erano state poste in pubblico le statue e l'altre memorie. Inoltre, per edificare le chiese all'usanza cristiana, non solamente distrusse i più onorati tempii degl'idoli; ma, per fare diventare più nobile e per adornare San Pietro, oltre gli ornamenti che da principio avuto avea, spogliò di colonne di pietra la mole d'Adriano, oggi detto Castello Sant'Agnolo, e molte altre, le quali veggiamo oggi guaste. Ed avvegnaché la religione cristiana non facesse questo per odio che ella avesse per le virtù, ma solo per contumelia ed abbattimento degli Dii de' gentili; non fu però che da questo ardentissimo zelo non seguisse tanta rovina a queste onorate professioni, che non se ne perdesse in tutto la forma. E, se niente mancava a questo grave infortunio, sopravvenne l'ira di Totila contra a Roma; che, oltre a sfasciarla di mura, e rovinar col ferro e col fuoco tutti i più mirabili e degni edificii di quella, universalmente la bruciò tutta; e spogliatala di tutti i viventi corpi, la lasciò in preda alle fiamme ed al fuoco; e, senza che in diciotto giorni continui si ritrovasse in quella vivente alcuno, abbatté e distrusse talmente le statue, le pitture, i musaici e gli stucchi maravigliosi che se ne perdé, non dico la maestà sola, ma la forma e l'essere stesso. Per il che, es-

her; but he didn't dare to declare himself for fear lest the Moor should notice and kill him on the spot. He tried various ways, as secretly as he could, to make the lady aware that he loved her; but she, who was completely devoted to the Moor, had no thoughts either for the ensign or any other man. And nothing he did to arouse love in her for him had any more effect than if it had been left undone. And so he imagined that this was happening because she was in love with the captain, and he determined to get him out of the way. [. . .]

## 25. Vasari (1511–1574): *The Lives*

(A) But that which, more than anything yet said, led to the infinite damage and destruction of the aforesaid artistic professions was the fervent zeal of the new Christian religion, which, after a long, bloody combat, had finally, through an abundance of miracles and the sincerity of its works, overturned and nullified the former faith of the pagans; while it was ardently striving with all diligence to remove and extirpate altogether even the slightest occasion that could give rise to a relapse, not only did it ruin or throw to the ground all the wondrous statues, sculptures, paintings, mosaics, and ornaments of the false gods of the pagans, but even the memory and honors of very many outstanding people to whom, for their eminent merits, the virtuous ancients had erected public statues and other memorials. Furthermore, in order to build churches for Christian use, not only did the new religion destroy the most esteemed temples of the idols, but, to make Saint Peter's more noble and to adorn it, beyond the ornaments it had had from the outset, it despoiled of their stone columns Hadrian's tomb, today called the Castel Sant'Angelo, and many other structures that we see in ruins today. And even though the Christian religion didn't do this out of hatred for virtues, but merely to dishonor and overturn the gods of the pagans, nevertheless this very ardent zeal resulted in such great ruin of these honored professions that they completely lost their form. And, as if there were nothing lacking to this grave misfortune, there then occurred Totila's wrath against Rome; besides destroying its walls and ravaging all its most noteworthy and meritorious buildings with steel and fire, he burned it entirely. Removing all living bodies from the city, he left it a prey to fire and flame; and, with no one left living in it after eighteen days on end, he overturned and destroyed its statues, paintings, mosaics, and wonderful stucco work so extensively that not only just its majesty, but its very form and existence were lost. Therefore, the ground-floor rooms of

sendo le stanze terrene, prima, de' palazzi o altri edificii, di stucchi, di pitture e di statue lavorate, con le rovine di sopra affogarono tutto il buono, che a' giorni nostri s'è ritrovato. E coloro che successer poi, giudicando il tutto rovinato, vi piantarono sopra le vigne: di maniera che, per essere le dette stanze terrene rimaste sotto terra, le hanno i moderni nominate grotto e grottesche le pitture che vi si veggono al presente. [. . .]

(B) Scoperto questo Giudizio, mostrò non solo Michelagnolo essere vincitore de' primi artefici che lavorato nella Sistina avevano, ma ancora nella volta, che egli tanto celebrata aveva fatta, volse vincere sé stesso; ed in quella di gran lunga passatosi, superò sé medesimo, avendosi egli imaginato il terrore di que' giorni, dove egli fa rappresentare, per più pena di chi non è ben vissuto, tutta la sua Passione; facendo portare in aria da diverse figure ignude la croce, la colonna, la lancia, la spugna, i chiodi e la corona, con diverse e varie attitudini molto dificilmente condotte a fine nella facilità loro. Evvi Cristo, il quale, sedendo, con faccia orribile e fiera ai dannati si volge, maladicendogli, non senza gran timore della Nostra Donna, che, ristrettasi nel manto, ode e vede tanta rovina. Sonvi infinitissime figure, che gli fanno cerchio, di Profeti, di Apostoli, e particolarmente Adamo e santo Pietro, i quali si stimano che vi sieno messi l'uno per l'origine prima delle genti al giudizio, l'altro per essere stato il primo fondamento della cristiana religione. A' piedi gli è un san Bartolomeo bellissimo, il qual mostra la pelle scorticata. Evvi similmente un ignudo di san Lorenzo; oltra che senza numero sono infinitissimi santi e sante, ed altre figure, maschi e femine intorno, appresso e discosto, i quali si abbracciano e fannosi festa, avendo per grazia di Dio, e guidardone delle opere loro, la beatitudine eterna. Sono sotto i piedi di Cristo i setti angeli scritti da san Giovanni evangelista, con le sette trombe, che, sonando a sentenza, fanno arricciare i capelli a chi li guarda, per la terribilità che essi mostrano nel viso; e fra gli altri vi sono due Angeli, che ciascuno ha il libro delle vite in mano; ed appresso, non senza bellissima considerazione, si veggono i setti peccati mortali da una banda combattere in forma di diavoli, e tirar giù allo inferno l'anime, che volano al cielo con attitudini bellissime, e scorti molto mirabili. Né ha restato nella resurrezione de' morti mostrare al mondo, come essi nella medesima terra ripiglion l'ossa e la carne, e come da altri vivi aiutati vanno volando al cielo, che da alcune anime già beate è loro porto aiuto; non senza vedersi tutte quelle parti di considerazioni, che a una tanta opera, come quella, si possa stimare che si convenga: perchè per lui si

the palaces or other buildings, above all, being decorated with stucco work, paintings, and statues, the ruins from above smothered all the fine things that have been rediscovered in our days. And the people who later settled there, believing that everything was ruined, planted vines above it; so that, because those ground-floor rooms had remained underground, the moderns called them grottoes and called the paintings now seen there "grotesques." [. . .]

(B) When this Last Judgment was unveiled, Michelangelo showed that he had not only surpassed the earlier artists who had worked in the Sistine Chapel, but had even outdone his own work on its ceiling, which he had made so famous; having surpassed himself by far on the ceiling, he now outdid himself here, having imagined the terror of those last days, where he depicts, for the greater punishment of those who have led a bad life, every element of the Passion, showing various nude figures hold aloft the cross, the column, the lance, the sponge, the nails, and the crown of thorns, in various different poses made with great pains to appear natural. There you have Christ, who, seated, turns His awe-inspiring, fierce face to the damned, cursing them, not without great fear on the part of the Madonna, who, huddling in her cloak, hears and sees such destruction. There you have an infinity of figures encircling Him: prophets, apostles, and especially Adam and Saint Peter, who may be thought to have been placed there, one because he was the original progenitor of the people being judged, the other because he was the primary base of the Christian religion. At His feet is a very fine Saint Bartholomew displaying his flayed skin. Likewise there is a nude Saint Lawrence, besides an infinite number of male and female saints, and other male and female figures around Him, near and far, embracing and congratulating one another because, by the grace of God, and, as a reward for their good works, they have gained eternal bliss. Beneath Christ's feet are the seven angels described by Saint John the Evangelist, with their seven trumpets, which, sounding judgment, make the onlookers' hair stand on end, their faces have such a frightening expression; among the others are two angels, each of whom holds the Book of Life; near them, not without a very fine planning, are seen the seven deadly sins on one side fighting in the guise of devils and pulling down to hell the souls that are flying to heaven in beautiful poses, with really remarkable foreshortenings. Nor did he neglect to show the world, in the resurrection of the dead, how, still under the earth, they take on flesh and bones again, and how, aided by other live people, they fly to heaven, with some souls already in bliss coming to their aid; not omitting all those considerations which can be thought to pertain to such a work as

è fatto studi e fatiche d'ogni sorte, apparendo egualmente per tutta l'opera, come chiaramente e particolarmente ancor nella barca di Caronte si dimostra; il quale con attitudine disperata l'anime tirate dai diavoli giù nella barca batte col remo, ad imitazione di quello che espresse il suo famigliarissimo Dante quando disse:

> *Caron demonio con occhi di bragia*
> *loro accennando, tutte le raccoglie:*
> *batte col remo qualunque s'adagia.*

Né si può immaginare quanto di varietà sia nelle teste di que' diavoli, mostri veramente d'inferno. Nei peccatori si conosce il peccato e la tema insieme del danno eterno. Ed oltre a ogni bellezza straordinaria è il vedere tanta opera sì unitamente dipinta e condotta che ella pare fatta in un giorno, e con quella fine che mai minio nessuno si condusse talmente. E nel vero, la moltitudine delle figure, la terribilità e grandezza dell'opera è tale, che non si può descrivere, essendo piena di tutti i possibili umani affetti, ed avendogli tutti maravigliosamente espressi. [. . .]

## 26. Stampa (ca 1523–1554): 3 sonetti

(A) Io assimiglio il mio signor al cielo
meco sovente. Il suo bel viso è 'l sole;
gli occhi, le stelle; e 'l suon de le parole
è l'armonia, che fa 'l signor di Delo.

Le tempeste, le piogge, i tuoni e 'l gelo
son i suoi sdegni, quando irar si suole;
le bonacce e 'l sereno è quando vuole
squarciar de l'ire sue benigne il velo.

La primavera e 'l germogliar de' fiori
è quando ei fa fiorir la mia speranza,
promettendo tenermi in questo stato.

L'orrido verno è poi, quando cangiato
minaccia di mutar pensieri e stanza,
spogliata me de' miei più ricchi onori.

(B) Io non v'invidio punto, angeli santi,
le vostre tante glorie e tanti beni,

this; because he made studies and efforts of all sorts, equally apparent throughout the work, as can be seen clearly and especially, for instance, in Charon's boat; with an attitude of despair Charon is beating with his oar the souls dragged down to his boat by the devils, in accordance with the description by Dante, very familiar to the artist, who writes:

> Demonic Charon, with eyes like live coals
> beckoning to them, gathers them all together:
> with his oar he beats anyone who tarries.

Nor can one imagine how much variety there is in the heads of those devils, true monsters from hell. In the sinners one can recognize both their sin and their fear of eternal damnation. And besides all the beauty, it's extraordinary to see so large a work painted and carried out so uniformly that it seems to have been done in a single day, and with a perfection that no paint has ever achieved before. Truly, the vast number of figures, the awesomeness, and the grandeur of the work are such that it can't be described, being full of all possible human emotions, all of them marvelously expressed. [. . .]

## 26. Stampa (ca. 1523–1554): 3 sonnets

(A) I liken my lord to the sky
in my mind frequently. His fair face is the sun;
his eyes, the stars; and the sound of his speech
is the harmony made by Apollo, lord of Delos.

The storms, the rains, the thunders, and the frost
are his fits of anger whenever he grows wrathful;
the sky is calm and clear when he wishes
to rend the veil of his beneficent anger.

It is springtime and flowers blossom
when he makes my hopes bloom,
promising to keep me in this condition.

Then, it's horrid winter when, changing,
he threatens to alter his mood and his abode,
stripping me of my richest honors.

(B) I envy you not at all, holy angels,
for your great glory and your great boons,

e que' disir di ciò che braman pieni,
stando voi sempre a l'alto Sire avanti;

perché i diletti miei son tali e tanti,
che non posson capire in cor terreni,
mentr'ho davanti i lumi almi e sereni,
di cui conven che sempre scriva e canti.

E come in ciel gran refrigerio e vita
dal volto Suo solete voi fruire,
tal io qua giù da la beltà infinita.

In questo sol vincete il mio gioire,
che la vostra è eterna e stabilita,
e la mia gloria può tosto finire.

(C) Come chi mira in ciel fisso le stelle,
sempre qualcuna nova ve ne scorge,
che, non più vista pria, fra tanti sorge
chiari lumi del mondo, alme fiammelle;

mirando fisso l'alte doti e belle
vostre, signor, di qualcuna s'accorge
l'occhio mio nova, che materia porge,
onde di lei si scriva e si favelle.

Ma, sì come non può gli occhi del cielo
tutti, perch'occhio vegga, raccontare
lingua mortal e chiusa in uman velo,

io posso ben i vostri onor mirare,
ma la più parte d'essi ascondo e celo,
perchè la lingua a l'opra non è pare.

## 27. Tasso (1544–1595): *Gerusalemme liberata*

Intanto Erminia infra l'ombrose piante
d'antica selva dal cavallo è scorta,
né più governa il fren la man tremante,
e mezza quasi par tra viva e morta.
Per tante strade si raggira e tante
il corridor ch'in sua balia la porta,
ch'al fin da gli occhi altrui pur si dilegua,
ed è soverchio omai ch'altri la segua.

nor for your desires which fully obtain what they yearn for,
since you are always in the presence of the high Lord;

because my delights are such and so numerous
that there's no room for them in earthly hearts
whenever I have before me the fine, clear eyes
that it behooves me always to write and sing about.

And just as in heaven you are wont to derive
great comfort and life from His countenance,
so do I on earth from his infinite beauty.

In this alone you surpass my joy:
your bliss is eternal and fixed,
while mine may soon be over.

(C) Just as one who gazes firmly at the stars in the sky
always discovers some new one
which, not seen before, emerges from among all those
bright lamps of the world, fine tongues of flame;

so, gazing firmly at your lofty and lovely talents,
my lord, my eyes discover
some new one, which offers me material
for writing and talking about it.

But, since all those eyes of heaven
can't be described, so that man's eye can see them,
by a mortal tongue enclosed in a human body,

I may very well gaze on your merits,
but most of them I hide and conceal
because my tongue isn't equal to the task.

## 27. Tasso (1544–1595): *Jerusalem Delivered*

Meanwhile, amid the shady trees of an age-old
forest, Erminia is led onward by her horse,
and her trembling hand can no longer control the bridle,
and she seems nearly halfway between living and dead.
The steed circles through so many, many paths,
transporting her and holding her in its power,
that finally she disappears from the eyes of the others,
and it's now useless for anyone to follow her.

Qual dopo lunga e faticosa caccia
tornansi mesti ed anelanti i cani
che la fera perduta abbian di traccia,
nascosa in selva da gli aperti piani,
tal pieni d'ira e di vergogna in faccia
riedono stanchi i cavalier cristiani.
Ella pur fugge, e timida e smarrita
non si volge a mirar s'anco è seguita.

Fuggì tutta la notte, e tutto il giorno
errò senza consiglio e senza guida,
non udendo o vedendo altro d'intorno
che le lagrime sue, che le sue strida.
Ma ne l'ora che 'l sol dal carro adorno
scioglie i corsieri e in grembo al mar s'annida,
giunse del bel Giordano a le chiare acque
e scese in riva al fiume, e qui si giacque.

Cibo non prende già, ché de' suoi mali
solo si pasce e sol di pianto ha sete;
ma 'l sonno, che de' miseri mortali
è co 'l suo dolce oblio posa e quiete,
sopì co' sensi i' suoi dolori, e l'ali
dispiegò sovra lei placide e chete;
né però cessa Amor con varie forme
la sua pace turbar mentre ella dorme.

Non si destò fin che garrir gli augelli
non sentì lieti e salutar gli albori,
e mormorar il fiume e gli arboscelli,
e con l'onda scherzar l'aura e co i fiori.
Apre i languidi lumi e guarda quelli
alberghi solitari de' pastori,
e parle voce udir tra l'acqua e i rami
ch'a i sospiri ed al pianto la richiami.

Ma son, mentr'ella piange, i suoi lamenti
rotti da un chiaro suon ch'a lei ne viene,
che sembra ed è di pastorali accenti
misto e di boscareccie inculte avene.
Risorge, e là s'indrizza a passi lenti,
e vede un uom canuto a l'ombre amene
tesser fiscelle a la sua greggia a canto
ed ascoltar di tre fanciulli il canto.

Just as, after a long, exhausting chase
the hounds return panting and unhappy
because they've lost the track of the wild animal,
which has left the open plain and hidden in the woods,
so, their faces full of anger and shame,
the Christian knights return wearily.
She keeps on fleeing and, timid and confused,
doesn't look back to see if she's still being followed.

She fled all night long, and all day long
she roamed by chance without a guide,
hearing or seeing nothing around her
but her own tears, her own outcries.
But at the hour when the sun unharnesses the steeds
from his beautiful chariot and nests in the lap of the sea,
she came to the clear waters of the lovely Jordan
and rode down to the riverbank, where she lay down.

She eats no food now, for on her woes alone
she nourishes herself, and is thirsty for tears alone;
but sleep, which for unhappy mortals
is repose and calm with its sweet oblivion,
soothed her grief along with her senses, and spread
its placid, still wings over her;
nor for that reason does Love cease to disturb her rest
with various visions while she sleeps.

She didn't awake until she heard the birds
chatter happily, welcoming the dawn,
and the river and shrubs murmur,
and the breeze sport with the waters and the flowers.
She opens her languid eyes and observes those
solitary dwellings of shepherds,
and she thinks she hears a voice amid the water and boughs
recalling her to sighs and tears.

But, while she weeps, her laments are
interrupted by a clear sound that comes to her,
which seems, and is, composed of pastoral songs
and of rustic woodland panpipes.
She rises, and walks there with slow steps,
and sees a white-haired man in the pleasant shade
weaving a wicker basket alongside his flock
and listening to the singing of three boys.

Vedendo quivi comparir repente
l'insolite arme, sbigottir costoro;
ma li saluta Erminia e dolcemente
gli affida, e gli occhi scopre e i bei crin d'oro:
—Seguite, —dice— aventurosa gente
al Ciel diletta, il bel vostro lavoro,
ché non portano già guerra quest'armi
a l'opre vostre, a i vostri dolci carmi—.

Soggiunse poscia: —O padre, or che d'intorno
d'alto incendio di guerra arde il paese,
come qui state in placido soggiorno
senza temer le militari offese?—
—Figlio, —ei rispose— d'ogni oltraggio e scorno
la mia famiglia e la mia greggia illese
sempre qui fur, né strepito di Marte
ancor turbò questa remota parte.

O sia grazia del Ciel che l'umiltade
d'innocente pastor salvi e sublime,
o che, sì come il folgore non cade
in basso pian ma su l'eccelse cime,
così il furor di peregrine spade
sol de' gran re l'altere teste opprime,
né gli avidi soldati a preda alletta
la nostra povertà vile e negletta. [. . .]

## 28. Bruno (1548–1600): *De la causa, principio e uno*

È dunque l'universo uno, infinito, inmobile. Una, dico, è la possibilità
assoluta, uno l'atto, una la forma o anima, una la materia o corpo, una
la cosa, uno lo ente, uno il massimo ed ottimo; il quale non deve
posser essere compreso, e però infinibile e interminabile, e per tanto
infinito e interminato, e per conseguenza inmobile. Questo non si
muove localmente, perché non ha cosa fuor di sé ove si trasporte, atteso che sia il tutto. Non si genera; perché non è altro essere, che lui
possa desiderare o aspettare, atteso che abbia tutto lo essere. Non si
corrompe; perché non è altra cosa in cui si cange, atteso che lui sia
ogni cosa. Non può sminuire o crescere, atteso che è infinito; a cui
come non si può aggiongere, così è da cui non si può suttrarre, per ciò
che lo infinito non ha parte proporzionabili. Non è alterabile in altra

Seeing weapons to which they're unaccustomed suddenly
appearing here, they got frightened;
but Erminia greets them and gently
reassures them, revealing her eyes and lovely golden hair:
"Continue," she says, "you lucky people
beloved of heaven, your lovely labors,
because these weapons do not now bring war
to your tasks or to your sweet songs."

Then she added: "O father, now that round about
the country blazes with the high flames of conflict,
how is it that you remain here in a calm abode
without fear of the dangers of war?"
"My son," he replied, "my family and my flock
have always been immune here from every
outrage and humiliation, nor has the noise of Mars
yet troubled this secluded place.

"Whether it's heavenly Grace that protects
and favors the humility of the innocent shepherd,
or, just as lightning falls not
on the lowly plain but on the lofty peaks,
so the frenzy of foreign swords
only oppresses the haughty heads of great kings,
and the greedy soldiers aren't enticed to plunder
by our humble, disdained poverty." [. . .]

## 28. Bruno (1548–1600): *Cause, Principle, and Unity*

Thus, the universe is one, infinite, without motion. One, I say, is the absolute possibility; the action is one; the form or soul is one; the matter or body is one; the thing is one; the being is one; the greatest and best is one. It cannot be contained, and so it's unendable and illimitable, and therefore infinite and unlimited, and consequently without motion. It has no local motion, because there's no place outside it that it could move to, seeing that it's the all. It doesn't beget, because there's no other being it can desire or await, seeing that it comprises all being. It isn't corrupted, because there's nothing else it can change into, seeing that it is everything. It can't diminish or grow, seeing that it's infinite; just as nothing can be added to it, so nothing can be subtracted from it, because the infinite doesn't have measurable parts. It can't be changed into another arrangement, because

disposizione, perché non ha esterno, da cui patisca e per cui venga in qualche affezione. Oltre che, per comprender tutte contrarietadi nell'esser suo in unità e convenienza, e nessuna inclinazione posser avere ad altro e novo essere, o pur ad altro e altro modo di essere, non può esser soggetto di mutazione secondo qualità alcuna, né può aver contrario o diverso, che lo alteri, perché in lui è ogni cosa concorde. Non è materia, perché non è figurato né figurabile, non è terminato né terminabile. Non è forma, perché non informa né figura altro, atteso che è tutto, è massimo, è uno, è universo. Non è misurabile né misura. Non si comprende, perché non è maggior di sé. Non si è compreso, perché non è minor di sé. Non si agguaglia, perché non è altro e altro, ma uno e medesimo. Essendo medesimo e uno, non ha essere ed essere; e perché non ha essere ed essere, non ha parte e parte; e per ciò che non ha parte e parte, non è composto. Questo è termine di sorte che non è termine, è talmente forma che non è forma, è talmente materia che non è materia, è talmente anima che non è anima: perché è il tutto indifferentemente, e però è uno, l'universo è uno.

In questo certamente non è maggiore l'altezza che la lunghezza e profondità; onde per certa similitudine si chiama, ma non è, sfera. Nella sfera, medesima cosa è lunghezza che larghezza e profondo, perché hanno medesimo termine; ma ne l'universo medesima cosa è larghezza, lunghezza e profondo, perché medesimamente non hanno termine e sono infinite. Se non hanno mezzo, quadrante e altre misure, se non vi è misura, non vi è parte proporzionale, né assolutamente parte che differisca dal tutto. Perché, se vuoi dir parte de l'infinito, bisogna dirla infinito; se è infinito, concorre in uno essere con il tutto: dunque l'universo è uno, infinito, impartibile. E se ne l'infinito non si trova differenza, come di tutto e parte, e come di altro e altro, certo l'infinito è uno. Sotto la comprensione de l'infinito non è parte maggiore e parte minore, perché alla proporzione de l'infinito non si accosta più una parte quantosivoglia maggiore che un'altra quantosivoglia minore; e però ne l'infinita durazione non differisce la ora dal giorno, il giorno da l'anno, l'anno dal secolo, il secolo dal momento; perché non son più gli momenti e le ore che gli secoli, e non hanno minor proporzione quelli che questi a la eternità. Similmente ne l'immenso non è differente il palmo dal stadio, il stadio da la parasanga; perché alla proporzione de la inmensitudine non più si accosta per le parasanghe che per i palmi. Dunque infinite ore non son più che infiniti secoli, e infiniti palmi non son di maggior numero che infinite parasanghe. Alla proporzione, similitudine, unione e identità de l'infinito non più ti accosti con essere uomo che formica, una stella

it has nothing outside it that could affect it or influence it in any way. Besides, because it contains all contraries in its being in oneness and harmony, and can have no inclination to be other and different or to acquire another, different mode of existence, it can't be subject to alteration in accordance with any quality; nor can there be an opposite or different force that could change it, because everything in it is harmonious. It isn't matter, because it has no shape and is unshapable, it isn't limited or limitable. It isn't form, because it doesn't inform or shape anything else, seeing that it's the all, the greatest, one, universal. It's neither measurable nor measure. It doesn't contain itself, because it isn't larger than itself. It hasn't been contained, because it isn't smaller than itself. It doesn't equal itself, because it isn't different things but one and the same. Being one and the same, it doesn't have a variety of being; and because it doesn't have a variety of being, it doesn't have various parts; and because it doesn't have various parts, it isn't composite. It's extent in such a way that it isn't extent; it's form in such a way that it isn't form; it's matter in such a way that it isn't matter; and it's soul in such a way that it isn't soul; because it's the undifferentiated whole, and thus it's one: the universe is one.

In it, surely, height isn't greater than length or depth; and so, by a certain resemblance, it's called a sphere, though it isn't. In a sphere, length, width, and depth are the same thing, because they have the same extent; but in the universe, width, length, and depth are the same thing because they're all unlimited and infinite. If they can't be halved, quartered, or otherwise subdivided, if there's no measure there, then there are no proportional parts, and absolutely no part that differs from the whole. Because, if you talk about a part of infinity, you must call it infinity; if it's infinite, it must concur with the whole in having one being; thus, the universe is one, infinite, indivisible. And if no difference is found in the infinite, such as between whole and part, or between one thing and another, then the infinite is certainly one. In the understanding of the infinite there's no larger or smaller part, because any one part, however much larger, doesn't approach the proportions of the infinite any more than another part, however smaller; and so, in infinite duration an hour isn't different from a day, a day from a year, a year from a century, a century from a moment, because moments and hours don't exist any more than centuries do, and neither the former nor the latter are any less in ratio to eternity. Similarly, in immensity a span doesn't differ from a stadion, or a stadion from a parasang, because the proportion of immensity isn't approached more closely by parasangs than by spans. Thus, infinite hours are no more numerous than infinite centuries, and infinite spans aren't more numerous than infinite parasangs. You can't get closer to the pro-

che un uomo; perché a quello essere non più ti avicini con esser sole, luna, che un uomo o una formica; e però nell'infinito queste cose sono indifferenti. E quello che dico di queste, intendo di tutte l'altre cose di sussistenza particulare.

Or, se tutte queste cose particulari ne l'infinito non sono altro e altro, non sono differenti, non sono specie, per necessaria consequenza non sono numero; dunque, l'universo è ancor uno immobile. Questo, perché comprende tutto, e non patisce altro e altro essere, e non comporta seco né in sé mutazione alcuna; per consequenza, è tutto quello che può essere; ed in lui (come dissi l'altro giorno) non è differente l'atto da la potenza. Se dalla potenza non è differente l'atto, è necessario che in quello il punto, la linea, la superficie e il corpo non differiscano: perché cossì quella linea è superficie, come la linea, movendosi, può essere superficie; cossì quella superficie è mossa ed è fatta corpo, come la superficie può moversi e, con il suo flusso, può farsi corpo. È necessario dunque che il punto ne l'infinito non differisca dal corpo, perché il punto, scorrendo da l'esser punto, si fa linea; scorrendo da l'esser linea, si fa superficie; scorrendo da l'esser superficie, si fa corpo; il punto, dunque, perché è in potenza ad esser corpo, non differisce da l'esser corpo dove la potenza e l'atto è una medesima cosa.

Dunque, l'individuo non è differente dal dividuo, il simplicissimo da l'infinito, il centro da la circonferenza. Perché dunque l'infinito è tutto quello che può essere, è inmobile; perché in lui tutto è indifferente, è uno; e perché ha tutta la grandezza e perfezione che si possa oltre e oltre avere, è massimo ed ottimo immenso. [. . .]

## 29. Galileo (1564–1642): *Il saggiatore*

Parmi d'aver per lunghe esperienze osservato, tale esser la condizione umana intorno alle cose intellettuali, che quanto altri meno e ne intende e ne sa, tanto più risolutamente voglia discorrerne; e che, all'incontro, la moltitudine delle cose conosciute ed intese renda più lento ed irresoluto al sentenziare circa qualche novità. Nacque già in un luogo assai solitario un uomo dotato da natura d'uno ingegno perspicacissimo e d'una curiosità straordinaria; e per suo trastullo allevandosi diversi uccelli, gustava molto del lor canto, e con grandissima meraviglia andava osservando con che bell'artificio, colla stess'aria con la quale respiravano, ad arbitrio loro formavano canti diversi, e tutti soavissimi. Accadde che una notte vicino a casa sua sentì un delicato

portion, similitude, oneness, and identity of the infinite by being a man than by being an ant, by being a star than by being a man, because you can't come closer to that essence by being the sun or moon than by being a man or an ant, because in the infinite there's no difference between these things. And what I say about them, I assert concerning everything else that has an individual existence.

Now, if all these individual things, in the infinite, aren't one and the other, aren't different, aren't specific, then as a necessary consequence they have no number; and so, the universe is still one and without motion. Because it comprises everything and doesn't admit of being one thing or another, and doesn't allow for any change with or in itself, therefore it's all that it can be; and in it (as I said the other day) actuality doesn't differ from potentiality. If the actual doesn't differ from the potential, of necessity point, line, plane, and solid don't differ within it: because that line is a plane, just as a line in motion can become a plane; thus, that plane progresses and becomes a solid, just as any plane can move and, by its progress, turn into a solid. Thus, of necessity a point in infinity isn't different from a solid, because a point, moving on a trajectory, becomes a line; the moving line becomes a plane; the moving plane becomes a solid; thus, because the point is a potential solid, it doesn't differ from a solid when potentiality and actuality are one and the same thing.

Therefore, the individual doesn't differ from the multiple, the simplest object from the infinite, the center from the circumference. So, because the infinite is all that it can be, it's without motion; because in it everything is undifferentiated and one; and, because it has all the size and perfection that can possibly be had, it is greatest and best in its immensity. [. . .]

## 29. Galileo (1564–1642): *The Assayer*

I believe that through long experience I have observed human nature, with regard to intellectual matters, to be such that, the less someone understands and knows of them, the more determinedly he wants to discourse on them; whereas, on the other hand, the great number of things a man knows and understands makes him slower and more irresolute to render judgments about anything new. Once in a very lonely place there was born a man endowed by nature with a very shrewd mind and unusual curiosity; raising various birds as a pastime, he greatly enjoyed their singing, and with very great amazement kept observing with what lovely skill, using the same air that they breathed, they formed different songs at will, all very sweet. It came about that one night he heard a delicate

suono, né potendosi immaginar che fusse altro che qualche uccelletto, si mosse per prenderlo; e venuto nella strada, trovò un pastorello, che soffiando in certo legno forato e movendo le dita sopra il legno, ora serrando ed ora aprendo certi fori che vi erano, ne traeva quelle diverse voci, simili a quelle d'un uccello, ma con maniera diversissima. Stupefatto e mosso dalla sua natural curiosità, donò al pastore un vitello per aver quel zufolo; e ritiratosi in sé stesso, e conoscendo che se non s'abbatteva a passar colui, egli non avrebbe mai imparato che ci erano in natura due modi da formar voci e canti soavi, volle allontanarsi da casa, stimando di potere incontrar qualche altra avventura. Ed occorse il giorno seguente, che passando presso a un piccol tugurio, sentì risonarvi dentro una simil voce; e per certificarsi se era un zufolo o pure un merlo, entrò dentro, e trovò un fanciullo che andava con un archetto, ch'ei teneva nella man destra, segando alcuni nervi tesi sopra certo legno concavo, e con la sinistra sosteneva lo strumento e vi andava sopra movendo le dita, e senz'altro fiato ne traeva voci diverse e molto soavi. Or qual fusse il suo stupore, giudichilo chi participa dell'ingegno e della curiosità che aveva colui; il qual, vedendosi sopraggiunto da due nuovi modi di formar la voce ed il canto tanto inopinati, cominciò a creder ch'altri ancora ve ne potessero essere in natura. Ma qual fu la sua meraviglia, quando entrando in certo tempio si mise a guardar dietro alla porta per veder chi aveva sonato, e s'accorse che il suono era uscito dagli arpioni e dalle bandelle nell'aprir la porta? Un'altra volta, spinto dalla curiosità, entrò in un'osteria, e credendo d'aver a veder uno che coll'archetto toccasse leggiermente le corde d'un violino, vide uno che fregando il polpastrello d'un dito sopra l'orlo d'un bicchiero, ne cavava soavissimo suono. Ma quando poi gli venne osservato che le vespe, le zanzare e i mosconi, non, come i suoi primi uccelli, col respirare formavano voci interrotte, ma col velocissimo batter dell'ali rendevano un suono perpetuo, quanto crebbe in esso lo stupore, tanto si scemò l'opinione ch'egli aveva circa il sapere come si generi il suono; né tutte l'esperienze già vedute sarebbono state bastanti a fargli comprendere o credere che i grilli, già che non volavano, potessero, non col fiato, ma collo scuoter l'ali, cacciar sibili così dolci e sonori. Ma quando ei si credeva non potere esser quasi possibile che vi fussero altre maniere di formar voci, dopo l'avere, oltre a i modi narrati, osservato ancora tanti organi, trombe, piffari, strumenti da corde, di tante e tante sorte, e sino a quella linguetta di ferro che, sospesa fra i denti, si serve con modo strano della cavità della bocca per corpo della risonanza e del fiato per veicolo del suono; quando, dico, ei credeva d'aver veduto il tutto, tro-

sound near his home and, unable to imagine that it could be anything but some songbird, he went out to capture it. Coming onto the path, he found a shepherd boy who, blowing into a certain perforated piece of wood and moving his fingers over it, now closing and now opening certain holes that were in it, drew from it those varied calls, similar to a bird's but created very differently. Dumbfounded and stirred by his inborn curiosity, he gave the shepherd a calf in order to obtain that flageolet; and reflecting on this and realizing that, if that boy hadn't chanced to pass by, he would never have learned that there existed in nature two ways of producing sweet calls and songs, he decided to leave home, feeling he would come across some other adventure. And it came about on the following day that, passing by a small hut, he heard a similar sound coming from inside it; and to ascertain whether it was a flageolet or a blackbird, he went in and found a boy who with a bow held in his right hand was rubbing a few sinews stretched over a certain concave piece of wood, while with his left he supported the instrument and moved his fingers over it, drawing various very sweet sounds from it without the use of breath. Now, judge of his amazement, if you share that man's mind and curiosity; seeing himself surprised by two new ways, so unexpected, of creating sounds and song, he began to believe there could be still others in nature. But what was his stupefaction when, entering a certain church, he began to look behind the door to see who had played, and observed that the sound had issued from the hinges and their straps when he opened the door! Another time, impelled by curiosity, he entered an inn, and thinking he'd find someone lightly touching the strings of a violin with a bow, saw a man who, rubbing the fleshy part of one fingertip on the rim of a glass, was drawing a very sweet sound from it. But when he later observed that wasps, gnats, and bluebottles didn't produce intermittent sounds with their breath, like his birds in the past, but emitted a constant sound by the very rapid beating of their wings, he was not only even more amazed, but he lost some of the high opinion he had about his knowledge of the generation of sound; nor would all his former experiences have sufficed to make him understand or believe that crickets, which didn't fly, could emit equally sweet and resonant sounds, not with their breath but by shaking their wings. But just when he thought it was nearly impossible for there to be other ways of producing sounds, after (in addition to the ways already described) having also observed many organs, trumpets, bagpipes, and string instruments of many, many kinds, and even that tiny iron rod which, held in one's teeth, makes an odd use of the mouth cavity as a soundbox and the breath as a carrier of the sound; when, I say, he thought he had seen it all, he found himself more wrapped in ignorance and amazement than ever

vossi più che mai rinvolto nell'ignoranza e nello stupore nel capitargli in mano una cicala, e che né per serrarle la bocca né per fermarle l'ali poteva né pur diminuire il suo altissimo stridore, né le vedeva muovere squamme né altra parte, e che finalmente, alzandole il casso del petto e vedendovi sotto alcune cartilagini dure ma sottili, e credendo che lo strepito derivasse dallo scuoter di quelle, si ridusse a romperle per farla chetare, e che tutto fu in vano, sin che, spingendo l'ago più a dentro, non le tolse, trafiggendola, colla voce la vita, sì che né anco poté accertarsi se il canto derivava da quelle: onde si ridusse a tanta diffidenza del suo sapere, che domandato come si generavano i suoni, generosamente rispondeva di sapere alcuni modi, ma che teneva per fermo potervene essere cento altri incogniti ed inopinabili.

Io potrei con altri molti essempi spiegar la ricchezza della natura nel produr suoi effetti con maniere inescogitabili da noi, quando il senso e l'esperienza non lo ci mostrasse, la quale anco talvolta non basta a supplire alla nostra incapacità; onde se io non saperò precisamente determinar la maniera della produzzion della cometa, non mi dovrà esser negata la scusa, e tanto più quant'io non mi son mai arrogato di poter ciò fare, conoscendo potere essere ch'ella si faccia in alcun modo lontano da ogni nostra immaginazione; e la difficoltà dell'intendere come si formi il canto della cicala, mentr'ella ci canta in mano, scusa di soverchio il non sapere come in tanta lontananza si generi la cometa. Fermandomi dunque su la prima intenzione del signor Mario e mia, ch'è di promuover quelle dubitazioni che ci è paruto che rendano incerte l'opinioni avute sin qui, e di proporre alcuna considerazione di nuovo, acciò sia essaminata e considerato se vi sia cosa che possa in alcun modo arrecar qualche lume ed agevolar la strada al ritrovamento del vero, anderò seguitando di considerar l'opposizioni fatteci dal Sarsi, per le quali i nostri pensieri gli sono paruti improbabili. [. . .]

## 30. Campanella (1568–1639): *La città del sole*

*Ospitalario*   Dimmi, di grazia, tutto quello che t'avvenne in questa navigazione.

*Genovese*   Già t'ho detto come girai il mondo tutto e poi come arrivai alla Taprobana, e fui forzato metter in terra, e poi, fuggendo la furia di terrazzani, mi rinselvai, ed uscii in un gran piano proprio sotto l'equinoziale.

*Osp.*   Qui che t'occorse?

*Gen.*   Subito incontrai un gran squadrone d'uomini e donne ar-

on coming across a cicada; neither by shutting its mouth nor by stopping its wings could he in the least diminish its very loud high-pitched sound; nor did he see it move scales or other body parts; finally, lifting the casing of its thorax and seeing beneath it some hard but thin cartilages, and thinking that the sound came from shaking them, he resorted to tearing them to make it be quiet. But it was all in vain, until, shoving his needle further in, he pierced the insect through and ended its call along with its life, so that he couldn't yet determine whether the sound came from them: whereupon he lapsed into so great a mistrust of his own knowledge that, when asked how sounds are produced, he nobly replied that he knew some ways but was sure that there could be a hundred others unknown and unguessable.

With many other examples I could explain the rich variety of nature in producing its effects in ways we can't imagine, unless our senses and experience show them to us; and at times even experience isn't enough to make up for our inadequacy; so that, if I'm unable to determine the precise way in which comets are formed, I shouldn't be denied an excuse, all the more so because I have never claimed to be able to do so, aware as I am that possibly it occurs in some way remote from all our imaginings; and the difficulty of understanding how the cicada's sound is produced, while it sings in our very hand, is an abundant excuse for not knowing how comets are formed at such a great distance. And so, maintaining the first intention of Mario and myself, which is to foster those doubts which we believed make the opinions held up to now uncertain, and to suggest some further reflection, so it can be examined and it can be seen whether there's anything that can in any way shed some light and smooth the path to the discovery of the truth, I shall continue to reflect on the opposition to our view put forward by Sarsi, because of which our ideas seemed unlikely to him. [. . .]

## 30. Campanella (1568–1639): *The City of the Sun*

HOSPITALER:   Please tell me everything that befell you on that voyage.

GENOESE:   I've already told you how I circled the whole world and then how I arrived in Ceylon and was forced to go ashore; then how, fleeing the frenzy of the natives, I entered the forest and emerged onto a wide plain right in the equatorial zone.

HOSP.:   What happened to you there?

GEN.:   I suddenly met a large troop of armed men and women; many of them understood my language and led me to the City of the Sun.

mate, e molti di loro intendevano la lingua mia, li quali mi condussero alla Città del Sole.

*Osp.*   Dì, come è fatta questa città? e come si governa?

*Gen.*   Sorge nell'ampia campagna un colle, sopra il quale sta la maggior parte della città; ma arrivano i suoi giri molto spazio fuor delle radici del monte, il quale è tanto, che la città fa due miglia di diametro e più, e viene ad essere sette miglia di circolo; ma, per la levatura, più abitazioni ha, che si fosse in piano.

È la città distinta in sette gironi grandissimi, nominati dalli sette pianeti, e s'entra dall'uno all'altro per quattro strade e per quattro porte, alli quattro angoli del mondo spettanti; ma sta in modo che, se fosse espugnato il primo girone, bisogna più travaglio al secondo e poi più; talché sette fiate bisogna espugnarla per vincerla. Ma io son di parere, che neanche il primo si può, tanto è grosso e terrapieno, ed ha valguardi, torrioni, artelleria e fossati di fuora.

Entrando dunque per la porta Tramontana, di ferro coperta, fatta che s'alza e cala con bello ingegno, si vede un piano di cinquanta passi tra la muraglia prima e l'altra. Appresso stanno palazzi tutti uniti per giro col muro, che puoi dir che tutti siano uno; e di sopra han li rivellini sopra a colonne, come chiostri di frati, e di sotto non vi è introito, se non dalla parte concava delli palazzi. Poi son le stanze belle con le fenestre al convesso ed al concavo, e son distinte con piccole mura tra loro. Solo il muro convesso è grosso otto palmi, il concavo tre, li mezzani uno o poco più.

Appresso poi s'arriva al secondo piano, ch'è dui passi o tre manco, e si vedono le seconde mura con li rivellini in fuora e passeggiatori; e della parte dentro, l'altro muro, che serra i palazzi in mezzo, ha il chiostro con le colonne di sotto, e di sopra belle pitture.

E così s'arriva fin al supremo e sempre per piani. Solo quando s'entran le porte, che son doppie per le mura interiori ed esteriori, si a-scende per gradi tali, che non si conosce, perché vanno obliquamente, e son d'altura quasi invisibile distinte le scale.

Nella sommità del monte vi è un gran piano ed un gran tempio in mezzo, di stupendo artifizio. [. . .]

È un Principe Sacerdote tra loro, che s'appella Sole, e in lingua no-stra si dice Metafisico: questo è capo di tutti in spirituale e temporale, e tutti li negozi in lui si terminano.

Ha tre Principi collaterali: Pon, Sin, Mor, che vuol dir: Potestà, Sapienza e Amore.

Il Potestà ha cura delle guerre e delle paci e dell'arte militare; è

HOSP.:  Tell me, what is that city like? How is it ruled?

GEN.:  There arises from the wide countryside a hill, on which most of the city is situated; but its circular zones extend beyond the roots of the mountain, which is so large that the city is two miles and more in diameter, and reaches seven miles in circumference; but, because of its elevation, it has more dwellings than if it were on the plain.

The city is divided into seven very large circular zones, called after the seven planets, and one passes from one to another by four roads and four gateways facing the four corners of the world; but the arrangement is such that, if the first zone were taken by storm, it would be harder to take the second, and so on; so that you'd need to besiege the city and take it seven times in order to conquer it. But it's my opinion that not even the first zone can be taken, it's so big and solid, and it has bulwarks, turrets, artillery, and moats outside it.

So, entering by the north gate, which is clad with iron, and can be raised and lowered with elegant machinery, one sees a level space of fifty paces between the first wall and the next. Nearby are palaces all built up against the wall in a circle, so continuous you could say there's just one; above, they have small detached forts on columns, like friary cloisters, and below there's no entrance except by the concave part of the palaces. Then, the dwellings are beautiful, with convex and concave windows, and they're separated by low walls. Only the convex wall is eight spans thick; the concave one, three; the partition walls, one or a little more.

Then you arrive at the second level space, which is two or three paces less, and you see the second walls with the lunettes outside and passageways; and on the interior, the next wall, which encloses the palaces in its midst, has a cloister with columns below, and beautiful paintings above.

And so you finally arrive at the highest zone, always through level spaces. Only when you enter the gates, which are double, with inner and outer walls, you ascend by such stairways that you don't notice them, because they are placed obliquely and the distance between the steps is all but nonexistent.

At the summit of the mountain there's a large level space with a great temple in the center, of amazing craftsmanship. [. . .]

They have a ruling priest among them called Sun; in our language you'd say Metaphysician: he is the religious and secular leader of them all, and all affairs are ultimately under his control.

He has three auxiliary princes, Pon, Sin, Mor (meaning Power, Wisdom, and Love).

Power is in charge of war and peace and military matters; he's the

supremo nella guerra, ma non sopra Sole; ha cura dell'offiziali, guerrieri, soldati, munizioni, fortificazioni ed espugnazioni.

Il Sapienza ha cura di tutte le scienze e delli dottori e magistrati dell'arti liberali e meccaniche, e tiene sotto di sé tanti offiziali quante son le scienze: ci è l'Astrologo, il Cosmografo, il Geometra, il Loico, il Rettorico, il Grammatico, il Medico, il Fisico, il Politico, il Morale; e tiene un libro solo, dove stan tutte le scienze, che fa leggere a tutto il popolo ad usanza di Pitagorici. E questo ha fatto pingere in tutte le muraglie, su li rivellini, dentro e di fuori, tutte le scienze.

Nelle mura del tempio esteriori e nelle cortine, che si calano quando si predica per non perdersi la voce, vi sta ogni stella ordinatamente con tre versi per una.

Nel dentro del primo girone tutte le figure matematiche, più che non scrisse Euclide ed Archimede, con la lor proposizione significante. Nel di fuore vi è la carta della terra tutta, e poi le tavole d'ogni provinzia con li riti e costumi e leggi loro, e con l'alfabeti ordinari sopra il loro alfabeto.

Nel dentro del secondo girone vi son tutte le pietre preziose e non preziose, e minerali, e metalli veri e pinti, con le dichiarazioni di due versi per uno. Nel di fuore vi son tutte sorti di laghi, mari e fiumi, vini ed ogli ed altri liquori, e loro virtù ed origini e qualità; e ci son le caraffe piene di diversi liquori di cento e trecento anni, con li quali sanano tutte l'infirmità quasi.

Nel dentro del terzo vi son tutte le sorti di erbe ed arbori del mondo pinte, e pur in teste di terra sopra il rivellino e le dichiarazioni dove prima si ritrovaro, e le virtù loro, e le simiglianze c'hanno con le stelle e con li metalli e con le membra umane, e l'uso loro in medicina. Nel di fuora tutte maniere di pesci di fiumi, laghi e mari, e le virtù loro, e 'l modo di vivere, di generarsi e allevarsi, e a che serveno; e le simiglianze c'hanno con le cose celesti e terrestri e dell'arte e della natura; sì che mi stupii, quando trovai pesce vescovo e catena e chiodo e stella, appunto come son queste cose tra noi. Ci sono ancini, rizzi, spondoli e tutto quanto è degno di sapere con mirabil arte di pittura e di scrittura che dichiara.

Nel quarto, dentro vi son tutte sorti di augelli pinti e lor qualità, grandezze e costumi, e la fenice è verissima appresso loro. Nel di fuora stanno tutte sorti di animali rettili, serpi, draghi, vermini, e l'insetti, mosche, tafani ecc., con le loro condizioni, veneni e virtuti; e son più che non pensamo. [. . .]

supreme leader in wartime, but not higher than Sun; he's in charge of the officers, warriors, soldiers, armaments, fortifications, and sieges.

Wisdom is in charge of all the sciences and professors and magistrates of the liberal and mechanical arts, and has below him an official for each of the sciences: there's the Astrologer, the Geographer, the Geometer, the Logician, the Rhetorician, the Grammarian, the Physician, the Physicist, the Politician, the Moralist; and he has a single book containing all the sciences, which he has read to the entire population, just as the followers of Pythagoras did. And he has had all the sciences depicted on every wall and on the small forts, inside and outside.

On the outer walls of the temple and on its curtains, which are lowered during sermons so the words remain audible, every star and planet is depicted in order, with three lines of verse for each one.

Inside the first circular zone are all the mathematical figures, more than those described by Euclid and Archimedes, with the chief theorem pertaining to each one. On the outside there's a map of the whole earth, as well as tablets for each province with their different rites, customs, and laws, and with the standard alphabets over their local alphabet.

Inside the second zone are all the precious and nonprecious stones, minerals, and metals real and depicted, with a two-verse explanation for each. Outside there are all sorts of lakes, seas, and rivers; wines, oils, and other fluids, with their powers, origins, and qualities; and there are carafes filled with various fluids a hundred to three hundred years old, with which they cure almost every illness.

Inside the third zone all the kinds of grasses and trees in the world are depicted, and also there are real ones in clay pots on the lunette with statements about where they were first found, and their powers, and the ways in which they correspond to the stars, metals, and parts of the human body, and their use in medicine. Outside there are all kinds of fish from rivers, lakes, and seas, and their powers, and the way they live, reproduce, and are raised, and what they're used for, and their correspondences to things heavenly and earthly, artificial and natural; so that I was amazed when I found the bishop fish, the chain fish, the nail fish, and the starfish just as they are in our part of the world. There are sea urchins, various marine mollusks, and everything worth knowing admirably painted and described in writing.

In the fourth zone, on the inside, are depicted all sorts of birds and their qualities, sizes, and habits; among them, the phoenix is very lifelike. On the outside are all kinds of crawling animals, snakes, dragons, and worms, and insects such as houseflies and gadflies, with their way of life, poisons, and powers; and there are more of them than we imagine. [. . .]

## 31. Marino (1569–1625): *L'Adone*

Ma sovr'ogni augellin vago e gentile
che più spieghi leggiadro il canto e 'l volo,
versa il suo spirto tremulo e sottile
la sirena de' boschi, il rosignuolo;
e tempra in guisa il peregrino stile
che par maestro de l'alato stuolo.
In mille fogge il suo cantar distingue,
e trasforma una lingua in mille lingue.

Udir musico mostro, oh meraviglia,
che s'ode sì ma si discerne apena,
come or tronca la voce, or la ripiglia,
or la ferma, or la torce, or scema, or piena,
or la mormora grave, or l'assottiglia,
or fa di dolci groppi ampia catena,
e sempre, o se la sparge o se l'accoglie,
con egual melodia la lega e scioglie.

Oh che vezzose, oh che pietose rime,
lascivetto cantor, compone e detta!
Pria flebilmente il suo lamento esprime,
poi rompe in un sospir la canzonetta.
In tante mute or languido, or sublime,
varia stil, pause affrena e fughe affretta,
ch'imita insieme e 'nsieme in lui s'ammira
cetra, flauto, liuto, organo e lira.

Fa de la gola lusinghiera e dolce
talor ben lunga articolata scala:
quinci quell'armonia che l'aura molce,
ondeggiando per gradi in alto essala;
e poi ch'alquanto si sostiene e folce,
precipitosa a piombo alfin si cala.
Alzando a piena gorga indi lo scoppio,
forma di trilli un contrapunto doppio.

Par ch'abbia entro le fauci e in ogni fibra
rapida rota o turbine veloce.
Sembra la lingua, che si volge e vibra,
spada di schermidor destro e feroce.

## 31. Marino (1569–1625): *Adonis*

But surpassing every other lovely, charming songbird
that most delightfully spreads its wings and song,
that siren of the groves, the nightingale,
pours forth its tremulous, ethereal spirit,
and so modulates its extraordinary art
that it seems like the master of the winged throng.
It divides its song into a thousand shapes
and transforms one tongue into a thousand tongues.

What a marvel, to hear a musical prodigy,
which is heard, to be sure, but scarcely discerned,
as it now cuts short its voice, now resumes it,
now stops it, now bends it, now abates it, now swells it,
now making it a deep murmur, now thinning it,
now creating a long chain of sweet grouped notes,
but always, whether scattering or gathering it,
binding and loosing it with equal melody.

Oh, what charming, oh, what tender rhymes
that lively singer composes and dictates!
First it expresses its lament tearfully,
then breaks off its ditty in a sigh.
Now languid, now sublime, into so many variations
it changes its note, slowing into pauses and rushing into flights,
that it imitates together, and one admires together in it,
the zither, flute, lute, organ, and lyre.

With its sweet, flattering throat
it sometimes makes a very long, articulated staircase,
then, in wavering steps it exhales skyward
that harmony which softens the air;
then, after sustaining and supporting the song a while,
it finally plummets downward precipitously.
Next, full-throatedly raising the outburst,
it forms a double counterpoint of trills.

It seems to have in its beak and in every fiber
a swift wheel or a rapid whirlwind.
Its tongue, turning and vibrating, resembles
the foil of a skillful, hotheaded fencer.

Se piega e 'ncrespa, o se sospende e libra
in riposati numeri la voce,
spirto il dirai del ciel, che 'n tanti modi
figurato e trapunto il canto snodi.

Chi crederà che forze accoglier possa
animetta sì picciola cotante?
e celar tra le vene e dentro l'ossa
tanta dolcezza un atomo sonante?
o ch'altro sia che la liev'aura mossa,
una voce pennuta, un suon volante?
e vestito di penne un vivo fiato,
una piuma canora, un canto alato?

Mercurio allor, che con orecchie fisse
vide Adone ascoltar canto sì bello:
—Deh, che ti pare— a lui rivolto disse
—de la divinità di quell'augello?
Diresti mai che tanta lena unisse
in sì poca sostanza un spiritello?
un spiritel, che d'armonia composto
vive in sì anguste viscere nascosto?

Mirabil arte in ogni sua bell'opra
(ciò negar non si può) mostra Natura,
ma qual pittor che 'ngegno e studio scopra
vie più che 'n grande in picciola figura,
ne le cose talor minime adopra
diligenza maggiore e maggior cura.
Quest'eccesso però sopra l'usanza
d'ogni altro suo miracolo s'avanza.

Di quel canto nel ver miracoloso
una istoria narrar bella ti voglio,
caso in un memorando e lagrimoso,
da far languir di tenerezza un scoglio.
Sfogava con le corde in suon pietoso
un solitario amante il suo cordoglio.
Tacean le selve, e dal notturno velo
era occupato in ogni parte il cielo. [. . .]

Its voice bends and curls, or suspends itself and balances
in reposeful rhythms;
you'd say it was a heavenly spirit, unloosing
its figured, embroidered song in so many modes.

Who'd believe that so tiny a soul
could contain such great forces;
that a resonant atom could conceal in its veins
and bones so much sweetness;
or that it's anything but a breath of the light breeze,
a feathered voice, a flying sound,
a living breath clad in feathers,
a singing plume, a winged song?

Then Mercury, who saw Adonis listening
to that lovely song with attentive ears,
addressed him, saying: "Well, what do you think
about that bird's excellence?
Would you ever say that a sprite could gather
so much vigor in so little substance?—
a sprite that, compounded of harmony,
lives hidden in such a narrow body?

"Nature displays (it cannot be denied)
amazing art in all her lovely works,
but like a painter who reveals his talent and skill
much more in a small figure than in a large one,
she sometimes employs in the smallest things
the greatest diligence and greatest care.
But this unusual creature, beyond the customary,
surpasses every other wonder of hers.

"Concerning that truly miraculous song
I want to tell you a lovely story,
an incident memorable and pitiable at the same time,
one that would make a rock melt with tenderness.
A lonely lover was giving vent to his grief
with the tender notes of his strings.
The woods were still, and the sky
was completely covered by the veil of night." [. . .]

## 32. Vico (1668–1744): *La Scienza nuova*

(A) La filosofia, per giovar al genere umano, dee sollevar e reggere l'uomo caduto e debole, non convellergli la natura né abbandonarlo nella sua corrozione.

Questa degnità allontana dalla scuola di questa Scienza gli stoici, i quali vogliono l'ammortimento de' sensi, e gli epicurei, che ne fanno regola, ed entrambi niegano la provvedenza, quelli faccendosi strascinare dal fato, questi abbandonandosi al caso, e i secondi oppinando che muoiano l'anime umane coi corpi, i quali entrambi si dovrebbero dire «filosofi monastici o solitari». E vi ammette i filosofi politici, e principalmente i platonici, i quali convengono con tutti i legislatori in questi tre principali punti: che si dia provvedenza divina, che si debbano moderare l'umane passioni e farne umane virtù, e che l'anime umane sien immortali. E, 'n conseguenza, questa degnità ne darà gli tre princìpi di questa Scienza.

(B) La legislazione considera l'uomo qual è, per farne buoni usi nell'umana società; come della ferocia, dell'avarizia, dell'ambizione, che sono gli tre vizi che portano a travverso tutto il gener umano, ne fa la milizia, la mercatanzia e la corte, e sì la fortezza, l'opulenza e la sapienza delle repubbliche; e di questi tre grandi vizi, i quali certamente distruggerebbero l'umana generazione sopra la terra, ne fa la civile felicità.

Questa degnità pruova esservi provvedenza divina e che ella sia una divina mente legislatrice, la quale delle passioni degli uomini tutti attenuti alle loro private utilità, per le quali viverebbono da fiere bestie dentro le solitudini, ne ha fatto gli ordini civili per gli quali vivano in umana società.

(C) [. . .] In tal densa notte di tenebre ond'è coverta la prima da noi lontanissima antichità, apparisce questo lume eterno, che non tramonta, di questa verità, la quale non si può a patto alcuno chiamar in dubbio: che questo mondo civile egli certamente è stato fatto dagli uomini, onde se ne possono, perché se ne debbono, ritruovare i princìpi dentro le modificazioni della nostra medesima mente umana. Lo che, a chiunque vi rifletta, dee recar maraviglia come tutti i filosofi seriosamente si studiarono di conseguire la scienza di questo mondo naturale, del quale, perché Iddio egli il fece, esso solo ne ha la scienza; e traccurarono di meditare su questo mondo delle nazioni, o sia mondo civile, del quale, perché l'avevano fatto gli uomini, ne pote-

## 32. Vico (1668–1744): *The New Science*

(A) Philosophy, if it is to aid the human race, must raise up and support fallen, weak man, and not distort his nature or desert him in his corrupt state.

This axiom removes from the school of this Science the Stoics, who wish for the deadening of the senses, and the Epicureans, who regulate themselves by the senses, while both of them deny Providence, the former believing that man is dragged along by fate, the latter abandoning themselves to chance and believing that human souls die with their bodies; both schools should be called "monastic or solitary philosophers." The axiom does admit the political philosophers, especially the Platonists, who agree with all legislators on these three principal points: that divine Providence exists, that human passions should be moderated and turned into human virtues, and that human souls are immortal. Consequently, this axiom will furnish us with the three basic principles of this Science.

(B) Legislation considers man as he is, to make good use of him in human society; just as of his fierceness, greed, and ambition, which are the three vices general to the whole human race, it makes soldiers, merchants, and courtiers; that is, the strength, wealth, and wisdom of the state; and it turns those three great vices, which would surely destroy the continuance of man on earth, into civic happiness.

This axiom proves that divine Providence exists and that it is a divine legislative mind which, out of the passions of men tightly clinging to their own private advantages, through which they'd live like wild beasts in wildernesses, has created the civic ranks through which they can live in human society.

(C) [. . .] In that very dense night of darkness with which that earliest and remotest antiquity is covered, there appears this eternal light which never sets, the light of this truth which can in no way be called into doubt: that this civic world was certainly created by men, so that they can, because they must, rediscover its principles within the modifications of our own human mind. It ought to astound anyone who reflects on it that all philosophers have seriously striven to obtain the knowledge of this world of nature, of which, since God created it, He alone has the knowledge; whereas they have neglected to meditate on this world of nations, or civic world, of which, since it had been created by men, men were able to obtain the knowledge. This bizarre result was caused by that wretchedness

vano conseguire la scienza gli uomini. Il quale stravagante effetto è provenuto da quella miseria, la qual avvertimmo nelle Degnità, della mente umana, la quale, restata immersa e seppellita nel corpo, è naturalmente inchinata a sentire le cose del corpo e dee usare troppo sforzo e fatiga per intendere se medesima, come l'occhio corporale che vede tutti gli obbietti fuori di sé ed ha dello specchio bisogno per vedere se stesso.

Or, poiché questo mondo di nazioni egli è stato fatto dagli uomini, vediamo in quali cose hanno con perpetuità convenuto e tuttavia vi convengono tutti gli uomini, perché tali cose ne potranno dare i princìpi universali ed eterni, quali devon essere d'ogni scienza, sopra i quali tutte le nazioni sursero e tutte vi si conservano in nazioni.

Osserviamo tutte le nazioni così barbare come umane, quantunque, per immensi spazi di luoghi e tempi tra loro lontane, divisamente fondate, custodire questi tre umani costumi: che tutte hanno qualche religione, tutte contraggono matrimoni solenni, tutte seppelliscono i loro morti; né tra nazioni, quantunque selvagge e crude, si celebrano azioni umane con più ricercate cerimonie e più consagrate solennità che religioni, matrimoni e seppolture. Ché, per la degnità che «idee uniformi, nate tra popoli sconosciuti tra loro, debbon aver un principio comune di vero», dee essere stato dettato a tutte: che da queste tre cose incominciò appo tutte l'umanità, e per ciò si debbano santissimamente custodire da tutte perché 'l mondo non s'infierisca e si rinselvi di nuovo. Perciò abbiamo presi questi tre costumi eterni ed universali per tre primi princìpi di questa Scienza.

(D) La sapienza poetica, che fu la prima sapienza della gentilità, dovette incominciare da una metafisica, non ragionata ed astratta qual è questa or degli addottrinati, ma sentita ed immaginata quale dovett'essere di tai primi uomini, siccome quelli ch'erano di niuno raziocinio e tutti robusti sensi e vigorosissime fantasie, com'è stato nelle *Degnità* stabilito. Questa fu la loro propia poesia, la qual in essi fu una facultà loro connaturale (perch'erano di tali sensi e di sì fatte fantasie naturalmente forniti), nata da ignoranza di cagioni, la qual fu loro madre di maraviglia di tutte le cose, che quelli, ignoranti di tutte le cose, fortemente ammiravano, come si è accennato nelle *Degnità*. Tal poesia incominciò in essi divina, perché nello stesso tempo ch'essi immaginavano le cagioni delle cose che sentivano ed ammiravano, essere dèi, come nelle *Degnità* il vedemmo con Lattanzio (ed ora il confermiamo con gli americani, i quali tutte le cose che superano la loro picciola capacità dicono esser dèi; a' quali aggiugniamo i Germani an-

of the human mind which we have pointed out in our axioms: our mind, remaining immersed and buried in our body, is naturally inclined to feel bodily things, and must make too much of a tiring effort to understand itself, just as our physical eye sees every object outside itself but needs a mirror to see itself.

Now, since this world of nations was made by man, let's see which things all men have always agreed upon, and still do, because such things can give us the universal, eternal principles, of the sort that should underlie every body of knowledge, on the basis of which all nations have arisen and maintain themselves as such.

We observe that all nations, both barbarian and civilized, no matter how greatly separated in space and time (and thus having had different foundations), retain these three human customs: they all have some form of religion, they all contract solemn marriages, they all conduct funerals for their dead; no matter how savage or crude the nations are, no human activities are celebrated with more intricate ceremonies and more consecrated solemnities than religion, marriage, and funerals. Because, according to the axiom stating that "Uniform ideas that have arisen among peoples unfamiliar with one another must have a common basis in truth," this must have been decreed to all of them: these three activities were at the basis of all human groups, and so must be scrupulously retained by all of them, so that the world doesn't return to wildness and savagery again. Thus, we have taken these three eternal and universal customs as three primary principles of this Science.

(D) Poetic wisdom, which was the first wisdom of the pagans, must have started with a metaphysics, not a reasoned, abstract one like the modern one of learned men, but a felt, imagined one of the kind men so primitive must have shared, seeing that they weren't addicted to reasoning but had robust senses and very lively imaginations, as has been established in our axioms. This was their own poetry, which in them was an inborn faculty (because they were naturally endowed with such senses and imaginations), arising from their ignorance of causation, which led them to marvel at all things, which they greatly wondered at in their ignorance of everything, as has been pointed out in the axioms. This poetry began among them as sacred poetry, because at the same time as they imagined that the causes of the things they felt and wondered at were gods, as we saw with Lactantius in our axioms (and now confirm it with reference to the natives of the New World, who call "gods" all things that are beyond their small capacity; to whom we add the ancient Germans who lived near

tichi, abitatori presso il Mar Agghiacciato, de' quali Tacito narra che dicevano d'udire la notte il Sole, che dall'occidente passava per mare nell'oriente, ed affermavano di vedere gli dèi: le quali rozzissime e semplicissime nazioni ci dànno ad intendere molto più di questi autori della gentilità, de' quali ora qui si ragiona); nello stesso tempo, diciamo, alle cose ammirate davano l'essere di sostanze dalla propia lor idea, ch'è appunto la natura de' fanciulli, che, come se n'è proposta una degnità, osserviamo prendere tra mani cose inanimate e trastullarsi e favellarvi come fusser, quelle, persone vive. [. . .]

## 33. Metastasio (1698–1782): 2 sonetti

(A)  Sogni e favole io fingo; e pure in carte
mentre favole e sogni orno e disegno,
in lor, folle ch'io son, prendo tal parte,
che del mal che inventai piango e mi sdegno.

Ma forse, allor che non m'inganna l'arte,
più saggio sono? l'agitato ingegno
forse allor più tranquillo? o forse parte
da più salda cagion l'amor, lo sdegno?

Ah! che non sol quelle ch'io canto o scrivo
favole son; ma quanto e temo e spero,
tutto è menzogna, e delirando io vivo.

Sogno della mia vita è il corso intero.
Deh tu, Signor, quando a destarmi arrivo,
fa ch'io trovi riposo in sen del vero.

(B)  Paride in giudicar l'aspra che insorse
nota contesa in fra le Dee maggiori,
s'abbagliò di Ciprigna ai bei splendori,
e dal suo labbro il frigio incendio scorse.

Ma del trono d'Assiria allor che sorse
la gran moglie di Nino ai primi onori,
con tal senno alternò l'armi e gli amori,
che all'Asia di stupor materia porse.

No, non han solo in due leggiadre stelle
tutte le donne il pregio lor racchiuso;
nè l'unico lor vanto è l'esser belle:

the Frozen Sea, of whom Tacitus tells that they said they heard the sun at night traveling through the sea from west to east, and asserted they could see the gods; these very rough and simple nations allow us to understand much more than do those pagan authors we're now discussing)—at that same time, I say, they lent those things at which they wondered a substantive existence based on their own imagination, which is just what children do: as one of our axioms has suggested, we see children pick up inanimate objects and play with them and talk to them as if they were living persons. [. . .]

## 33. Metastasio (1698–1782): 2 sonnets

(A) I make up dreams and tales; yet while I adorn
and design tales and dreams on paper,
I take such part in them, madman that I am,
that I weep and get angry at woes of my own invention.

But am I perhaps more wise at times when my art
isn't deceiving me? Is my agitated mind
perhaps calmer then? Or do that love,
that anger, arise from a more solid cause?

Ah! it's because not only the things I sing or write
are fables, but all my fears and hopes
are lies as well, and I live in a delirium.

The entire course of my life is a dream.
Oh, Lord, when I come to awaken,
let me find rest in the bosom of truth!

(B) When Paris was judging that well-known
fierce contest which arose among the major goddesses,
he was dazzled by Aphrodite of the lovely splendors,
and from his lips the burning of Troy flowed.

But when from the throne of Assyria the great wife
of Ninus ascended to the highest of honors,
with such wisdom did she alternate between war and love
that she offered Asia matter for amazement.

No, not all women have confined their worth
to two lovely starry eyes alone;
nor is being beautiful their only boast:

che vide il Termodonte a maggior uso
troncar Pentesilea la mamma imbelle,
ed in asta cangiar la rocca e il fuso.

## 34. Gozzi (1713–1786): 2 sonetti

**Dell'ortolano e dell'asino**

Nel più fresco mattin, carco di fiori
coll'Ortolano un Asinel sen gìa;
e passo passo tutta empiea la via
e l'aere intorno di graditi odori.

Seguiano l'orme sue ninfe e pastori,
per la fragranza che del carco uscia,
ma sulla sera ognun da lui fuggìa
con atti schifi e detti ancor peggiori.

Non ti maravigliar de' novi torti,
disse il Villan; chè sul mattino onore
faceano i fior. Sai che letame or porti?

Chi correa dietro all'odoroso fiore
fugge ora il puzzo. In odio a' vivi e a' morti
vien quei che perde il suo gradito odore.

**Della gamberessa e sua figlia**

Vede la Gamberessa, che sua figlia
nel camminare mal move le piante;
ed in cambio d'andar col capo avante,
va con la coda; onde ella la ripiglia;

e dice: Oh che vegg'io! che maraviglia!
cervellaccio balordo e stravagante,
va ritta, innanzi: che fai tu, furfante,
tu vai rovescia? di', chi ti consiglia?

Ma la figlia rispose a' detti suoi:
Io sempre d'imitarvi ebbi desio,
e non mi par che siam varie fra noi.

Da voi appresi ogni costume mio:
andate ritta, se potete voi;
e cercherò di seguitarvi anch'io.

for the river Thermodon saw Penthesilea cut off
her unwarlike breast for greater advantage,
and exchange her distaff and spindle for a spear.

## 34. Gozzi (1713–1786): 2 sonnets

### Of the Market Gardener and the Donkey

Very early in the morning, a little donkey
burdened with flowers set off with the market gardener;
at each step he filled the entire road
and the air around with pleasant fragrances.

Nymphs and shepherds followed in his steps
because of the aroma emitted by his burden,
but at evening everyone shunned him
with gestures of disgust and words worse still.

"Don't be surprised at this new bad treatment,"
the rustic told him, "for this morning it was the flowers
that honored you. Do you know that you're now carrying manure?

"Those who were running after the fragrant flower
are now avoiding the stench. Hated by the living and the dead
is the fellow who loses his good odor."

### Of the Crayfish and Her Daughter

The mother crayfish sees that her daughter,
when walking, moves her feet badly
and, instead of going with her head forward,
goes tail first; for which she reprimands her,

saying: "What's this I see! What a marvel!
You dull-witted, bizarre, brainless thing,
walk straight forward! What are you doing, scamp,
walking backwards? Tell me, who ordered you to?"

But her daughter replied to her words:
"I have always wanted to imitate you,
and I don't think we're different from each other.

"From you I learned all my habits:
*you* walk straight if you can,
and I'll try to follow you myself!"

## 35. Parini (1729–1799): sonetto

Quell'io che già con lungo amaro carme
Amor derisi, e il suo regno potente,
e tutta osai chiamar l'Itala gente
col mio riso maligno ad ascoltarme;

or sento anch'io sotto a le indomit' arme
tra la folla del popolo imminente
dietro a le rote del gran carro lente
dall'offeso tiranno strascinarme.

Ognun per osservar l'infame multa
preme urta e grida al suo propinquo: È quei!
e il beffator comun beffa ed insulta.

Io scornato abbassando gli occhi rei
seguo il mio fato; e il fier nemico esulta.
Imparate a deridere gli Dei.

## 36. Alfieri (1749–1803): 3 sonetti

(A) S'io t'amo? oh donna! io nol diria volendo.
Voce esprimer può mai quanta m'ispiri
dolcezza al cor, quando pietosa giri
ver me le luci, ove alti sensi apprendo?

S'io t'amo? E il chiedi? e nol dich'io tacendo?
E non tel dicon miei lunghi sospiri;
e l'alma afflitta mia, che par che spiri,
mentre dal tuo bel ciglio immobil pendo?

E non tel dice ad ogni istante il pianto,
cui di speranza e di temenza misto,
versare a un tempo, e raffrenare io bramo?

Tutto tel dice in me: mia lingua intanto
sola tel tace, perchè il cor s'è avvisto,
ch'a quel ch'ei sente, è un nulla il dirti: Io t'amo.

(B) L'Arno già, l'Appennino, e il Po mi lasso
dietro le spalle; e l'Alpi negre a fronte

## 35. Parini (1729–1799): sonnet

I, the man who once in a long, bitter song
laughed at Love and his mighty sway,
daring to summon the whole Italian nation
to listen to me and my slanderous laughter—

now I, too, feel myself, below his invincible weapons,
amid the threatening crowd of people,
behind the slow wheels of his great chariot,
being dragged along by the insulted tyrant.

Everyone who views the degrading penalty
pushes, pokes, and cries to his neighbor: "It's him!"
and mocks and insults the public mocker.

I, humiliated, lowering my guilty eyes,
follow my destiny, and my savage enemy is exultant.
Now go and laugh at the gods!

## 36. Alfieri (1749–1803): 3 sonnets

(A) Do I love you? My lady! I wouldn't say it even if I wanted.
Can words ever express what great sweetness
you inspire in my heart, when you tenderly turn
those eyes to me in which I learn lofty meanings?

Do I love you? You ask? Don't I say so, keeping silent?
Don't my long sighs tell you so,
and my grieving soul, which seems to expire
while I hang motionless from your lovely eyelashes?

Don't my tears tell you so at every moment,
tears compounded of hope and fear,
which I yearn to shed and hold back at the same time?

Everything in me tells you so: meanwhile, my tongue
alone doesn't tell you, because my heart is aware
that, to what it feels, saying "I love you" is nothing.

(B) Now I leave the Arno, the Apennines, and the Po
behind me; and the black Alps in front of me

già mi mostran l'angusto ed erto passo,
per cui convien che al Tirolese io monte.

L'amoroso pensiero agili e pronte
l'ali ha così, ch'oltre quei massi al basso,
là dove il Reno è assai già lungi al fonte,
io fortemente immaginando passo,

e del gran fiume in su la manca riva
trovo, tra vespro e sera, entro un bel bosco,
sola e pensosa una terrena Diva.

Già, per le folte piante, è l'aer fosco;
non visto, odo che dice: or non arriva
gente ancor qui dal bel paese Tosco?

(C)  Presso al loco ove l'Istro è un picciol fonte,
nell'atto io d'esser dal mio ben diviso,
di un gelato sudor sentia la fronte
molle, e di ardente lagrimare il viso.

E in flebil suono di pietà, che un monte
avria spezzato, un parlare interciso
udia di voci a saettar sì pronte,
ch'io sperai che il dolor mi avrebbe ucciso.

In quel punto, non so quel ch'io dicessi;
nulla, credo: io piangeva; e piango ancora;
nè sapea dov'io m'era, o che mi fessi.

Vedea lei sola; e l'ho negli occhi ognora:
a un cenerino drappo avea commessi
gli omeri, e il crin copria color d'aurora.

## 37. Monti (1754–1828): 2 sonetti

### Sopra la morte

Morte, che se' tu mai? Primo dei danni
l'alma vile e la rea ti crede e teme;
e vendetta del Ciel scendi ai tiranni,
che il vigile tuo braccio incalza e preme.

Ma l'infelice, a cui de' lunghi affanni
grave è l'incarco, e morta in cuor la speme,

now show me the narrow, steep pass
I must ascend to reach the Tyrol.

Lovers' thoughts have such agile, ready
wings that, in my strong imagination I am passing
beyond those masses of rock onto the lowlands
where the Rhine is already very far from its source,

and finding, on the left bank of the great river,
between dusk and night, within a lovely grove,
an earthly goddess alone and pensive.

Now, amid the dense trees, the air is murky;
myself unseen, I hear her ask: "Does no one
still come here from the fair land of Tuscany?"

(C) Near the spot where the Danube is a little spring,
at the moment of being parted from my sweetheart,
I felt my brow moist with a cold sweat,
and my eyes wet with ardent tears.

And in a lamenting tone of pity that would have
cracked a mountain, I heard an intermittent
sound of voices so ready to dart arrows
that I hoped my grief would kill me.

At that moment I don't know what I may have said;
nothing, I think; I was weeping, and still am;
nor did I know where I was, or what I was doing.

I saw *her* alone; and I still have her in my eyes;
she had entrusted her shoulders to an ash-colored
cloth, and the color of dawn covered her hair.

## 37. Monti (1754–1828): 2 sonnets

### On Death

Death, what are you, anyway? A base, criminal soul
thinks you're the worst of evils, and fears you;
and as vengeance from heaven you descend on tyrants,
whom your vigilant arm pursues and oppresses.

But the unhappy man, to whom the burden of long
woes is heavy, and in whose heart hope is dead,

quel ferro implora troncator degli anni,
e ride all'appressar dell'ore estreme.

Fra la polve di Marte e le vicende
ti sfida il forte, che ne' rischi indura;
e il saggio senza impallidir ti attende.

Morte, che se' tu dunque? Un'ombra oscura,
un bene, un male, che diversa prende
dagli affetti dell'uom forma e natura.

**Per un dipinto dell'Agricola rappresentante la figlia sua**

Più la contemplo, più vaneggio in quella
mirabil tela: e il cor, che ne sospira,
sì nell'obbietto del suo amor delira,
che gli amplessi n'aspetta e la favella.

Ond'io già corro ad abbracciarla. Ed ella
labbro non move, ma lo sguardo gira
vêr me sì lieto, che mi dice: Or mira,
diletto genitor, quanto son bella.

Figlia, io rispondo, d'un gentil sereno
ridon tue forme; e questa imago è diva
sì che ogni tela al paragon vien meno.

Ma un'imago di te vegg'io più viva,
e la veggo sol io; quella che in seno
al tuo tenero padre Amor scolpiva.


## 38. Foscolo (1778–1827): 5 sonetti

### Alla sera

Forse perché della fatal quïete
Tu sei l'immago a me sì cara vieni
O sera! E quando ti corteggian liete
Le nubi estive e i zeffiri sereni,

E quando dal nevoso aere inquïete
Tenebre e lunghe all'universo meni
Sempre scendi invocata, e le secrete
Vie del mio cor soavemente tieni.

prays for that steel which cuts short the years
and smiles at the approach of his final hour.

Amid the dust and vicissitudes of war
the strong man, who grows hard in danger, defies you;
and the wise man awaits you without turning pale.

Death, what are you, then? A dark shadow,
a boon, an evil, which takes on different forms
and natures based on man's emotions.

### On a Portrait of His Daughter by Agricola

The more I contemplate it, the more I rave about
that wonderful canvas; and my heart, sighing over it,
is so delirious over the object of its love
that it expects embraces and speech from it.

And so I already run to hug her. But she
doesn't move her lips, yet turns her gaze
toward me so gaily that she says: "Now see,
beloved father, how beautiful I am!"

"Daughter," I reply, "with a noble calm
your forms are smiling, and this image is so divine
that no other picture can stand comparison with it."

But I see a more living image of it,
one that I alone see; the one which has been engraved
in your loving father's heart by Love.

## 38. Foscolo (1778–1827): 5 sonnets

### To Evening

Perhaps because you are the image
of death's repose you are so dear when you come to me,
O evening! Both when you're cheerfully escorted
by summer clouds and calm zephyrs,

and when you bring long, unquiet darkness
to the universe from the snowy air,
you always descend at my call, and gently
guard the secret paths of my heart.

Vagar mi fai co' miei pensier su l'orme
Che vanno al nulla eterno; e intanto fugge
Questo reo tempo, e van con lui le torme

Delle cure onde meco egli si strugge;
E mentre io guardo la tua pace, dorme
Quello spirto guerrier ch'entro mi rugge.

## Di sé stesso

Non son chi fui; perì di noi gran parte:
Questo che avanza è sol languore e pianto.
E secco è il mirto, e son le foglie sparte
Del lauro, speme al giovenil mio canto.

Perché dal dì ch'empia licenza e Marte
Vestivan me del lor sanguineo manto,
Cieca è la mente e guasto il core, ed arte
L'umana strage, arte è in me fatta, e vanto.

Che se pur sorge di morir consiglio,
A mia fiera ragion chiudon le porte
Furor di gloria, e carità di figlio.

Tal di me schiavo, e d'altri, e della sorte,
Conosco il meglio ed al peggior mi appiglio,
E so invocare e non darmi la morte.

## Di sé stesso all'amata

Così gl'interi giorni in lungo incerto
Sonno gemo! ma poi quando la bruna
Notte gli astri nel ciel chiama e la luna,
E il freddo aer di mute ombre è coverto;

Dove selvoso è il piano e più deserto
Allor lento io vagando, ad una ad una
Palpo le piaghe onde la rea fortuna
E amore, e il mondo hanno il mio core aperto.

Stanco mi appoggio or al troncon d'un pino,
Ed or prostrato ove strepitan l'onde,
Con le speranze mie parlo e deliro.

You make me roam in thought on the tracks
that lead to eternal nothingness; and meanwhile
this evil time rushes by, and with it go the swarms

of troubles that consume it along with me;
but while I behold your peace, that warlike
spirit roaring within me sleeps.

## On Himself

I'm no longer the man I was; much of me has perished:
what survives is only languor and weeping.
The myrtle is withered, and the laurel leaves
scattered which were the hope of my youthful song.

Because since the day that impious license and war
clad me in their bloodstained mantle,
my mind has been blind, my heart a ruin; and a trade—
slaughtering people has become my trade and boast.

For, even if the decision to die is taken,
the doors to my savage reason are shut
by a rage for fame and by filial piety.

Thus, a slave to myself, others, and fate,
I know what's right but cling to what's wrong,
and I can summon death but not give it to myself.

## On Himself, to His Beloved

Thus I moan away whole days in a long,
uncertain slumber! But then, when brown
night calls the stars and moon to the sky,
and the cold air is covered with mute shadows,

where the plain is wooded and most deserted,
then, roaming slowly, I touch one by one
the wounds with which my evil fortune,
love, and the world have laid my heart open.

Wearily I now lean on the trunk of a pine,
and now lying prostrate where the waters murmur,
I speak to my hopes and I rave.

Ma per te le mortali ire e il destino
Spesso obbliando, a te, donna, io sospiro:
Luce degli occhi miei chi mi t'asconde?

## A Zacinto

Né più mai toccherò le sacre sponde
Ove il mio corpo fanciulletto giacque,
Zacinto mia, che te specchi nell'onde
Del greco mar da cui vergine nacque

Venere, e fea quelle isole feconde
Col suo primo sorriso, onde non tacque
Le tue limpide nubi e le tue fronde
L'inclito verso di colui che l'acque

Cantò fatali, ed il diverso esiglio
Per cui bello di fama e di sventura
Baciò la sua petrosa Itaca Ulisse.

Tu non altro che il canto avrai del figlio,
O materna mia terra; a noi prescrisse
Il fato illacrimata sepoltura.

## In morte del fratello Giovanni

Un dì, s'io non andrò sempre fuggendo
Di gente in gente, mi vedrai seduto
Su la tua pietra, o fratel mio, gemendo
Il fior de' tuoi gentili anni caduto.

La madre or sol, suo dì tardo traendo,
parla di me col tuo cenere muto:
Ma io deluse a voi le palme tendo;
E se da lunge i miei tetti saluto,

Sento gli avversi Numi, e le secrete
Cure che al viver tuo furon tempesta,
E prego anch'io nel tuo porto quïete.

Questo di tanta speme oggi mi resta!
Straniere genti, l'ossa mie rendete
Allora al petto della madre mesta.

But for your sake often forgetting my mortal
rage and my destiny, I sigh, lady, to you:
light of my eyes, who is hiding you from me?

## To Zante

Never again shall I touch the sacred shores
where my boyish body lay,
my Zante, you that mirror yourself in the waters
of the Grecian sea from which was born in youthful glory

Venus, who made those islands fertile
with her first smile, so that your limpid clouds
and your foliage were sure to be mentioned
in the famous poetry of the bard who sang

of the fateful sea and the diversified exile
because of which, handsome in fame and misfortune,
Ulysses kissed his rocky Ithaca.

You will have no more from your son than his song,
O my motherland; for us fate has ordained
a burial place that no one will weep over.

## On the Death of His Brother Giovanni

One day, if I won't always continue to flee
from country to country, you will see me seated
on your tombstone, O my brother, moaning for
the fallen flower of your noble years.

Alone now, drawing out her slow days, our mother
speaks of me to your mute ashes;
but I hold out to you my disappointed hands,
and if I greet my home from afar,

I feel the enmity of the gods, and the secret
troubles that created a storm in your life,
and I, too, pray for calm in your harbor.

From such great hopes only this remains to me today!
Foreign people, restore my bones
at that time to the bosom of my sorrowful mother.

## 39. Manzoni (1785–1873): *I promessi sposi*

Andava un giorno per una strada della sua città, seguito da due bravi, e accompagnato da un tal Cristoforo, altre volte giovine di bottega e, dopo chiusa questa, diventato maestro di casa. Era un uomo di circa cinquanta anni, affezionato dalla gioventú a Lodovico, che aveva veduto nascere, e che, tra salario e regali, gli dava non solo da vivere, ma di che mantenere e tirar su una numerosa famiglia. Vide Lodovico spuntar da lontano un signor tale, arrogante e soverchiatore di professione, col quale non aveva mai parlato in vita sua, ma che gli era cordiale nemico, e al quale rendeva, pur di cuore, il contraccambio: giacché è uno dei vantaggi di questo mondo, quello di poter odiare ed essere odiati, senza conoscersi. Costui, seguito da quattro bravi, s'avanzava diritto, con passo superbo, con la testa alta, con la bocca composta all'alterigia e allo sprezzo. Tutt'e due camminavan rasente al muro: ma Lodovico (notate bene) lo strisciava col lato destro; e ciò secondo una consuetudine, gli dava il diritto (dove mai si va a ficcare il diritto!) di non istaccarsi dal detto muro, per dar passo a chi si fosse; cosa della quale allora si faceva gran caso. L'altro pretendeva, all'opposto, che quel diritto competesse a lui, come a nobile, e che a Lodovico toccasse d'andar nel mezzo; e ciò in forza d'un'altra consuetudine. Perocché, in questo, come accade in molti affari, erano in vigore due consuetudine contrarie; senza che fosse deciso qual delle due fosse la buona; il che dava opportunità di fare una guerra ogni volta che una testa dura s'abbattesse in un'altra della stessa tempra. Que' due si venivano incontro, ristretti alla muraglia, come due figure di basso rilievo ambulanti. Quando si trovarono viso a viso, il signor tale, squadrando Lodovico, a capo alto, col cipiglio imperioso, gli disse, in un tono corrispondente di voce: —Fate luogo.

—Fate luogo voi, —rispose Lodovico.— La diritta è mia.

—Co' vostri pari, è sempre mia.

—Sì, se l'arroganza de' vostri pari fosse legge per i pari miei.

I bravi dell'uno e dell'altro eran rimasti fermi, ciascuno dietro al suo padrone, guardandosi in cagnesco, con le mani alle daghe, preparati alla battaglia. La gente che arrivava di qua e di là, si teneva in distanza a osservare il fatto; e la presenza di quegli spettatori animava sempre più il puntiglio de' contendenti.

—Nel mezzo, vile meccanico; o ch'io t'insegno una volta come si tratta co' gentiluomini.

—Voi mentite ch'io sia vile.

## 39. Manzoni (1785–1873): *The Betrothed*

One day he was walking down a street in his city, followed by two body-guards and accompanied by a certain Cristoforo, formerly a shop clerk and, now that the shop was closed, his steward. He was a man of about fifty, fond of Lodovico since his boyhood, having seen him born. Between salary and presents, Lodovico gave him not only enough to live on, but enough to keep and raise a numerous family. Lodovico saw appearing in the distance a certain lord, arrogant and overbearing by profession, to whom he had never spoken in his life, but who was his bitter enemy, and whom he hated reciprocally, and wholeheartedly—because it's one of this world's advantages to be able to hate and be hated without knowing the other person. This lord, followed by four bodyguards, was advancing straight ahead, his step prideful, his head high, his lips expressive of haughtiness and contempt. Both were walking right up against the wall, but (note this well) Lodovico was brushing it with his right side, and this, in accordance with a social convention, gave him the right (the situations people's "rights" get them into!) not to detach himself from the aforesaid wall to make way for anyone; a matter to which people gave great impor-tance at that time. The other man claimed, on the contrary, that that right belonged to him, inasmuch as he was a nobleman, and that it was Lodovico's place to walk in the middle; this was based on a different con-vention. Because in this matter as in many, two opposing conventions were valid, though no one had decided which of the two was the opera-tive one; this lent the opportunity to go to war whenever one hard head came across another of the same nature. Those two confronted each other, hugging the wall like two bas-reliefs walking. When they found themselves face to face, the lord, scrutinizing Lodovico, his head high, with an imperious frown, said, in a corresponding tone of voice: "Make way!"

"Make way yourself!" Lodovico replied. "I have the right of way."

"With the likes of you, it's always mine."

"Yes, if the arrogance of the likes of you were a law to the likes of me."

The bodyguards on either side had remained still, each one behind his own master, exchanging surly looks, their hands on their daggers, ready for battle. The people arriving here and there kept at a distance to watch the incident, and the presence of those spectators kept fueling the obsti-nacy of the rivals.

"In the middle, base merchant, or I'll teach you once and for all how to behave to noblemen!"

"It's a lie that I'm base!"

—Tu menti ch'io abbia mentito. —Questa risposta era di prammatica.— E se, tu fossi cavaliere, come son io, —aggiunse quel signore,— ti vorrei far vedere, con la spada e con la cappa, che il mentitore sei tu.

—È un buon pretesto per dispensarvi di sostener co' fatti l'insolenza delle vostre parole.

—Gettate nel fango questo ribaldo, —disse il gentiluomo, voltandosi a' suoi.

—Vediamo! —disse Lodovico, dando subitamente un passo indietro, e mettendo mano alla spada.

—Temerario! —gridò l'altro, sfoderando la sua:— io spezzerò questa, quando sarà macchiata del tuo vil sangue.

Così s'avventarono l'uno all'altro; i servitori delle due parti si slanciarono alla difesa de' loro padroni. Il combattimento era disuguale, e per il numero, e anche perché Lodovico mirava piuttosto a scansare i colpi, e a disarmare il nemico che ad ucciderlo; ma questo voleva la morte di lui ad ogni costo. Lodovico aveva già ricevuta al braccio sinistro una pugnalata d'un bravo, e una sgraffiatura leggera in una guancia, e il nemico principale gli piombava addosso per finirlo; quando Cristoforo, vedendo il suo padrone nell'estremo pericolo, andò col pugnale addosso al signore. Questo, rivolta tutta la sua ira contro di lui, lo passò con la spada. A questa vista Lodovico, come fuor di sé, cacciò la sua nel ventre del feritore, il quale cadde moribondo, quasi a un punto col povero Cristoforo. I bravi del gentiluomo, visto ch'era finita, si diedero alla fuga, malconci: quelli di Lodovico, tartassati e sfregiati anche loro, non essendovi più a chi dare, e non volendo trovarsi impicciati nella gente, che già accorreva, scantonarono dall'altra parte; e Lodovico si trovò solo, con que' due funesti compagni ai piedi, in mezzo a una folla.

«Com'è andata? —È uno.— Son due. —Gli ha fatto un occhiello nel ventre.— Chi è stato ammazzato? —Quel prepotente.— Oh santa Maria, che sconquasso! —Chi cerca trova.— Una le paga tutte. —Ha finito anche lui.— Che colpo! Vuol essere una faccenda seria. —E quell'altro disgraziato!— Misericordia! che spettacolo! —Salvatelo, salvatelo.— Sta fresco anche lui. —Vedete com'è concio! butta sangue da tutte le parti.— Scappi, scappi. Non si lasci prendere.»

Queste parole, che più di tutte si facevano sentire nel frastuono confuso di quella folla, esprimevano il voto comune; e, col consiglio, venne anche l'aiuto. Il fatto era accaduto vicino a una chiesa di cappuccini, asilo, come ognun sa, impenetrabile allora a' birri, e a tutto quel complesso di cose e di persone, che si chiamava la giustizia. L'uccisore fe-

"You lie when you say that I do." This was a standard retort. "And if you were a knight like me," the lord added, "I'd show you, with cape and sword, that the liar is you."

"That's a good excuse to get out of supporting the insolence of your words with real actions."

"Throw this scoundrel into the mud!" the nobleman said, addressing his men.

"We'll see!" Lodovico said, suddenly taking a step backward and laying hand on his sword.

"Rash fellow!" the other shouted, unsheathing his own. "I'll smash this after it's stained with your base blood."

And so the two hurled themselves at each other; the servants on both sides dashed to their masters' defense. The fight was uneven, both in numbers and also because Lodovico sought rather to parry the blows and disarm his enemy than to kill him; but the lord wanted his death at all costs. Lodovico had already received a dagger blow from one bodyguard in his left arm and a light scratch on one cheek, and his chief enemy was falling upon him to finish him off, when Cristoforo, seeing his master in extreme danger, attacked the lord with his dagger. The lord, turning all his wrath onto him, thrust him through and through with his sword. At that sight Lodovico, as if beside himself, plunged his own into the slayer's belly; the man fell, dying, almost at the same moment as poor Cristoforo. The nobleman's bodyguards, seeing it was all over, ran off in bad shape; Lodovico's, they, too, ill-treated and slashed in the face, having no one left to assail, and not wishing to be obstructed by the people, who were already running up, turned the corner in the other direction; and Lodovico found himself alone, with those two direful companions at his feet, in the middle of a crowd.

"How did it go?" "It's one man." "It's two." "He made a hole in his belly." "Who got killed?" "That high-and-mighty." "Oh, blessed Virgin, what a to-do!" "If you ask for it, you get it." "You pay for all your crimes at one time." "This one's a goner, too." "What a blow! It looks like a serious business." "And that other poor guy!" "Mercy, what a sight!" "Save him, save him!" "He's in a fix, too." "See what bad shape he's in! He's bleeding everywhere." "Run away, run away! Don't get caught!"

These words, which were most clearly heard amid that crowd's confused uproar, expressed their general wishes; and, with the advice, came aid, as well. The incident had occurred near a Capuchin church, an asylum, as everyone knows, which couldn't be entered by the police at that time, and was barred to that whole complex of things and persons which was known as "justice." The wounded slayer was led or carried there by

rito fu qui condotto o portato dalla folla, quasi fuori di sentimento; e i frati lo ricevettero dalle mani del popolo, che glielo raccomandava dicendo: «è un uomo dabbene che ha freddato un birbone superbo: l'ha fatto per sua difesa: c'è stato tirato per i capelli.»[. . .]

## 40. Pellico (1789–1854): *Le mie prigioni*

Il venerdí 13 ottobre 1820 fui arrestato a Milano, e condotto a Santa Margherita. Erano le tre pomeridiane. Mi si fece un lungo interrogatorio per tutto quel giorno e per altri ancora. Ma di ciò non dirò nulla. Simile ad un amante maltrattato dalla sua bella e dignitosamente risoluto di tenerle broncio, lascio la politica ov'ella sta, e parlo d'altro.

Alle nove della sera di quel povero venerdí, l'attuario mi consegnò al custode, e questi, condottomi nella stanza a me destinata, si fece da me rimettere con gentile invito, per restituirmeli a tempo debito, orologio, danaro e ogni altra cosa ch'io avessi in tasca, e m'augurò rispettosamente la buona notte.

—Fermatevi, caro voi, —gli dissi;— oggi non ho pranzato; fatemi portare qualche cosa.

—Subito: la locanda è qui vicina; e sentirà, signore, che buon vino!

—Vino, non ne bevo.

A questa risposta, il signor Angiolino mi guardò spaventato, e sperando ch'io scherzassi. I custodi di carcere che tengono bettola i-norridiscono d'un prigioniero astemio.

—Non ne bevo, davvero.

—M'incresce per lei; patirà al doppio la solitudine . . .

E vedendo ch'io non mutava proposito, uscí; ed in meno di mez-z'ora ebbi il pranzo. Mangiai pochi bocconi, tracannai un bicchier d'acqua, e fui lasciato solo.

La stanza era a pian terreno e metteva sul cortile. Carceri di qua, carceri di là, carceri di sopra, carceri di rimpetto. M'appoggiai alla finestra e stetti qualche tempo ad ascoltare l'andare e venire de' carcerieri, ed il frenetico canto di parecchi de' rinchiusi.

Pensava: «Un secolo fa, questo era un monastero: avrebbero mai le sante e penitenti vergini che lo abitavano, immaginato che le loro celle suonerebbero oggi, non più di femminei gemiti e d'inni divoti, ma di bestemmie e di canzoni invereconde, e che conterrebbero uomini d'ogni fatta, e per lo piú destinati agli ergastoli o alle forche? E fra un secolo, chi respirerà in queste celle? Oh fugacità del tempo! oh mobilità perpetua delle cose! Può chi vi considera affliggersi, se fortuna

the crowd, almost unconscious, and the friars received him from the hands of the people, who urged them to take care of him, saying: "He's a decent man who has rubbed out a haughty rogue; he did it in self-defense; he was dragged into it." [. . .]

## 40. Pellico (1789–1854): *My Prisons*

On Friday, October 13, 1820, I was arrested in Milan and taken to Santa Margherita. It was three in the afternoon. I was interrogated at length that whole day, and for a few more. But I'll say nothing about it. Like a lover badly treated by his sweetheart and proudly determined to sulk over it, I leave politics aside, and speak of other things.

At nine P.M. on that unhappy Friday, the officer handed me over to the guard, who, leading me to the room assigned to me, asked me politely to give him my watch, money, and everything else I had in my pocket; it would be returned to me at the proper time. Then he respectfully wished me a good night.

"Stop, my good man!" I said. "I haven't dined today; have me brought something."

"At once! The inn is nearby. You'll see, sir, how good the wine is!"

"I don't drink wine."

At that reply, Mr. Angiolino looked at me in alarm, in hopes I was joking. Prison guards who keep taverns shudder at a prisoner who's a teetotaler.

"I don't drink it, honestly."

"I'm sorry for you; you'll suffer doubly from the loneliness . . ."

But seeing that I wasn't changing my mind, he went out; and in less than half an hour I had my meal. I ate just a few mouthfuls, I gulped down a glass of water, and I was left to myself.

The room was on the ground floor, overlooking the courtyard. Cells here, cells there, cells overhead, cells opposite. I leaned on the window and stood there a while listening to the coming and going of the jailers and the frenetic singing of several of the detainees.

I thought: "A century ago, this was a convent: would those holy, penitent virgins living here ever have imagined that today their cells would echo, no longer with female moans and devout hymns, but with curses and indecent songs, and would contain men of all sorts, most of them fated to be imprisoned or hanged? And in another century, who will be breathing in these cells? Oh, the fleetingness of time! Oh, the perpetual changeableness of things! Can a man who reflects on you be saddened if

cessò di sorridergli, se vien sepolto in prigione, se gli si minaccia il patibolo? Ieri, io era uno de' piú felici mortali del mondo: oggi non ho piú alcuna delle dolcezze che confortavano la mia vita; non piú libertà, non piú consorzio d'amici, non piú speranze! No; il lusingarsi sarebbe follía. Di qui non uscirò se non per essere gettato ne' piú orribili covili, o consegnato al carnefice! Ebbene, il giorno dopo la mia morte, sarà come s'io fossi spirato in un palazzo, e portato alla sepoltura co' piú grandi onori».

Cosí il riflettere alla fugacità del tempo mi invigoriva l'animo. Ma mi risorsero alla mente il padre, la madre, due fratelli, due sorelle, un'altra famiglia ch'io amava quasi fosse la mia; ed i ragionamenti filosofici nulla piú valsero. M'intenerii, e piansi come un fanciullo.

Tre mesi prima io ero andato a Torino ed avea riveduto dopo parecchi anni di separazione i miei cari genitori, uno de' fratelli e le due sorelle. Tutta la nostra famiglia s'era sempre tanto amata! Niun figliolo era stato piú di me colmato di benefizi dal padre e dalla madre! Oh come al rivedere i venerati vecchi io m'era commosso, trovandoli notabilmente piú aggravati dall'età che non m'immaginava! Quanto avrei allora voluto non abbandonarli piú, consacrarmi a sollevare colle mie cure la loro vecchiaia! Quanto mi dolse, ne' brevi giorni che io stetti a Torino, di aver parecchi doveri che mi portavano fuori del tetto paterno, e di dare cosí poca parte del mio tempo agli amati congiunti! La povera madre diceva con melanconica amarezza: «Ah! il nostro Silvio non è venuto a Torino per veder noi!». Il mattino che ripartii per Milano, la separazione fu dolorosissima. Il padre entrò in carrozza con me, e m'accompagnò per un miglio; poi tornò indietro soletto. Io mi voltava a guardarlo, e piangeva, e baciava un anello che la madre mi avea dato, e mai non mi sentii cosí angosciato di allontanarmi da' parenti. Non credulo a' presentimenti, io stupiva di non poter vincere il mio dolore, ed era sforzato a dire con ispavento: «D'onde questa mia straordinaria inquietudine?». Pareami pur di prevedere qualche grande sventura.

Ora, nel carcere, mi risovvenivano quello spavento, quell'angoscia; mi risovvenivano tutte le parole udite, tre mesi innanzi, da' genitori. Quel lamento della madre: «Ah! il nostro Silvio non è venuto a Torino per veder noi!», mi ripiombava sul cuore. Io mi rimproverava di non essermi mostrato loro mille volte piú tenero. «Li amo cotanto, e ciò dissi loro cosí debolmente! Non dovea mai piú vederli e mi saziai cosí poco de' loro cari volti! e fui cosí avaro delle testimonianze dell'amor mio!». Questi pensieri mi straziavano l'anima. [. . .]

fortune has ceased to smile upon him, if he's buried in a prison, if he's threatened by the gallows? Yesterday I was one of the happiest mortals in the world; today I no longer have any of the sweet things that comforted my life: no more freedom, no more company of friends, no more hopes! No, to flatter oneself would be madness. I'll only get out of here to be thrown into the most horrible dens or to be handed over to the executioner! Very well, the day after my death it will be as if I had expired in a palace and had been borne to my grave with the greatest honors."

Thus, reflecting on the fleetingness of time lent vigor to my mind. But there returned to my thoughts my father, my mother, my two brothers, my two sisters, and another family I loved as if it were my own; and my philosophical reasonings did me no further good. I weakened, and wept like a child.

Three months earlier, I had gone to Turin and had seen again, after several years of separation, my dear parents, one of my brothers, and my two sisters. Our whole family had always loved one another so! No son had ever had more kindness heaped on him by his father and mother! Oh, how moved I had been on seeing the venerated old couple again, finding them noticeably more burdened by age than I had imagined! How much I would have wanted then not to desert them again, to devote myself to comfort their old age with my care! How it grieved me, in those brief days I remained in Turin, that I had several duties which took me out of my parents' house, so that I could give so small a part of my time to my beloved relatives! My poor mother kept saying with melancholy bitterness: "Ah! It's not us that our Silvio came to Turin to see!" The morning I left again for Milan, the parting was very painful. My father got in the coach with me and accompanied me for a mile; then he turned back alone. I looked back to watch him, and wept, and kissed a ring my mother had given me; never had I felt so anguished at leaving my relatives. Though not superstitious about forebodings, I was amazed at being unable to overcome my sorrow, and I was compelled to say in alarm: "Where is this unusual nervousness of mine coming from?" I even felt I was foreseeing some great disaster.

Now, in jail, I recalled that alarm, that anguish; I remembered all the words I had heard from my parents three months previously. That lament of my mother's, "Ah! It's not us that our Silvio came to Turin to see!," kept falling on my heart. I reproached myself for not having shown myself a thousand times more tender to them. "I love them so, and told them I did in such a feeble way! I was never to see them again and I feasted so little on their dear faces! And I was so stingy with tokens of my love!" Those thoughts were lacerating my soul. [. . .]

## 41. Leopardi (1798–1837): 2 liriche

L'infinito

Sempre caro mi fu quest'ermo colle,
e questa siepe, che da tanta parte
dell'ultimo orizzonte il guardo esclude.
Ma sedendo e mirando, interminati
spazi di là da quella, e sovrumani
silenzi, e profondissima quïete
io nel pensier mi fingo; ove per poco
il cor non si spaura. E come il vento
odo stormir tra queste piante, io quello
infinito silenzio a questa voce
vo comparando: e mi sovvien l'eterno,
e le morte stagioni, e la presente
e viva, e il suon di lei. Cosí tra questa
immensità s'annega il pensier mio:
e il naufragar m'è dolce in questo mare.

Le ricordanze

Vaghe stelle dell'Orsa, io non credea
tornare ancor per uso a contemplarvi
sul paterno giardino scintillanti,
e ragionar con voi dalle finestre
di questo albergo ove abitai fanciullo,
e delle gioie mie vidi la fine.
Quante immagini un tempo, e quante fole
creommi nel pensier l'aspetto vostro
e delle luci a voi compagne! allora
che, tacito, seduto in verde zolla,
delle sere io solea passar gran parte
mirando il cielo, ed ascoltando il canto
della rana rimota alla campagna!
E la lucciola errava appo le siepi
e in su l'aiuole, sussurrando al vento
i viali odorati ed i cipressi
là nella selva; e sotto al patrio tetto
sonavan voci alterne, e le tranquille
opre de' servi. E che pensieri immensi,
che dolci sogni mi spirò la vista

# 41. Leopardi (1798–1837): 2 lyric poems

### The Infinite

I've always been fond of this solitary hill
and this hedge, which cuts off one's view
from such a great part of the farthest horizon.
But, as I sit and gaze, limitless
spaces beyond the hedge, and superhuman
silences, and the most profound repose
I create in my imagination; at which my heart
is nearly frightened. And when I hear
the wind rustling through these trees, I compare
that infinite silence to its voice,
and I call to mind eternity
and the dead seasons, and the present,
living one, and its sounds. Thus, in that
immensity my thoughts are drowned,
and shipwreck in this sea is sweet to me.

### Remembrances

Beautiful stars of the Dippers, I didn't expect
to contemplate you again as I used to,
twinkling above my parents' garden,
or to speak to you from the windows
of this house I dwelt in as a boy,
seeing the end of my joys.
How many images in those days, and how many fantasies
were created in my thoughts by the sight of you
and of the stars that accompany you, then,
when silently seated on the green turf,
I used to spend a large part of the night
gazing at the sky and listening to the call
of the frogs, far away in the countryside!
And the firefly would roam near the hedges
and over the flower beds, as the fragrant garden walks
whispered in the wind, as did the cypresses
there in the grove; and beneath my parents' roof
voices sounded in alternation, as did the calm
tasks of the servants. And what immense thoughts,
what sweet dreams were inspired in me by the sight

di quel lontano mar, quei monti azzurri,
che di qua scopro, e che varcare un giorno
io mi pensava, arcani mondi, arcana
felicità fingendo al viver mio!
ignaro del mio fato, e quante volte
questa mia vita dolorosa e nuda
volentier con la morte avrei cangiato.
    Né mi diceva il cor che l'età verde
sarei dannato a consumare in questo
natio borgo selvaggio, intra una gente
zotica, vil; cui nomi strani, e spesso
argomento di riso e di trastullo,
son dottrina e saper; che m'odia e fugge,
per invidia non già, che non mi tiene
maggior di sé, ma perché tale estima
ch'io mi tenga in cor mio, sebben di fuori
a persona giammai non ne fo segno.
Qui passo gli anni, abbandonato, occulto,
senz'amor, senza vita; ed aspro a forza
tra lo stuol de' malevoli divengo:
qui di pietà mi spoglio e di virtudi,
e sprezzator degli uomini mi rendo,
per la greggia ch'ho appresso: e intanto vola
il caro tempo giovanil; più caro
che la fama e l'allor, più che la pura
luce del giorno, e lo spirar: ti perdo
senza un diletto, inutilmente, in questo
soggiorno disumano, intra gli affanni,
o dell'arida vita unico fiore.
    Viene il vento recando il suon dell'ora
dalla torre del borgo. Era conforto
questo suon, mi rimembra, alle mie notti,
quando fanciullo, nella buia stanza,
per assidui terrori io vigilava,
sospirando il mattin. Qui non è cosa
ch'io vegga o senta, onde un'immagin dentro
non torni, e un dolce rimembrar non sorga.
Dolce per sé; ma con dolor sottentra
il pensier del presente, un van desio
del passato, ancor tristo, e il dire: io fui. [. . .]

of that distant sea, those blue mountains,
which I detect from here, and which I thought about
crossing some day, imagining worlds unknown,
happiness unknown to my life,
ignorant of my fate, and of how many times
I would gladly have exchanged this sad
and empty life of mine for death!
   Nor did my heart tell me I'd be condemned
to waste my verdant years in this
savage town where I was born, among a rough,
low populace; to whom learning and knowledge
are strange names, and often a cause for laughter
and amusement; people who hate and shun me,
not out of envy, because they don't consider me
greater than they, but because they think
I secretly consider myself to be superior, though outwardly
I never give an indication of it to anyone.
Here I spend my years, abandoned, obscure,
without love, without life; and I necessarily become
harsh amid the throng of ill-wishers:
here I divest myself of pity and virtues,
turning into a despiser of mankind,
because of the herd I have near me; meanwhile
my dear youth flies away, more dear
than fame and laurels; more than the pure
light of the day, and breath: I'm losing you
without any pleasure, uselessly, in this
inhuman abode, amid anguish,
O you sole flower of my arid life!
   The wind comes, bearing the sound of the hour
from the town clock tower. That sound,
I remember, was a comfort to my nights
when, as a boy, in my dark room,
I lay awake, constantly in terror,
yearning for the morning. Here there's nothing
I see or hear that doesn't bring back an image
to my mind, some sweet recollection arising.
Sweet in itself; but painfully there mingle with it
thoughts of the present, a vain regret
for the past, also sad, and the words: "I exist no more." [. . .]

## 42. De Sanctis (1817–1883): *Storia della letteratura italiana*

Si può ora comprendere il meccanismo del dramma metastasiano. Sta in cima l'eroe o l'eroina, Zenobia o Issipile, Temistocle o Tito. L'eroe ha tutte le perfezioni che la poesia ha collocate nell'età dell'oro, e sveglia l'eroismo intorno a sé, rende eroici anche i personaggi secondari. Piú l'età è prosaica, piú esagerato è l'eroismo, abbandonato a una immaginazione libera, che ingrandisce le proporzioni a arbitrio, con non altro scopo che di eccitare la maraviglia. Il maraviglioso è in questo, che l'eroe è un'antitesi accentuata e romorosa alla vita comune, offrendo in olocausto alla virtú tutt'i sentimenti umani, come Abramo pronto a uccidere il figlio. Cosí Enea abbandona Didone per seguire la gloria, Temistocle e Regolo vanno incontro a morte per amor della patria, Catone si uccide per la libertà, Megacle offre la vita per l'amico, e Argene per l'amato. Questa forza di soffocare i sentimenti umani e naturali, che regolano la vita comune, era detta generosità o magnanimità, forza o grandezza di animo, com'è il perdono delle offese, il sacrificio dell'amore o della vita. Situazione tragica se mai ce ne fu, anzi il fondamento della tragedia. Ma qui rimane per lo piú elegiaca, feconda di emozioni superficiali, momentanee e variate, che in ultimo sgombrano a un tratto e lasciano il cielo sereno. La generosità degli uni provoca la generosità degli altri, l'eroismo opera come corrente elettrica, guadagna tutt'i personaggi, e tutto si accomoda come nel migliore de' mondi, tutti eroi e tutti contenti. Di questa superficialità che resta ne' confini dell'idillio e dell'elegia, e di rado si alza alla commozione tragica, la ragione è questa, che la virtú vi è rappresentata non come il sentimento di un dovere preciso e obbligatorio per tutti, corrispondente alla vita pratica, ma come un fatto maraviglioso, che per la sua straordinarietà tolga il pubblico alla contemplazione della vita comune. Perciò è una virtú da teatro, un eroismo da scena. Piú le combinazioni sono straordinarie, piú le proporzioni sono ingrandite, e piú cresce l'effetto. I personaggi posano, si mettono in vista, sentenziano, si atteggiano, come volessero dire: — Attenti! ora viene il miracolo—. Temistocle dice:

> *Sentimi, o Serse;*
> *Lisimaco, m'ascolta; udite, o voi,*
> *Popoli spettatori,*
> *Di Temistocle i sensi; e ognun ne sia*
> *Testimonio e custode.*

In questo meccanismo trovi sempre la collisione, il contrasto tra l'eroi-

## 42. De Sanctis (1817–1883): *History of Italian Literature*

Now we can understand the mechanism of Metastasio's drama. At the summit is the hero or heroine, Zenobia or Hypsipile, Themistocles or Titus. The hero has every perfection that poets have assigned to the Golden Age, and arouses heroism all around him, making even the secondary characters heroic. The more prosaic the age is, the more exaggerated the heroism, left prey to a free imagination which enlarges the proportions at will, with no other aim than to excite wonder. The wonder lies in this: that the hero is an emphatic, loud antithesis to normal life, sacrificing all human feeling to virtue, like Abraham ready to kill his son. Thus, Aeneas deserts Dido in order to seek fame, Themistocles and Regulus face death for love of country, Cato commits suicide for freedom, Megacles offers his life for his friend, and Argene for her lover. This power to stifle the natural human feelings that regulate everyday life was called nobility or magnanimity, strength or greatness of mind, such as the forgiveness of offenses, or the sacrifice of love or life. A tragic situation if there ever was one; in fact, the very basis of tragedy. But here it generally remains elegiac, rich in superficial, ephemeral, and varied emotions, which ultimately clear the sky all at once, leaving it calm. The noble actions of some call forth the noble actions of the others, heroism acts like a electric current, affecting all the characters, and everything is arranged as if in the best of possible worlds: everyone's a hero and everyone's contented. The reason for this superficiality, which remains on the borderline between idyll and elegy and seldom rises to the level of stirring tragedy, is that virtue is depicted there, not as the feeling of a precise duty incumbent on everyone, in accordance with practical life, but as a wondrous deed, the unusualness of which takes the audience out of its contemplation of everyday life. Therefore it's a theatrical virtue, a stage heroism. The more out of the ordinary the combinations are, the more the proportions are enlarged and the effect magnified. The characters pose, they put themselves forward, they speak in epigrams, they assume attitudes, as if they wanted to say: "Watch out! Here comes the miracle!" Themistocles says:

> "Hear me, O Xerxes;
> Lysimachus, heed me; listen, you
> onlooking nations,
> to Themistocles' opinion; and let everyone be
> a witness and guardian!"

In this mechanism you always find a clash, a conflict between heroism and

smo e la natura. L'eroismo ha la sua sublimità nello splendore delle sentenze. La natura ha il suo patetico nelle tenere effusioni de' sentimenti. Ne nasce un urto vivace di sentimenti e di sentenze, con alterna vittoria e con crescente sospensione, come nel soliloquio di Tito, insino a che natura ed eroismo fanno la loro riconciliazione in un modo cosí inaspettato e straordinario, com'è tutto l'intrigo. Tito fa condurre Sesto all'arena, deliberato già di perdonargli: non gli basta la virtú, vuole lo spettacolo e la sorpresa. Questa, che a noi pare una moralità da scena, era a quel tempo una moralità convenuta, ammessa in teoria, ammirata, applaudita, a quel modo che le romane battevano le mani ai gladiatori che morivano per i loro begli occhi. Si direbbe che Tito facesse il possibile per meritarsi gli applausi del pubblico. Appunto perché questo eroismo non aveva una vera serietà di motivi interni e non veniva dalla coscienza, quel mondo atteggiato all'eroica aveva del comico, ed era possibile che vi penetrasse senza stonatura la società contemporanea nelle sue parti anche buffe e volgari. Prendiamo l'*Adriano*. Vincitore de' Parti, proclamato imperatore, Adriano si trova in una delle situazioni piú strazianti, promesso sposo di Sabina, amante di Emirena figlia del suo nemico, e rivale di Farnaspe, l'amato di Emirena. Situazione molto avviluppata, e che diviene intricatissima per opera di un quarto personaggio, Aquilio, confidente di Adriano, amante secreto di Sabina, e che perciò fomenta la passione del suo padrone. Emirena per salvare il padre offre la mano ad Adriano. La generosità di Emirena eccita la generosità di Sabina, che scioglie Adriano dalla data fede. La generosità di Sabina eccita la generosità di Adriano, che libera il padre di Emirena, rende costei al suo amato, e sposa Sabina. E tutti felici, e il coro intuona le lodi di Adriano. Ma guardiamo in fondo a questi personaggi eroici. Adriano è una buona natura d'uomo, tutt'altro che eroica, voltato in qua e in là dalle impressioni, mobile, superficiale, credulo, insomma un buon uomo che rasenta l'imbecille. Non è lui che opera; egli è il paziente, anzi che l'agente del melodramma, e come colui che dà ragione a chi ultimo parla, dà sempre ragione all'ultima impressione. Si trova eroe per occasione, un eroe cosí equivoco, che impedisce ad Emirena di baciargli la mano, tremando di una nuova impressione. [. . .]

## 43. Collodi (1826–1890): *Le avventure di Pinocchio*

C'era una volta . . .

—Un re!— diranno subito i miei piccoli lettori.

nature. Heroism finds its sublimity in the splendor of the epigrams. Nature finds its pathetic quality in the tender outpourings of feeling. From this there arises a lively clash between feelings and epigrams, with an alternation of victories and growing suspense, as in Titus's soliloquy, until nature and heroism are reconciled in a manner as unexpected and unusual as the whole plot is. Titus has Sextus led to the arena, already intending to pardon him; virtue isn't enough for him, he wants spectacle and surprise. This, which appears to us to be a theatrical morality, was at that time an agreed-on morality, admitted in theory, admired, applauded, in the same way that the Roman ladies clapped for the gladiators who were dying "for their beautiful eyes." You'd say that Titus was doing everything possible to earn the audience's applause. Precisely because this heroism failed to possess a true seriousness of inner motives and didn't spring from the conscience, that world, with its show of the heroic, had something comic in it, and it was possible for contemporary society to enter into it without incongruity, even in its funny, vulgar aspects. Let's take the drama *Adriano*. Victor over the Parthians, hailed as emperor, Hadrian finds himself in one of the most agonizing situations: engaged to Sabina, he's in love with Emirena, his enemy's daughter, and thus he's the rival of Pharnaspes, whom Emirena loves. A very entangled situation, which is made extremely complicated by a fourth character, Aquilius, Hadrian's confidant, who is secretly in love with Sabina and therefore fosters his master's passion for Emirena. She, to save her father, offers her hand to Hadrian. Her noble action arouses the noble feelings of Sabina, who releases Hadrian from his plighted troth. Sabina's noble action arouses the noble feelings of Hadrian, who frees Emirena's father, restores her to the man she loves, and marries Sabina. And they're all happy, and the chorus intones the praises of Hadrian. But let's take a hard look at these heroic characters. Hadrian is a good-natured chap, anything but heroic, who's tossed back and forth by his impressions, changeable, superficial, gullible: in short, a kindly man who's not far from being a fool. It isn't he who takes action; he's the passive one, not the active one, in the melodrama, and like a man who always agrees with the last person who has spoken, he always yields to the latest impression he has received. He is made a hero by circumstances, a hero so equivocal that he stops Emirena from kissing his hand, fearing to receive a fresh impression. [. . .]

## 43. Collodi (1826–1890): *The Adventures of Pinocchio*

Once upon a time there was . . .
    "A king!" my little readers will immediately say.

No, ragazzi, avete sbagliato. C'era una volta un pezzo di legno.

Non era un legno di lusso, ma un semplice pezzo da catasta, di quelli che d'inverno si mettono nelle stufe e nei caminetti per accendere il fuoco e per riscaldare le stanze.

Non so come andasse, ma il fatto gli è che un bel giorno questo pezzo di legno capitò nella bottega di un vecchio falegname, il quale aveva nome mastr'Antonio, se non che tutti lo chiamavano maestro Ciliegia, per via della punta del suo naso, che era sempre lustra e paonazza, come una ciliegia matura.

Appena maestro Ciliegia ebbe visto quel pezzo di legno, si rallegrò tutto e dandosi una fregatina di mani per la contentezza, borbottò a mezza voce:

—Questo legno è capitato a tempo: voglio servirmene per fare una gamba di tavolino.

Detto fatto, prese subito l'ascia arrotata per cominciare a levargli la scorza e a digrossarlo, ma quando fu lì per lasciare andare la prima asciata, rimase col braccio sospeso in aria, perché sentì una vocina sottile, che disse raccomandandosi:

—Non mi picchiar tanto forte!

Figuratevi come rimase quel buon vecchio di maestro Ciliegia!

Girò gli occhi smarriti intorno alla stanza per vedere di dove mai poteva essere uscita quella vocina, e non vide nessuno! Guardò sotto il banco, e nessuno; guardò dentro un armadio che stava sempre chiuso, e nessuno; guardò nel corbello dei trucioli e della segatura, e nessuno; aprì l'uscio di bottega per dare un'occhiata anche sulla strada, e nessuno! O dunque? . . .

—Ho capito;— disse allora ridendo e grattandosi la parrucca, —si vede che quella vocina me la sono figurata io. Rimettiamoci a lavorare.

E ripresa l'ascia in mano, tirò giù un solennissimo colpo sul pezzo di legno.

—Ohi! tu m'hai fatto male!— gridò rammaricandosi la solita vocina.

Questa volta maestro Ciliegia restò di stucco, cogli occhi fuori del capo per la paura, colla bocca spalancata e colla lingua giù ciondoloni fino al mento, come un mascherone da fontana. Appena riebbe l'uso della parola, cominciò a dire tremando e balbettando dallo spavento:

—Ma di dove sarà uscita questa vocina che ha detto ohi? . . . Eppure qui non c'è anima viva. Che sia per caso questo pezzo di legno che abbia imparato a piangere e a lamentarsi come un bambino? Io non lo posso credere. Questo legno eccolo qui; è un pezzo di legno da caminetto, come tutti gli altri, e a buttarlo sul fuoco, c'è da far bollire una pentola di fagioli . . . O dunque? Che ci sia nascosto dentro qual-

No, children, you're wrong. Once upon a time there was a piece of wood.

It wasn't luxurious wood, but a simple piece out of the stack, one of those that are placed in stoves and fireplaces in wintertime to light the fire and heat the rooms.

I don't know how it came about, but the fact is that, one fine day, this piece of wood found its way into the workshop of an elderly carpenter whose name was Master Antonio, except that everyone called him Master Cherry because of the tip of his nose, which was always shiny and bright red as a ripe cherry.

As soon as Master Cherry saw that piece of wood, he was completely delighted and, rubbing his hands with satisfaction, he muttered in quiet tones:

"This wood has come into my hands opportunely: I'll use it to make the leg of a small table."

No sooner said than done: at once he picked up his sharpened hatchet to begin removing the bark from it and trimming it, but when he was about to deliver the first hatchet blow, he remained with his arm suspended in the air, because he heard a faint little voice, which said beseechingly:

"Don't hit me so hard!"

Just imagine how amazed that good old man Master Cherry was!

He cast his confused eyes all around the room to see where that little voice could possibly have come from, but he saw nobody! He looked under the bench: nobody. He looked inside an armoire that was always shut: nobody. He looked in the basket of shavings and sawdust: nobody. He opened the workshop door to glance at the street as well: nobody! Or else? . . .

"I've got it," he then said, laughing and scratching his wig. "Obviously I imagined that little voice. Let's get back to work!"

And, picking up the hatchet again, he gave the piece of wood a tremendous blow.

"Ouch, you've hurt me!" the same little voice called out complainingly.

This time Master Cherry was struck dumb, his eyes bulging from his head with fear, his mouth gaping, and his tongue hanging down to his chin, like a grotesque face on a fountain. As soon as he regained his power of speech, he began to say, trembling and stammering with fright:

"But where can that little voice have come from that said, 'Ouch'? . . . After all, there isn't a living soul here. Can this piece of wood by chance have learned to cry and whimper like a baby? I can't believe it. Here's this wood in front of me; it's a piece of firewood like all the rest, and if you

cuno? Se c'è nascosto qualcuno, tanto peggio per lui. Ora l'accomodo io!

E così dicendo, agguantò con tutt'e due le mani quel povero pezzo di legno e si pose a sbatacchiarlo senza carità contro le pareti della stanza.

Poi si messe in ascolto, per sentire se c'era qualche vocina che si lamentasse. Aspettò due minuti, e nulla; cinque minuti, e nulla; dieci minuti, e nulla!

—Ho capito,— disse allora sforzandosi di ridere e arruffandosi la parrucca, —si vede che quella vocina che ha detto ohi, me la sono figurata io! Rimettiamoci a lavorare.

E perché gli era entrata addosso una gran paura, si provò a canterellare per farsi un po' di coraggio.

Intanto, posata da una parte l'ascia, prese in mano la pialla, per piallare e tirare a pulimento il pezzo di legno; ma nel mentre che lo piallava in su e in giù, sentì la solita vocina che gli disse ridendo:

—Smetti! tu mi fai il pizzicorino sul corpo!

Questa volta il povero maestro Ciliegia cadde giù come fulminato. Quando riaprì gli occhi, si trovò seduto per terra.

Il suo viso pareva trasfigurato, e perfino la punta del naso, di paonazza come era quasi sempre, gli era diventata turchina dalla gran paura.

In quel punto fu bussato alla porta.

—Passate pure,— disse il falegname, senza aver la forza di rizzarsi in piedi.

Allora entrò in bottega un vecchietto tutto arzillo, il quale aveva nome Geppetto; ma i ragazzi del vicinato, quando lo volevano far montare su tutte le furie, lo chiamavano col soprannome di *Polendina,* a motivo della sua parrucca gialla che somigliava moltissimo alla polendina di granturco.

Geppetto era bizzosissimo. Guai a chiamarlo Polendina! Diventava subito una bestia e non c'era più verso di tenerlo. ·

—Buon giorno, mastr'Antonio,— disse Geppetto. —Che cosa fate costì per terra?

—Insegno l'abbaco alle formicole.

—Buon pro vi faccia!

—Chi vi ha portato da me, compar Geppetto?

—Le gambe. Sappiate, mastr'Antonio, che son venuto da voi, per chiedervi un favore. [. . .]

threw it on the fire, you could manage to set a pot of beans boiling . . . Or what? Can someone be hidden inside it? If someone's hiding, too bad about him! Now I'm going to fix him!"

And, with those words, he gripped that poor piece of wood with both hands and began to bang it mercilessly against the walls of the room.

Then he stopped to listen, to hear if there was any little voice sorry for itself. He waited two minutes: nothing. Five minutes: nothing. Ten minutes: nothing.

"I've got it," he then said, forcing himself to laugh and ruffling his wig. "Obviously that little voice which said 'Ouch' was in my imagination. Let's get back to work!"

And because he had had a great fright, he tried to hum to give himself a little courage.

Meanwhile, putting the hatchet aside, he picked up the plane to plane and smooth the piece of wood; but while he was planing it to and fro, he heard the same little voice saying to him with a laugh:

"Stop! You're tickling me all over!"

This time poor Master Cherry fell down as if struck by lightning. When he opened his eyes again, he found himself sitting on the floor.

His face looked transfigured, and even the tip of his nose had changed from bright red, as it nearly always was, to a deep blue, because of his big scare.

At that moment there was a knock at the door.

"Come right in," said the carpenter, lacking the strength to stand up.

Then there entered into the workshop a very sprightly little old man whose name was Geppetto; but the neighborhood children, when they wanted him to become enraged, called him by the nickname "Polenta," because of his yellow wig, which greatly resembled polenta made from Indian corn.

Geppetto was extremely irritable. Woe to you if you called him Polenta! He'd immediately become a wild beast, and there was no longer any way to restrain him.

"Good day, Master Antonio," said Geppetto. "What are you doing there on the floor?"

"I'm teaching the little ants the multiplication table."

"Much good may it do you!"

"What's brought you to me, friend Geppetto?"

"My legs. If you must know, Master Antonio, I've come to you to ask a favor of you." [. . .]

## 44. Nievo (1831–1861): *Le confessioni di un italiano*

Io nacqui veneziano ai 18 ottobre del 1775, giorno dell'Evangelista Luca; e morrò per la grazia di Dio italiano quando lo vorrà quella Provvidenza che governa misteriosamente il mondo. Ecco la morale della mia vita. E siccome questa morale non fui io ma i tempi che l'hanno fatta, così mi venne in mente, che descrivere ingenuamente quest'azione dei tempi sopra la vita d'un uomo potesse recare qualche utilità a coloro, che da altri tempi son destinati a sentire le conseguenze meno imperfette di quei primi influssi attuati.

Sono vecchio, oramai, più che ottuagenario nell'anno che corre dell'Era Cristiana 1858; e pur giovine di cuore forse meglio che nol fossi mai nella combattuta giovinezza, e nella stanchissima virilità. Molto vissi e soffersi; ma non mi vennero meno quei conforti, che, sconosciuti le più volte di mezzo alle tribolazioni che sempre paiono soverchie alla smoderatezza e cascaggine umana, pur sollevano l'anima alla serenità della pace e della speranza, quando tornano poi alla memoria quali veramente sono, talismani invincibili contro ogni avversa fortuna. Intendo quegli affetti e quelle opinioni, che anzichè prender norma dalle vicende esteriori comandano vittoriosamente ad esse e se ne fanno agone di operose battaglie. La mia indole, l'ingegno, la prima educazione e le operazioni e le sorti progressive furono, come ogni altra cosa umana, miste di bene e di male: e se non fosse sfoggio indiscreto di modestia potrei anco aggiungere, che in punto a merito abbondò piuttosto il male che il bene. Ma in tutto ciò nulla sarebbe di strano o degno di esser narrato, se la mia vita non correva a cavalcione di questi due secoli che resteranno un tempo assai memorabili, massime nella storia italiana. Infatti fu in questo mezzo che diedero primo frutto di fecondità reale quelle speculazioni politiche che dal milletrecento al millesettecento traspirarono dalle opere di Dante, di Macchiavelli, di Vico e di tanti altri che non soccorrono ora alla mia mediocre coltura e quasi ignoranza letteraria. La circostanza, altri direbbe la sventura, di aver vissuto in questi anni, mi ha dunque indotto nel divisamento di scrivere quanto ho veduto, sentito, fatto e provato dalla prima infanzia al cominciare della vecchiaia, quando gli acciacchi dell'età, la condiscendenza ai più giovani, la temperanza delle opinioni senili e, diciamolo anche, l'esperienza di molte e molte disgrazie in questi ultimi anni mi ridussero a quella dimora campestre, dove aveva assistito all'ultimo e ridicolo atto del gran dramma feudale. Nè il mio semplice racconto rispetto alla storia ha di-

## 44. Nievo (1831–1861): *The Confessions of an Italian*

I was born a Venetian citizen on October 18, 1775, the day of the Evangelist Luke; and, by the grace of God, I shall die an Italian when that is desired by the Providence which mysteriously rules the world.

That's the moral of my life. And just as it wasn't I, but the times, that created that moral, so it has occurred to me that to describe frankly this effect of the times on a man's life might be of some utility to those who are destined by other times to feel the less imperfect consequences of those influences first set in motion.

I'm old by now, over eighty in this current year of the Christian era, 1858; but still perhaps younger at heart than I ever was during my agitated youth and very weary prime of life. I lived through and suffered a great deal; but I wasn't deprived of those comforts which, most often unrecognized amid the tribulations which always seem excessive to human intemperance and lassitude, nevertheless uplift the soul to the serenity of peace and hope when they later return to one's memory as they really are: invincible talismans against all adverse fortune. I mean those emotions and opinions which, instead of taking outside events as a model, command them victoriously and make them the arena of industrious combats. My nature, my intellect, my early upbringing, and my progressive actions and destinies were, like every other human matter, a mixture of good and bad; and if it weren't an indiscreet display of modesty, I could also add that, with regard to merit, the bad was rather more plentiful than the good. But in all this there'd be nothing strange or worth narrating if my life didn't straddle these two centuries, which for some time will remain quite memorable, especially in the history of Italy. Indeed, it was in this milieu that the first fruits of real fecundity were borne by those political speculations which, from the fourteenth century to the eighteenth, transpired from the works of Dante, Machiavelli, Vico, and so many others who at the moment don't come to the aid of my mediocre learning and my all but ignorance of literature. The circumstance (others would say the misfortune) of having lived through those years has therefore induced me into the decision to set down all I've seen, heard, done, and experienced from earliest childhood to the onset of old age, when the infirmities of the elderly, obligingness to those younger, the moderateness of old folks' opinions, and, let's add, the experience of very many disasters in these last years, reduced me to live in this rustic abode, where I had participated in the final ridiculous act of the great feudal drama. Nor does my simple narrative about history have any other importance than a marginal note would have that was affixed by an unknown contemporary

versa importanza di quella che avrebbe una nota, apposta da ignota mano contemporanea alle rivelazioni d'un antichissimo codice. L'attività privata d'un uomo che non fu nè tanto avara da trincerarsi in se stessa contro le miserie comuni, nè tanto stoica da opporsi deliberatamente ad essa, nè tanto sapiente da trascurarla disprezzandola, mi pare debba in alcun modo riflettere l'attività comune e nazionale che l'assorbe; come il cader d'una goccia rappresenta la direzione della pioggia. Così l'esposizione de' casi miei sarà quasi un esemplare di quelle innumerevoli sorti individuali, che dallo sfasciarsi dei vecchi ordinamenti politici al raffazzonarsi dei presenti composero la gran sorte nazionale italiana. Mi sbaglierò forse, ma meditando dietro essi potranno alcuni giovani sbaldanzirsi dalle pericolose lusinghe, e taluni anche infervorarsi nell'opera lentamente ma durevolmente avviata, e molti poi fermare in non mutabili credenze quelle vaghe aspirazioni, che fanno loro tentare cento vie prima di trovare quell'una che li conduca nella vera pratica del ministero civile. Così almeno parve a me in tutti i nove anni nei quali a sbalzi, e come suggerivano l'estro e la memoria, venni scrivendo queste note. Le quali incominciate con fede pertinace alla sera d'una grande sconfitta e condotte a termine traverso una lunga espiazione in questi anni di rinata operosità, contribuirono alquanto a persuadermi del maggior nerbo, e della più legittima speranza nei presenti, con lo spettacolo delle debolezze e delle malvagità passate.

Ed ora, prima di prendere a trascriverle, volli con queste poche righe di proemio definire e sanzionar meglio quel pensiero che a me, già vecchio e non letterato, cercò forse indarno insegnare la malagevole arte dello scrivere. Ma già la chiarezza delle idee, la semplicità dei sentimenti, e la verità della storia mi saranno scusa e più supplimento alla mancanza di retorica: la simpatia dei buoni lettori mi terrà vece di gloria.

Al limitare della tomba, già omai solo nel mondo, abbandonato così dagli amici che dai nemici, senza timori e senza speranze che non siano eterne, libero per l'età da quelle passioni che sovente pur troppo deviarono dal retto sentiero i miei giudizi, e dalle caduche lusinghe della mia non temeraria ambizione, un solo frutto raccolsi della mia vita, la pace dell'animo. In questa vivo contento, in questa mi affido; questa io addito ai miei fratelli più giovani come il più invidiabile tesoro, e l'unico scudo per difendersi contro gli adescamenti dei falsi amici, le frodi dei vili, e le soperchierie dei potenti. [. . .]

hand to the revelations of a very old manuscript. The private activity of a man who was neither so selfish as to entrench himself in solitude in the face of public unhappiness, nor so stoical as to combat it deliberately, nor so wise as to ignore it contemptuously, ought in some way, it seems to me, to reflect the public and national activity that absorbs him; just as the falling of one drop points out the direction of the rain. Thus, the exposition of my experiences will be like an exemplary model of those innumerable individual destinies which, from the undoing of the old political structures up to the renewal of the present ones, made up the great national Italian destiny. Maybe I'm mistaken, but, meditating on these things, some young men will be able to lose their faith in dangerous illusions, and some even become excited by the task which has been slowly but lastingly set in motion; many, then, will solidify into unchangeable beliefs those vague aspirations which make them try out a hundred paths before finding that single one which will lead them to the proper practice of government service. At least that's how it seemed to me in all the nine years in which, almost jerkily, as my caprice and memory prompted, I wrote down these notes. Begun with persistent faith on the night of a great defeat and completed during a long expiation in these years of reborn activity, they contributed somewhat to convince me of the greater sinew and more legitimate hope of the present years lent by the spectacle of bygone weaknesses and malevolence.

And now, before beginning to transcribe them, I wished, in these few prefatory lines, to define and better confirm that idea which, perhaps in vain, tried to teach me, already old and not literary, the difficult art of writing. But the clarity of ideas, the simplicity of feelings, and the truth of the history will surely afford me an excuse and make up for the lack of rhetoric: the kindness of my good readers will be a substitute for fame.

On the brink of the tomb, now alone in the world, abandoned by friends as well as enemies, without fear and without hope except of eternity, freed by age from those passions which, unfortunately, often led my judgments off the right track, and from those ephemeral illusions of my not rash ambition, I have gathered but one fruit from my life: peace of mind. In it I live contentedly, in it I trust; I point it out to my younger brothers as the most enviable treasure, and the sole shield to defend oneself from the allurements of false friends, the frauds of base people, and the haughtiness of the powerful. [. . .]

# 45. Carducci (1835–1907): 2 liriche e una prosa

## (A) Pianto antico

L'albero a cui tendevi
la pargoletta mano,
il verde melograno
da' bei vermigli fior,

nel muto orto solingo
rinverdí tutto, or ora,
e giugno lo ristora
di luce e di calor.

Tu, fior della mia pianta
percossa e inaridita,
tu, dell'inutil vita
estremo unico fior,

sei nella terra fredda,
sei nella terra negra
né il sol piú ti rallegra
né ti risveglia amor.

## (B) Mezzogiorno alpino

Nel gran cerchio de l'alpi, su 'l granito
squallido e scialbo, su' ghiacciai candenti,
regna sereno intenso ed infinito
nel suo grande silenzio il mezzodí.
Pini ed abeti senza aura di venti
si drizzano nel sol che gli penetra,
sola garrisce in picciol suon di cetra
l'acqua che tenue tra i sassi fluí.

## (C) Le cicale

Oh tra il grigio polveroso dei rami, e nei crepacci gialli delle colline
cretacee, e nelle fenditure ferrigne de' riarsi maggesi, oh care bestio-
line brune co' due grossi occhi fissi e co' tre occhi piccoli vivi sul dosso
cartilaginoso! Esse cantano quanto dura la perfezione del loro essere,
cioè fin che amano: cantano i maschi, le femmine no: le donne sono
sempre senza poesia. Cominciano agli ultimi di giugno; nelle splen-

## 45. Carducci (1835–1907): two lyric poems and a prose passage

(A) Ancient Lament

The tree to which you reached out
your tiny hand,
the green pomegranate tree
with the lovely red flowers,

standing alone in the silent garden,
has just put forth new green all over,
and June is strengthening it
with light and warmth.

But you, blossom of my stricken,
withered tree,
you, my useless life's
final, sole flower,

you are in the cold ground,
you are in the black ground;
the sun no longer cheers you,
love no longer awakens you.

(B) Noon in the Alps

In the great circle of the Alps, on the bare,
colorless granite, on the shining glaciers,
noon reigns serene, intense, and infinite
in its great silence.
Pines and firs, without a breath of wind,
stand upright in the sunshine that penetrates them;
alone there murmurs in a low, lyre-like tone,
the thin stream that has flowed between the rocks.

(C) The Cicadas

Oh, amid the dusty gray of the boughs, and in the yellow clefts of the
chalk hills, and in the ironlike cracks of the scorched fallow fields; oh, dear
little brown creatures with two big fixed eyes and three small lively eyes
on your cartilaginous backs! They sing for as long as the perfection of their
being lasts; that is, for as long as they love. The males sing, not the fe-
males: women are always without poetry. They begin in the final days of

dide mattinate, quando la clemenza del sole nel suo primo salire, sor-
ride ancora agli odoranti vezzi della giovane estate, cominciano ad ac-
cordare in lirica monotonia le voci argute e squillanti. Prima una, due,
tre, quattro, da altrettanti alberi; poi dieci, venti, cento, mille, non si
sa di dove, pazze di sole, come le sentí il greco poeta, poi tutto un gran
coro, che aumenta d'intonazione e d'intensità col calore e col luglio, e
canta, canta, canta su' capi, d'attorno, a' piedi dei mietitori. Finisce la
mietitura, ma non il coro. Nelle fiere solitudini del solleone pare che
tutta la pianura canti, e tutti i monti cantino, e tutti i boschi cantino;
pare che essa, la terra, dalla perenne gioventú del suo seno, espanda
in un inno immenso il giubilo de' suoi sempre nuovi amori col sole. A
me in quel nirvana di splendori e di suoni avviene e piace di annegare
la coscienza di uomo, e confondermi alla gioia della mia madre Terra:
mi pare che tutte le mie fibre e tutti i miei sensi fremano, esultino,
cantino in amoroso tumulto, come altrettante cicale. Non è vero che
io sia serbato ai freddi silenzi del sepolcro! Io vivrò e canterò, atomo
a parte della mia madre immortale. Oh felice Titone, uscito cicala
dagli amplessi dell'Aurora! E felicissimi voi, uomini antichi, i quali,
come la Grecia imaginò e come raccontò il senno divino di Platone,
tutte le vostre vite spendeste dietro la voce delle Muse, e per la voce
delle Muse tutto obliaste, anche l'alimento e l'amore, sin che gli Dei,
impietositi, vi trasformarono in brune cicale!

In Toscana e in Romagna le cicale durano a cantare, piú sempre
rade, è vero, e via via piú discordi, fino in settembre; e a me è
avvenuto di sentirne qualcuna appunto dopo le prime piogge settem-
brine. Come s'affaticava, quasi per un senso di dovere, la figlia della
Terra a pur cantare! Ma come era triste quello stridore di cicala unica
tra il ridesto sussurrio de' venti freschi e la dolcezza del verde rin-
tenerito! E anch'io sono ormai una cicala di settembre: non rimpiango
né richiamo né invidio. Soltanto, tra le brezze d'autunno ricordo gli
ardori del luglio 1857, e le estati della dolce Toscana.

## 46. Verga (1840–1922): *Mastro-don Gesualdo*

Masi, il garzone, corse a svegliare don Gesualdo prima dell'alba, con
una voce che faceva gelare il sangue nelle vene:
    «Alzatevi, vossignoria; ch'è venuto il manovale da Fiumegrande e
vuol parlarvi subito! . . .»
    «Da Fiumegrande? . . . a quest'ora? . . .» Mastro-don Gesualdo an-

June; in the splendid mornings when the clemency of the just rising sun still smiles on the fragrant charms of the young summer, they begin to tune in a lyrical monotone their high-pitched, shrill voices. First one, two, three, four, from the same number of trees; then ten, twenty, a hundred, a thousand, from who knows where, maddened by sunshine, just as the Greek poet heard them; then an entire large chorus, increasing in tone and intensity with the heat and July, singing, singing, singing overhead, all around, at the feet of the reapers. The harvest ends, but not the chorus. In the fierce solitudes of the dog days the entire plain seems to be singing, and all the mountains, and all the groves; it seems as if the earth itself, from the eternal youth of its bosom, is proclaiming in an immense hymn the exultation of its ever-new romance with the sun. In that nirvana of splendors and sounds, I manage pleasingly to drown my human consciousness and mingle with the joy of my mother Earth: I feel as if all my fibers and senses were trembling, exulting, singing in a tumult of love, like so many cicadas. It isn't true that I'm destined for the cold silence of the grave! I shall live and sing, an atom detached from my immortal mother. O happy Tithonus, who emerged as a cicada from the embraces of Aurora! And extremely happy you, men of antiquity, who, as Greece imagined and the divine mind of Plato recounted, spent all your life listening to the Muses, and because of their voice, forgot everything else, even food and love, until the gods, taking pity, transformed you into brown cicadas!

In Tuscany and Romagna the cicadas go on singing, their numbers constantly thinning, it's true, and becoming more discordant, until September; and I have happened to hear one right after the first September rains. How that daughter of Earth tired itself out, continuing to sing, almost through a sense of duty! But how sad was that sound of a single cicada amid the reawakened whispering of the cool breezes and the sweetness of the refreshed greenery! And I, too, by now am a September cicada: I have no regrets, no complaints, no envy. Only, amid the autumn breezes I recall the heat of July 1857, and the summers of sweet Tuscany.

## 46. Verga (1840–1922): *Master Gesualdo*

Masi the farmhand ran to awaken Master Gesualdo before dawn, with a voice that froze the blood in one's veins:

"Get up, sir, for the laborer has come from Fiumegrande and wants to talk to you at once! . . ."

"From Fiumegrande? . . . At this hour? . . ." Master Gesualdo was

dava raccattando i panni tastoni, al buio, ancora assonnato, con un guazzabuglio nella testa. Tutt'a un tratto gridò:

«Il ponte! . . . Deve essere accaduta qualche disgrazia! . . .»

Giú nella stalla trovò il manovale seduto sulla panchetta, fradicio di pioggia, che faceva asciugare i quattro cenci a una fiammata di strame. Appena vide giungere il padrone, cominciò a piagnucolare di nuovo:

«Il ponte! . . . Mastro Nunzio, vostro padre, disse che era ora di togliere l'armatura! . . . Nardo vi è rimasto sotto! . . .»

Era un parapiglia per tutta la casa: Speranza, la sorella, che scendeva a precipizio, intanto che suo marito s'infilava le brache; Santo, ancora mezzo ubbriaco, ruzzoloni per la scaletta della botola, urlando quasi l'accoppassero. Il manovale, a ciascuno che capitava, tornava a dire:

«Il ponte! . . . l'armatura! . . . Mastro Nunzio dice che fu il cattivo tempo! . . .»

Don Gesualdo andava su e giú per la stalla, pallido senza dire una parola, senza guardare in viso nessuno, aspettando che gl'insellassero la mula, la quale spaventata anch'essa sparava calci, e Masi dalla confusione non riusciva a metterle il basto. A un certo punto gli andò coi pugni sul viso, cogli occhi che volevano schizzargli dall'orbita.

«Quando? Santo e santissimo! . . . Non la finisci piú, peste che ti venga!»

«Colpa vostra! Ve l'avevo detto! Non sono imprese per noialtri!» sbraitava la sorella in camicia, coi capelli arruffati, una furia tale e quale! Massaro Fortunato, piú calmo, approvava la moglie, con un cenno del capo, silenzioso, seduto sulla panchetta, simile a una macina di mulino. «Voi non dite nulla! state lí come un allocco!»

Adesso Speranza inveiva contro suo marito: «Quando si tratta d'aiutar voi, che pure siete suo cognato! . . . carico di figliuoli anche! . . . allora saltano fuori le difficoltà! . . . denari non ce ne sono! . . . i denari che si son persi nel ponte della malora!»

Gesualdo da principio si voltò verso di lei inviperito, colla schiuma alla bocca. Poscia mandò giú la bile, e si mise a canterellare mentre affibbiava la testiera della mula: un'allegria che gli mangiava il fegato. Si fece il segno della croce, mise il piede alla staffa; infine di lassú, a cavallo, che toccava quasi il tetto col capo, sputò fuori il fatto suo, prima d'andarsene:

«Avete ragione! M'ha fatto fare dei bei negozi, tuo marito! La semenza che abbiamo buttato via a Donninga! La vigna che m'ha fatto piantare dove non nasce neppure erba da pascolo! . . . Testa fine tuo marito! . . . M'è toccato pagarle di tasca mia le vostre belle specu-

gathering up his clothes gropingly, in the dark, still drowsy, with his head in a muddle. All at once he shouted:

"The bridge! . . . Some disaster must have happened! . . ."

Down in the stable he found the laborer sitting on the bench, soaked with rain, drying out his few rags at a straw fire. As soon as he saw his boss coming, he started to whimper again:

"The bridge! . . . Master Nunzio, your father, said it was time to remove the scaffolding! . . . Nardo was trapped under it! . . ."

There was a hubbub all over the house: Speranza, the Master's sister, who was hurtling downstairs, while her husband was pulling up his trousers; Santo, still half drunk, tumbling down the trapdoor ladder and howling as if being murdered. To everyone who came by, the laborer repeated:

"The bridge! . . . The scaffolding! . . . Master Nunzio says it was the bad weather! . . ."

Master Gesualdo was walking to and fro in the stable, pale, without saying a word, without looking anyone in the face, waiting for them to saddle his mule, which, also frightened, was kicking out; and in his confusion Masi was unable to put on its packsaddle. At one point Gesualdo raised his fists to the man's face, his eyes nearly darting out of their sockets.

"When will it be? Damn and double damn! . . . You never finish, may the plague take you!"

"Your fault! I told you so! These aren't jobs for the like of us!" his sister was yelling. In her nightgown, her hair rumpled, she was just like a Fury! The bailiff Fortunato, calmer, was agreeing with his wife by nodding his head as he sat silently on the bench like a millstone. "You say nothing! You stand there like a dunce!"

Now Speranza was railing at her husband: "When it's a question of *your* helping out—after all, you're his brother-in-law! . . . and loaded down with children! . . . then the difficulties jump up! . . . there's no money! . . . the money that was lost on that damned bridge!"

Gesualdo first turned toward her in a rage, his mouth foaming. Then he swallowed his anger and began to hum while fastening the mule's headstall: a cheerfulness that gnawed at his liver. He crossed himself, put his foot in the stirrup; finally, mounted, from the saddle, nearly touching the ceiling with his head, he spat out his feelings before leaving:

"You're right! Your husband has got me into some fine deals! The seed we threw away at Donninga! The vines he had me plant where not even grazing grass grows! . . . A real brain, your husband! . . . I've had to pay for your fine speculations out of my own pocket! But I'm tired of

lazioni! Ma son stanco, veh, di portare la soma! L'asino quand'è stanco si corica in mezzo alla via e non va piú avanti . . .»

E spronò la mula, che borbottava ancora; la sorella sbraitandogli dietro, dall'uscio della stalla, finché si udirono i ferri della cavalcatura sui ciottoli della stradicciuola, nel buio. Il manovale si mise a correre, affannato, zoppicando; ma il padrone, che aveva la testa come un mulino, non se ne avvide. Soltanto allorché furono giunti alla chiusa del Carmine, volse il capo all'udire lo scalpiccío di lui nella mota, e lo fece montare in groppa. Il ragazzo, colla voce rotta dall'andatura della mula, ripeteva sempre la stessa cosa:

«Mastro Nunzio disse che era tempo di togliere l'armatura . . . Era spiovuto dopo il mezzogiorno . . . "No, vossignoria" disse mastro Nardo; "lasciamo stare ancora sino a domani . . ." Disse mastro Nunzio: "Tu parli cosí per papparti un'altra giornata di paga . . .". Io intanto facevo cuocere la minestra per gli uomini . . . Dal monte si udiva gridare: "La piena! cristiani! . . .". Mentre Nardo stava sciogliendo l'ultima fune . . .»

Gesualdo, col viso al vento, frustato dalla burrasca, spronava sempre la mula colle calcagna, senza aprir bocca. «Eh? . . . Che dite, don Gesualdo? . . . Non rispondete? . . .»

«Che non ti casca mai la lingua?» rispose infine il padrone.

Cominciava ad albeggiare prima di giungere alla Torretta. Un contadino che incontrarono spingendo innanzi l'asinello, pigliandosi l'acquazzone sotto la giacca di cotonina, col fazzoletto in testa e le mani nelle tasche, volle dire qualche cosa; accennava laggiú, verso il fiume, mentre il vento si portava lontano la voce. Piú in là una vecchierella raggomitolata sotto un carrubio si mise a gridare:

«Non potete passare, no! . . . Il fiume! . . . badate! . . .»

In fondo, nella nebbia del fiume e della pioggia, si scorgeva confusamente un enorme ammasso di rovine, come un monte franato in mezzo al fiume, e sul pilone rimasto in piedi, perduto nella bruma del cielo basso, qualcosa di nero che si muoveva, delle braccia che accennavano lontano. Il fiume, di qua e di là dei rottami, straripava in larghe pozze fangose. [. . .]

## 47. Boito (1842–1918): "L'alfier nero"

Chi sa giocare a scacchi prenda una scacchiera, la disponga in bell'ordine davanti a sé ed immagini ciò che sto per descrivere.

Immagini al posto degli scacchi bianchi un uomo dal volto intelli-

carrying the burden, see? When a donkey is tired it lies down in the middle of the road and refuses to go onward . . ."

And he spurred the mule, still grumbling; his sister kept yelling after him from the stable door for as long as the mule's horseshoes could be heard on the cobbles of the narrow lane, in the dark. The laborer began running, panting, limping; but his boss, whose head was spinning like a windmill, didn't notice. It was only when they reached the church of Mount Carmel that he turned his head on hearing the fellow's scuffling through the mud, and he made him mount behind him. The boy, his voice shaken up by the mule's gait, kept repeating the same thing:

"Master Nunzio said it was time to remove the scaffolding . . . It had stopped raining after midday. 'No, sir,' said Master Nardo, 'let it still stand until tomorrow.' Master Nunzio said: 'You say that to wangle another day's pay. . . .' Meanwhile I was cooking the soup for the men . . . From the mountain we heard them yell: 'The flood! Christians! . . .' While Nardo was untying the last rope . . ."

Gesualdo, his face in the wind, whipped by the storm, kept spurring his mule with his heels, not opening his mouth. "Eh? . . . What do you say, Master Gesualdo? . . . You don't answer? . . ."

"Doesn't your tongue ever stop?" his boss finally replied.

Dawn was beginning to break before they reached La Torretta. A farmer they met pushing his donkey forward, receiving the shower beneath his light cotton jacket, his handkerchief on his head and his hands in his pockets, tried to say something; he pointed down yonder, toward the river, while the wind carried away his words. Farther along, a little old woman huddled under a carob tree began to yell:

"You can't pass, no! . . . The river! . . . Watch out! . . ."

In the background, in the mist from the river and the rain, could be vaguely discerned an enormous mass of ruins, like a mountain that had slid into the middle of the river; and on the pylon that had remained standing, lost in the murk of the low sky, something black that was moving, arms that were pointing far away. The river, on either side of the wreckage, was overflowing and forming wide, muddy pools. [. . .]


# 47. Boito (1842–1918): "The Black Chess Bishop"

Let whoever knows how to play chess take a chessboard, set up the pieces properly in front of himself, and picture what I'm about to describe.

Picture on the side of the white pieces a man with an intelligent face;

gente; due forti gibbosità appaiono sulla sua fronte, un po' al disopra
delle ciglia, là dove Gall mette la facoltà del calcolo; porta un collare
di barba biondissima ed ha i mustacchi rasi com'è costume di molti
americani. È tutto vestito di bianco e, benché sia notte e giuochi al
lume della candela, porta un *pince-nez* affumicato e guarda attraverso
quei vetri la scacchiera con intensa concentrazione. Al posto degli
scacchi neri c'è un negro, un vero etiopico, dalle labbra rigonfie, senza
un pelo di barba sul volto e lanuto il crine come una testa d'ariete;
questi ha pronunziatissime le *bosses* dell'astuzia, della tenacità; non si
scorgono i suoi occhi perché tien china la faccia sulla partita che sta
giuocando coll'altro. Tanto sono oscuri i suoi panni che pare vestito a
lutto. Quei due uomini di colore opposto, muti, immobili, che com-
battono col loro pensiero, il bianco con gli scacchi bianchi, il negro coi
neri, sono strani e quasi solenni e quasi fatali. Per sapere chi sono
bisogna saltare indietro sei ore e stare attenti ai discorsi che fanno alcuni forestieri nella sala di lettura del principale albergo d'uno fra i
più conosciuti luoghi d'acque minerali in Isvizzera. L'ora è quella che
i francesi chiamano *entre chien et loup*. I camerieri dell'albergo non
avevano ancora accese le lampade; i mobili della sala e gli individui
che conversavano, erano come sommersi nella penombra sempre più
folta del crepuscolo; sul tavolo dei giornali bolliva un *samovar* su
d'una gran fiamma di spirito di vino. Quella semi-oscurità facilitava il
moto della conversazione; i volti non si vedevano, si udivano soltanto
le voci che facevano questi discorsi:

«Sulla lista degli arrivati ho letto quest'oggi il nome barbaro di un
nativo del Morant-Bay».

«Oh! un negro! chi potrà essere?»

«Io l'ho veduto, milady; pare Satanasso in persona.»

«Io l'ho preso per un *ourang-outang*.»

«Io l'ho creduto, quando m'è passato accanto, un assassino che si
fosse annerita la faccia».

«Ed io lo conosco, signori, e posso assicurarvi che quel negro è il
miglior galantuomo di questa terra. Se la sua biografia non vi è nota,
posso raccontarvela in poche parole. Quel negro nativo del Morant-
Bay venne portato in Europa fanciullo ancora da uno speculatore, il
quale, vedendo che la tratta degli schiavi in America era incomoda e
non gli fruttava abbastanza, pensò di tentare una piccola tratta di
*grooms* in Europa; imbarcò segretamente una trentina di piccoli negri,
figliuoli dei suoi vecchi schiavi, e li vendé a Londra, a Parigi, a Madrid
per duemila dollari l'uno. Il nostro negro è uno di questi trenta *grooms*.
La fortuna volle ch'egli capitasse in mano d'un vecchio lord senza

two prominent bumps can be seen on his forehead, a little above the eyebrows, where Gall locates the power of calculation; he wears a fringe of very blonde beard and he has shaved off his mustache, as many Americans do. He's dressed all in white and, though it's nighttime and he's playing by candlelight, he wears a pince-nez with dark lenses, through which he studies the board with intense concentration. On the side of the black pieces is a black man, a real "Ethiop," with thick lips, not a wisp of beard on his face, and with hair as woolly as a ram's head; this man shows very pronounced bumps of shrewdness and tenacity; his eyes aren't seen because his face is bent over the game he's playing with the other man. His clothes are so dark that he seems to be in mourning. Those two men of contrasting color, silent, motionless, battling with their minds, the white man with the white pieces, the black man with the black, are strange and almost solemn and almost fateful. To know who they are we must jump back six hours and pay attention to the conversation between some foreigners in the reading room of the main hotel in one of the best-known watering places in Switzerland. It's that twilight hour the French call *entre chien et loup*. The hotel servants had not yet lit the lamps; the furniture in the room and the individuals conversing were as if submerged in the penumbra of dusk, which was steadily increasing; on the newspaper table a samovar was boiling, over a high flame of spirits of wine. That semidarkness gave impetus to the conversation; the people's faces couldn't be seen; only their voices were heard, speaking as follows:

"I read today on the list of new arrivals the barbaric name of a native of Morant Bay."

"Oh, a black! Who can he be?"

"I saw him, my lady; he looks like Satan in person."

"I took him for an orangutan."

"When he passed by me, I thought he was an assassin who had blackened his face."

"But I know him, ladies and gentlemen, and I can assure you that that black is the greatest gentleman on earth. If his life story isn't known to you, I can recount it in very few words. That black, a native of Morant Bay, was brought to Europe while still a boy by a speculator who, seeing that the slave trade in America was troublesome and not sufficiently profitable, got the idea of trying out a little trade in grooms in Europe; he secretly embarked some thirty young blacks, sons of his old slaves, and sold them in London, Paris, and Madrid for two thousand dollars each. Our black is one of those thirty grooms. As fortune decreed, he came into the hands of a elderly lord with no family, who

famiglia, il quale dopo averlo tenuto cinque anni dietro la sua carrozza, accortosi che il ragazzo era onesto ed intelligente, lo fece suo domestico, poi suo segretario, poi suo amico e, morendo, lo nominò erede di tutte le sue sostanze. Oggi questo negro (che alla morte del suo lord abbandonò l'Inghilterra e si recò in Isvizzera) è uno dei più ricchi possidenti del cantone di Ginevra, ha delle mirabili coltivazioni di tabacco e per un certo suo segreto nella concia della foglia, fabbrica i migliori zigari del paese; anzi guardate: questi *vevay* che fumiamo ora, vengono dai suoi magazzeni, li riconosco pel segno triangolare che v'è impresso verso la metà del loro cono. I ginevrini chiamano questo bravo negro *Tom* o *l'Oncle Tom* perché è caritatevole, magnanimo; i suoi contadini lo venerano, lo benedicono. Del resto egli vive solo, sfugge amici e conoscenti; gli rimane al Morant-Bay un unico fratello, nessun altro congiunto; è ancora giovine, ma una crudele etisia lo uccide lentamente; viene qui tutti gli anni per far la cura delle acque.»

«Povero *Oncle Tom*! Quel suo fratello a quest'ora potrebbe già essere stato decapitato dalla ghigliottina di Monklands. Le ultime notizie delle colonie narrano d'una tremenda sollevazione di schiavi furiosamente combattuta dal governatore britannico. Ecco intorno a ciò cosa narra l'ultimo numero del *Times*: "I soldati della regina inseguono un negro di nome Gall-Ruck che si era messo a capo della rivolta con una banda di 600 uomini ecc. ecc.".»

«Buon Dio!» esclamò una voce di donna «e quando finiranno queste lotte mortali fra i bianchi ed i negri?!»

«Mai!» rispose qualcuno dal buio.

Tutti si rivolsero verso la parte di chi aveva profferito quella sillaba. Là v'era sdraiato su d'una poltrona, con quella elegante disinvoltura che distingue il vero *gentleman* dal *gentleman* di contraffazione, un signore che spiccava dall'ombra per le sue vesti candidissime.

«Mai» riprese quando si sentì osservato «mai, perché Dio pose odio fra la razza di Cam e quella di Iafet, perché Dio separò il colore del giorno dal color della notte. Volete udire un esempio di questo antagonismo accanito fra i due colori?» [. . .]

### 48. Fogazzaro (1842–1911): *Malombra*

Uno dopo l'altro, gli sportelli dei vagoni sono chiusi con impeto; forse, pensa un viaggiatore fantastico, dal ferreo destino che, ormai senza rimedio, porterà via lui e i suoi compagni nelle tenebre. La locomotiva fischia, colpi violenti scoppiano di vagone in vagone sino all'ul-

after keeping him behind his carriage for five years, noticing that the boy was honest and bright, made him his valet, then his secretary, then his friend, and, dying, named him as heir to all his property. Today this black (who on his lord's death left England and came to Switzerland) is one of the richest landowners in the canton of Geneva, has marvelous tobacco plantations, and by a certain secret way of tanning the leaves, manufactures the best cigars in the country; just look: these Vevey cigars we're now smoking come from his storehouses; I recognize them by the triangular mark stamped near the middle of their tips. The Genevans call this excellent black Tom or Uncle Tom because he's charitable and generous; his farmers venerate and bless him. For the rest, he lives alone, avoids friends and acquaintances; he still has one brother in Morant Bay, no other relative; he's still young, but a cruel tuberculosis is killing him slowly; he comes here every year to take the waters."

"Poor Uncle Tom! At this date, that brother of his might already have been beheaded by Monklands's guillotine. The last news from the colonies mention a terrible slave uprising furiously combated by the British governor. Here's what the latest issue of the *Times* says about it: 'The soldiers of the Queen are pursuing a black called Gall-Ruck, who led the revolt with a band of 600 men, etc., etc.'"

"My Lord!" a woman's voice exclaimed. "When will these mortal combats between whites and blacks ever end?"

"Never!" replied someone out of the darkness.

Everyone turned in the direction of the utterer of those syllables. There, sprawling on an armchair, with that elegant nonchalance which distinguishes a real gentleman from an imitation one, was a man who stood out from the shadows by his very white attire.

"Never," he repeated on sensing he was observed, "never, because God set hatred between the race of Ham and that of Japhet, because God separated the color of the day from the color of the night. Do you want to hear an example of that tenacious antagonism between the two colors?" [. . .]

## 48. Fogazzaro (1842–1911): *Malombra*

One after the other, the doors of the railway cars are slammed shut; perhaps, an imaginative passenger thinks, by the stern destiny which will now irremediably carry off him and his fellow travelers into the darkness. The locomotive whistles, violent shocks break out from car to car until the last

timo: il convoglio va lentamente sotto l'ampia tettoia, esce dalla luce dei fanali nell'ombra della notte, dai confusi rumori della grande città nel silenzio delle campagne addormentate: si svolge sbuffando mostruoso serpente, tra il labirinto delle rotaie, sinché, trovata la via, precipita per quella ed urla, tutto battiti dal capo alla coda, tutto un tumulto di polsi viventi.

V'ha poca probabilità d'indovinare che cosa pensasse poi quel viaggiatore fantastico, rapito tra fiotti di fumo, stormi di faville, oscure forme d'alberi e di casolari. Forse studiava il senso riposto dei bizzarri ed incomprensibili geroglifici ricamati sopra una borsa da viaggio ritta sul sedile di fronte a lui; poiché vi teneva fissi gli occhi, di tanto in tanto moveva le labbra, come chi tenta un calcolo, e quindi alzava le sopracciglia, come chi trova di riuscire all'assurdo.

Eran già passate alcune stazioni, quando un nome gridato, ripetuto nella notte, lo scosse. Una folata d'aria fresca gli disperse le fila sottili del ragionamento; il convoglio era fermo e lo sportello aperto. Egli discese in fretta; era il solo viaggiatore per . . .

«Signore» disse una voce rauca e vibrata «è Lei che va dai signori del Palazzo?»

Questa domanda gli fu tratta a bruciapelo da un uomo che gli si piantò di fronte con la sinistra al cappello e una frusta nella destra.

«Ma . . .»

«Oh, per bacco» disse colui, grattandosi la nuca «chi dev'essere allora?»

«Ma come si chiamano questi signori del Palazzo?»

«Ecco, vede, da noi si dice i *signori del Palazzo* e non si dice altro. Per esempio, a dire così, per un dieci miglia tutto all'ingiro, capiscono; Lei, mettiamo, viene da Milano, è un'altra storia. Queste sono sciocchezze, io lo so benissimo il nome; ma adesso, piglialo! Noi povera gente non abbiamo tanta memoria. È poi un nome tanto fuori di proposito!».

«Sarebbe . . .»

«Aspetti; Lei che taccia e che non mi confonda. Ehi, dalla lanterna!»

Un guardiano si avvicinò lentamente con le braccia penzoloni, facendo dondolare la sua lanterna a fior di terra.

«Non bruciarti i calzoni, che Vittorio non te li paga» disse il giovinotto di poca memoria. «Tira su quell'empiastro di una lanterna. Qua, prestamela un momento.»

E, dato di piglio alla lanterna, la sbatté quasi sul viso al forestiere.

one: the train moves slowly under the wide station canopy, emerges from the light of the lamps into the shade of night, from the jumbled sounds of the big city into the silence of the sleeping countryside. Puffing, it unwinds like a gigantic snake through the maze of rails until, finding the right track, it hurtles down it howling, all throbs from head to tail, all a tumult of living pulsations.

There's little probability of guessing what that imaginative passenger thought next, snatched away amid gusts of smoke, swarms of sparks, and dark shapes of trees and cottages. Maybe he was musing on the hidden meaning of the bizarre, incomprehensible hieroglyphics embroidered on a traveling bag that stood upright on the seat opposite him, because he kept staring at it, moving his lips from time to time like someone trying to reckon up some figures, then raising his brows like a man who finds he has ended up in absurdity.

A few stations had already been passed when a name that was called out, repeated in the night, shook him. A gust of fresh air dispersed the thin threads of his meditation; the train had stopped and the door was open. He got off hastily; he was the only passenger for ——.

"Sir," said a hoarse, vibrant voice, "is it you that's going to the gentlemen in the Palace?"

This question was directed at him point blank by a man who took a stand opposite him, his left hand touching his hat and his right hand holding a whip.

"But . . ."

"Oh, goodness," the man said, scratching the back of his neck, "who else can it be?"

"But what's the name of those gentlemen in the Palace?"

"Look, you see, around here people say 'the gentlemen in the Palace' and nothing else. For example, when you say that, for ten miles round about, they understand; *you* come from Milan, let's say, and it's a different matter. This is all foolishness, I know their name perfectly—but right now, go find it! We poor folk don't have such a great memory. Besides, it's such an out-of-the-way name!"

"Would it be . . ."

"Wait; be still and don't confuse me. Hey, you with the lantern!"

A guard approached slowly with his arms dangling, swinging his lantern just above the ground.

"Don't burn your trousers, because Vittorio won't pay you for them," said the young man with the bad memory. "Hold up that devil of a lantern! Here, lend it to me for a minute!"

And, grasping the lantern, he almost dashed it in the stranger's face.

«Ah, è lui, è lui, è lui tal e quale come mi hanno detto. Un giovinotto, occhi neri, capelli neri, nera mica male anche la faccia. Bravo signore.»

«Ma chi ti ha detto? . . .»

«Lui, il signore, il conte!»

"Oh, diavolo" pensò colui, "un uomo che non ho mai visto e che mi scrive di non avermi mai visto!"

«To'!» esclamò l'altro lasciando cader la frusta e cacciandosi la mano in tasca. «Proprio vero che più asino di così la mia vecchia non mi poteva fare neanche a volere. Il signor conte non mi ha dato un coso per farmi riconoscere? Ce l'ho ben qui. Tolga!»

Era un biglietto di visita profumato di tabacco e di monete sucide. Portava questo nome:

CESARE D'ORMENGO

«Andiamo» disse il forestiere.

Fuori della stazione c'era un calessino scoperto. Il cavallo, legato alla palizzata, col muso a terra, aspettava rassegnato il suo destino.

«S'accomodi, signore; non c'è troppo morbido, ma capisce, siamo in campagna. Ih!»

Il lesto vetturale, afferrate le redini, balzò d'un salto a cassetto e cacciò il cavallo a suon di frusta per una stradicciola oscura, così tranquillamente come se fosse stato mezzogiorno.

«Abbia mica paura, vede» diss'egli «benché sia scuro come in bocca al lupo. Questa strada la cavalla e io l'abbiamo sulla punta delle dita. Ih! Ho menato giù due forestieri anche la notte passata, due signori di Milano, come Lei. Gran brava persona il signor conte!» soggiunse poi, tirandosi a sedere di sghembo e cacciandosi sotto le coscie il manico della frusta. «Che brav'uomo! E signore, ehi! Ha amici in tutte le sette parti del mondo. Oggi ne capita uno, domani un altro, tutti fior di gente, gran signori, sapienti, che so io. Già Lei sarà pratico!»

«Io? È la prima volta che vengo qua.» [. . .]

## 49. Pascoli (1855–1912): 3 liriche

### Alba festiva

Che hanno le campane,
che squillano vicine,
che ronzano lontane?

"Ah, it's him, it's him, exactly as they told me. A young man, dark eyes, black hair, his face pretty swarthy, too. Good, sir!"

"But who told you all this?"

"He, the master, the count!"

"Oh, damn," the traveler thought, "a man I've never seen and who writes saying he's never seen me!"

"Ho!" the other man exclaimed, dropping his whip and plunging his hand in his pocket. "It's the actual truth that my old lady couldn't have had a son dumber than me even if she had wanted to! Didn't the count give me a thingamajig to make myself recognized? I have it right here. Take it!"

It was a visiting card that smelled of tobacco and dirty coins. It bore this name:

CESARE D'ORMENGO

"Let's go!" said the stranger.

Outside the station was a small open gig. The horse, tied to the paling, its muzzle to the ground, was waiting, resigned to its fate.

"Get in, sir; it's none too soft, but you realize, we're in the country. Ah!"

The nimble driver, seizing the reins, reached the box at one bound and drove the horse by the cracking of his whip down a dark lane as calmly as if it had been midday.

"Don't be afraid, see," he said, "even if it's as dark as a wolf's mouth. The mare and I have this road at our fingertips. Ah! Just last night I brought two strangers down, two gentlemen from Milan, like you. A very fine man, the count is!" he then added, turning till he sat obliquely, and thrusting the whip handle under his thighs. "What a fine man! And a gentleman?—ho! He's got friends in all seven parts of the world. Today one drops in, tomorrow another, all of them the cream of society, great gentlemen, scholars, as far as I know. You must already be aware of all this!"

"I? It's my first time here." [. . .]

# 49. Pascoli (1855–1912): 3 lyric poems

Festive Dawn

What's the matter with the bells
that they jangle nearby,
that they drone in the distance?

È un inno senza fine,
or d'oro, ora d'argento,
nell'ombre mattutine.

Con un dondolìo lento
implori, o voce d'oro,
nel cielo sonnolento.

Tra il cantico sonoro
il tuo tintinno squilla,
voce argentina — Adoro,

adoro — Dilla, dilla,
la nota d'oro — L'onda
pende dal ciel, tranquilla.

Ma voce più profonda
sotto l'amor rimbomba,
par che al desìo risponda:

la voce della tomba.

### Pianto

Più bello il fiore cui la pioggia estiva
lascia una stilla dove il sol si frange;
più bello il bacio che d'un raggio avviva
                occhio che piange.

### In cammino

Siede sopra una pietra del cammino,
a notte fonda, nel nebbioso piano:
e tra la nebbia sente il pellegrino
le foglie secche stridere pian piano:
il cielo geme, immobile, lontano,
e l'uomo pensa: Non sorgerò più.

Pensa: un'occhiata quale passeggero,
vana, ha gettata a passeggero in via,
è la sua vita, e impresse nel pensiero
l'orma che lascia il sogno che s'oblìa;
un'orma lieve, che non sa se sia
spento dolore o gioia che non fu.

It's an endless hymn,
now golden, now silvery,
in the morning shadows.

With a slow swinging
you implore, O golden voice,
in the drowsy sky.

Amid the resonant canticle
your jingling blares,
a silvery voice: "I adore,

I adore." Speak it, speak it,
the golden note! The wave of sound
is suspended in the air, calmly.

But a deeper voice
booms beneath that love,
seeming to respond to desire:

the voice of the tomb.

## Lament

More beautiful the flower on which the summer rain
leaves a drop where the sunlight is refracted;
more lovely the kiss that is enlivened by a ray
from weeping eyes.

## On the Road

He sits on a wayside stone,
in the deep night, on the misty plain:
and in the mist the pilgrim hears
the dry leaves rustling very quietly;
the sky moans, motionless, distant,
and the man thinks: "I won't arise anymore."

He thinks: a glance such as one wayfarer
has cast at another along the way, an empty glance—
such is his life, and it has stamped on his mind
merely the trace left by a dream that one forgets,
a slight trace: he doesn't know whether it's
grief that has ended or joy that never existed.

Ed ecco — quasi sopra la sua tomba
siede, tra l'invisibile caduta —
passa uno squillo tremulo di tromba
che tra la nebbia, nel passar, saluta;
squillo che viene d'oltre l'ombra muta,
d'oltre la nebbia: di più su: più su,

dove serene brillano le stelle
sul mar di nebbia, sul fumoso mare
in cui t'allunghi in pallide fiammelle
tu, lento Carro, e tu, Stella polare,
passano squilli come di fanfare,
passa un nero triangolo di gru.

Tra le serene costellazïoni
vanno e la nebbia delle lande strane;
vanno incessanti a tiepidi valloni
a verdi oasi, ad isole lontane,
a dilagate cerule fiumane,
vanno al misterïoso Timbuctù.

Sono passate . . . Ma la testa alzava
dalla sua pietra intento il pellegrino
a quella voce, e tra la nebbia cava
riprese il suo bordone e il suo destino:
tranquillamente seguitò il cammino
dietro lo squillo che vanìa laggiù.

## 50. Svevo (1861–1928): *Senilità*

Subito, con le prime parole che le rivolse, volle avvisarla che non intendeva compromettersi in una relazione troppo seria. Parlò cioè a un
dipresso così: —T'amo molto e per il tuo bene desidero ci si metta
d'accordo di andare molto cauti.— La parola era tanto prudente
ch'era difficile di crederla detta per amore altrui, e un po' più franca
avrebbe dovuto suonare così: —Mi piaci molto, ma nella mia vita non
potrai essere giammai più importante di un giocattolo. Ho altri doveri
io, la mia carriera la mia famiglia.

La sua famiglia? Una sorella non ingombrante né fisicamente né
moralmente, piccola e pallida, di qualche anno più giovane di lui, ma
più vecchia per carattere o forse per destino. Dei due, era lui l'egoista,

And lo!—it's as if he were sitting on his tomb
amid the invisible falling of the leaves—
there passes a tremulous sound like a trumpet blast
which, as it passes by in the mist, he greets;
a blast that comes from beyond the mute shadows,
from beyond the mist: from higher up, higher up,

where the stars are shining calmly
on the sea of mist, on the vague sea
in which you extend with pale tongues of flame,
slow Wain, and you, pole star,
there pass trumpet blasts like fanfares,
there passes a black triangle of cranes.

Amid the serene constellations
they fly, and the mist of the unfamiliar regions;
they fly uninterruptedly to warm valleys,
green oases, remote islands,
to swollen, overflowing blue rivers,
they fly to mysterious Timbuctoo.

They have passed by . . . But the pilgrim
had raised his head from his stone, intent
on that sound, and amid the concave mist
he has taken up his staff and his destiny:
calmly he has continued his journey
following the trumpet blare that was vanishing in the distance.

## 50. Svevo (1861–1928): *Old Age*

At once, with the first words he addressed to her, he meant to let her
know that he didn't intend to get involved in a relationship that was too
serious. That is, he spoke more or less as follows: "I love you a lot, and for
your own good I want us to agree to proceed very cautiously." His words
were so prudent that it was hard to believe them spoken out of love for
another; expressed a little more frankly, they would have run: "I like you
a lot, but in my life you'll never be able to be more important than a play-
thing. I have other duties: my career, my family."

His family? A sister who was no encumbrance either physically or mentally, a small, pale woman a few years younger than he but older in character, or perhaps through destiny. Of the two, he was the selfish one, the

il giovane; ella viveva per lui come una madre dimentica di se stessa, ma ciò non impediva a lui di parlarne come di un altro destino importante legato al suo e che pesava sul suo, e così, sentendosi le spalle gravate di tanta responsabilità, egli traversava la vita cauto, lasciando da parte tutti i pericoli ma anche il godimento, la felicità. A trentacinque anni si trovava nell'anima la brama insoddisfatta di piaceri e di amore, e già l'amarezza di non averne goduto, e nel cervello una grande paura di se stesso e della debolezza del proprio carattere, invero piuttosto sospettata che saputa per esperienza.

La carriera di Emilio Brentani era più complicata perché intanto si componeva di due occupazioni e due scopi ben distinti. Da un impieguccio di poca importanza presso una società di assicurazioni, egli traeva giusto il denaro di cui la famigliuola abbisognava. L'altra carriera era letteraria e, all'infuori di una riputazioncella, —soddisfazione di vanità più che d'ambizione— non gli rendeva nulla, ma lo affaticava ancora meno. Da molti anni, dopo di aver pubblicato un romanzo lodatissimo dalla stampa cittadina, egli non aveva fatto nulla, per inerzia non per sfiducia. Il romanzo, stampato su carta cattiva, era ingiallito nei magazzini del libraio, ma mentre alla sua pubblicazione Emilio era stato detto soltanto una grande speranza per l'avvenire, ora veniva considerato come una specie di rispettabilità letteraria che contava nel piccolo bilancio artistico della città. La prima sentenza non era stata riformata, s'era evoluta.

Per la chiarissima coscienza ch'egli aveva della nullità della propria opera, egli non si gloriava del passato, però, come nella vita così anche nell'arte, egli credeva di trovarsi ancora sempre nel periodo di preparazione, riguardandosi nel suo più segreto interno come una potente macchina geniale in costruzione, non ancora in attività. Viveva sempre in un'aspettativa, non paziente, di qualche cosa che doveva venirgli dal cervello, l'arte, di qualche cosa che doveva venirgli di fuori, la fortuna, il successo, come se l'età delle belle energie per lui non fosse tramontata.

Angiolina, una bionda dagli occhi azzurri grandi, alta e forte, ma snella e flessuosa, il volto illuminato dalla vita, un color giallo di ambra soffuso di rosa da una bella salute, camminava accanto a lui, la testa china da un lato come piegata dal peso del tanto oro che la fasciava, guardando il suolo ch'ella ad ogni passo toccava con l'elegante ombrellino come se avesse voluto farne scaturire un commento alle parole che udiva. Quando credette di aver compreso disse: —Strano— timidamente guardandolo sottecchi. —Nessuno mi ha mai parlato così.— Non aveva compreso e si sentiva lusingata al vederlo assumere

young one; she lived for him like a mother forgetful of herself, but that didn't keep him from speaking of her as another important destiny linked to his own and weighing on his own; and thus, feeling his shoulders burdened by such great responsibility, he went through life cautiously, leaving aside all dangers but also enjoyment, happiness. At thirty-five, he found in his soul the unsatisfied longing for pleasures and love, and, already, the bitterness of not having enjoyed them, and in his brain a great fear of himself and of the weakness of his own character, a weakness, in truth, rather suspected than known from experience.

Emilio Brentani's career was more complicated, because at the moment it was made up of two occupations and two goals that were clearly distinguished. From a petty little job with an insurance firm he derived just the amount of money his little family needed. The other career was literary and, beyond a minor reputation (which satisfied his vanity more than his ambition), brought him in nothing, but tired him out even less. For many years, after publishing a novel highly praised in the local press, he had done nothing, out of inertia, not for lack of self-confidence. The novel, printed on cheap paper, had yellowed in the publisher's warehouse, but whereas upon its publication, Emilio had been called only a great hope for the future, now he was considered as a sort of respectable literary figure who counted as part of the city's small artistic assets. The earlier judgment hadn't been revised, it had evolved.

Because of his very clear awareness of the worthlessness of his own work, he didn't boast about the past, but (as in his life, so in his art) he thought he was still in a period of preparation, viewing himself in his inmost thoughts as a powerful machine of ingenious construction not yet in full operation. He constantly lived in the (not patient) expectancy of something that would spring from his brain (art) or something that would come to him from outside (luck, success), as if the day of lively energy had not come to a close for him.

Angiolina, a blonde with big blue eyes, tall and sturdy, but lithe and supple, her face glowing with life, her amber complexion suffused with pink thanks to her good health, was walking beside him, her head leaning to one side as if bent by the weight of all the gold that encircled it, looking at the ground which at every step she touched with her elegant parasol, as if she wanted to elicit from it a commentary to the words she was hearing. When she thought she had understood, she said, timidly and furtively looking at him: "Odd. No one has ever spoken to me like that." She hadn't understood and she felt flattered to see him assume a role that

un ufficio che a lui non spettava, di allontanare da lei il pericolo. L'affetto ch'egli le offriva ne ebbe l'aspetto di fraternamente dolce. Fatte quelle premesse, l'altro si sentì tranquillo e ripigliò un tono più adatto alla circostanza. Fece piovere sulla bionda testa le dichiarazioni liriche che nei lunghi anni il suo desiderio aveva maturate e affinate, ma, facendole, egli stesso le sentiva rinnovellare e ringiovanire come se fossero nate in quell'istante, al calore dell'occhio azzurro di Angiolina. Ebbe il sentimento che da tanti anni non aveva provato, di comporre, di trarre dal proprio intimo idee e parole: un sollievo che dava a quel momento della sua vita non lieta, un aspetto strano, indimenticabile, di pausa, di pace. La donna vi entrava! Raggiante di gioventù e bellezza ella doveva illuminarla tutta facendogli dimenticare il triste passato di desiderio e di solitudine e promettendogli la gioia per l'avvenire ch'ella, certo, non avrebbe compromesso.

Egli s'era avvicinato a lei con l'idea di trovare un'avventura facile e breve, di quelle che egli aveva sentito descrivere tanto spesso e che a lui non erano toccate mai o mai degne di essere ricordate. Questa s'era annunziata proprio facile e breve. L'ombrellino era caduto in tempo per fornirgli un pretesto di avvicinarsi ed anzi —sembrava malizia!— impigliandosi nella vita trinata della fanciulla, non se n'era voluto staccare che dopo spinte visibilissime. Ma poi, dinanzi a quel profilo sorprendentemente puro, a quella bella salute —ai rétori corruzione e salute sembrano inconciliabili— aveva allentato il suo slancio, timoroso di sbagliare e infine s'incantò ad ammirare una faccia misteriosa dalle linee precise e dolci, già soddisfatto, già felice. [. . .]

## 51. D'Annunzio (1863–1938): *L'innocente* e versi

(A) Mancava quasi un'ora al mezzogiorno. Era una mattina calda, d'un caldo precoce, azzurra ma navigata da qualche nuvola molle. I frutici, deliziosi, che davano il nome alla villa —*Villalilla*— fiorivano per ogni dove, signoreggiavano tutto il giardino, facevano un bosco appena interrotto qua e là da cespugli di rose gialle e da mucchi di giaggioli. Qua e là le rose si arrampicavano su per i fusti, s'insinuavano tra i rami, ricadevano miste in catene, in ghirlande, in festoni, in corimbi; a piè dei fusti le iridi fiorentine elevavano di tra le foglie simili a lunghe spade glauche le forme ampie e nobili dei loro fiori; i tre profumi si mescevano in un accordo profondo che io riconoscevo

wasn't his duty: to remove her from danger. The affection he was offering her sounded like something fraternally sweet.

After that preamble, he felt calm and resumed a tone more suited to the situation. He showered onto her blonde head the lyrical declarations that through the long years his desire had ripened and refined, but, as he made them, he himself felt them become renewed and rejuvenated as if they had just been born, in the warmth of Angiolina's blue eyes. He had the feeling he hadn't experienced for so many years: that of putting together words and ideas out of his own inner resources—a feeling of relief which gave that moment of his far from happy life a strange, unforgettable aspect of repose and peace. Woman was entering it! Radiant with youth and beauty, she would brighten it entirely, making him forget the sad past days of longing and solitude, and promising him joy for the future, which she, surely, wouldn't jeopardize.

He had drawn near her with the thought of finding an easy, brief adventure, one of those he had heard described so often but which had never befallen him, at least none worth remembering. This one had promised to be really easy and brief. Her parasol had fallen opportunely, offering him an excuse for approaching; and, in fact (it seemed like a stratagem!), once entangling himself in the girl's lace-covered life, he hadn't wanted to detach himself until being very visibly urged to do so. But later, in the presence of that surprisingly pure profile and that healthy body (to rhetoricians corruptness and good health seem irreconcilable), he had slackened his impetus, fearing to make a mistake; finally he was delighted to admire a mysterious face with precise, sweet lines. Now he was contented, now he was happy. [. . .]

## 51. D'Annunzio (1863–1938): *The Innocent One* and verse

(A) It was almost an hour till noon. It was a warm morning, one of premature warmth, blue but sailed-through by a few soft clouds. The shrubs, delightful ones, that gave the villa its name—Villa Lilac—were blossoming everywhere, they dominated the whole garden, they formed a grove scarcely interrupted here and there by bushes of yellow roses and clumps of iris. Here and there the roses climbed up the stems, made their way between the branches and hung down, intermingled in chains, garlands, festoons, and clusters; at the foot of the stems the Florentine irises raised aloft, amid their leaves, which resembled long, blue-green swords, the ample, noble forms of their blossoms; the three fragrances mingled in a

perché dal tempo lontano era rimasto nella mia memoria distinto
come un accordo musicale di tre note. Nel silenzio non si udiva se
non il garrire delle rondini. La casa a pena s'intravedeva tra i coni dei
cipressi, e le rondini vi accorrevano innumerevoli come le api al-
l'alveare. [. . .]

(B) Il giardino non aveva piú le sue miriadi di grappoli turchinicci;
non aveva piú la sua delicata selva di fiori, né il suo profumo triplice,
armonioso come una musica, né il suo riso aperto, né il clamore continuo delle sue rondini. Non altro aveva di lieto, se non le voci e le
corse di due bambine inconsapevoli. Molte rondini erano partite; altre
partivano. Eravamo giunti in tempo per salutare l'ultimo stormo.
    Tutti i nidi erano abbandonati, vacui, esanimi. Qualcuno era in-
franto, e sugli avanzi della creta tremolava qualche penna esile.
L'ultimo stormo era adunato sul tetto lungo le gronde, e aspettava ancora qualche compagna dispersa. Le migratrici stavano in fila sull'orlo
del canale, talune rivolte col becco, altre col dorso, per modo che le
piccole code forcute e i piccoli petti candidi si alternavano. E cosí, a-
spettando, gittavano nell'aria calma i richiami. E di tratto in tratto, a
due, a tre, giungevano le compagne in ritardo. E s'approssimava l'ora
della dipartita. I richiami cessavano, un'occhiata di sole languida scendeva sulla casa chiusa, sui nidi deserti. Nulla era piú triste di quelle
esili piume morte, che qua e là, trattenute dalla creta, tremolavano.
    Come sollevato da un colpo di vento subitaneo, da una raffica, lo
stormo si levò con un gran frullo d'ali, sorse nell'aria in guisa d'un vor-
tice, rimase un istante a perpendicolo sulla casa; senza incertezze,
quasi che davanti gli si fosse disegnata una traccia, si mise compatto in
viaggio, s'allontanò, si dileguò, disparve. [. . .]

(C) Consolazione

Non pianger piú. Torna il diletto figlio
alla tua casa. È stanco di mentire.
Vieni, usciamo. Tempo è di rifiorire.
Troppo sei bianca: il volto è quasi un giglio.

Vieni, usciamo. Il giardino abbandonato
serba ancora per noi qualche sentiero.
Ti dirò come sia dolce il mistero
che vela certe cose del passato.

Ancora qualche rosa è ne' rosai,
ancora qualche timida erba odora.

deep harmony which I recognized because from far-off days it had remained in my memory as distinctly as a musical chord of three notes. In
the silence nothing was heard but the twittering of the swallows. The
hours could scarcely be glimpsed through the conical cypresses, and the
swallows were flying to it as numerous as bees to their hive. [. . .]

(B)  The garden no longer had its myriads of purple clusters; it no longer
had its delicate forest of flowers or its threefold fragrance, harmonious as
a piece of music, or its open smile, or the continuous call of its swallows.
It had nothing joyous except the voices and scampering of two innocent
baby girls. Many swallows had departed; others were about to. We had arrived in time to greet the last flock of them.

All the nests were deserted, empty, lifeless. Some were broken, and on
the remains of the clay a few thin feathers trembled. The last flock had
assembled on the roof along the eaves, and was still awaiting a few scattered companions. The migrants stood in a row on the rim of the gutter,
some beak forward, some tail forward, so that their little forked tails and
their little white breasts alternated. And thus, waiting, they flung their
cries into the calm air. And from time to time, in twos, in threes, the tardy
companions arrived. And the time for departure drew near. The cries
ceased, a languid glimpse of sunshine descended upon the shut-up house,
on the deserted nests. Nothing was sadder than those thin dead feathers
which were trembling here and there, stuck in the clay.

As if uplifted by a sudden rush of wind, by a gust, the flock rose with a
great rustling of wings, ascended into the air like a whirlwind, hovered for
a moment perpendicularly to the house; without uncertainties, as if its
route had been traced before it, it set off compactly on its journey, grew
distant, became lost to sight, disappeared. [. . .]

(C) Consolation

Weep no more. Your beloved son is returning
to your house. He's tired of dissimulating.
Come, let's go out. It's time to blossom anew.
You're too pale: your face is almost a lily.

Come, let's go out. The deserted garden
still reserves some path for us.
I shall tell you how sweet is the mystery
that veils certain things from the past.

There are still a few roses on their bushes,
some timid herb still sheds its fragrance.

Ne l'abbandono il caro luogo ancora
sorriderà, se tu sorriderai.

Ti dirò come sia dolce il sorriso
di certe cose che l'oblío afflisse.
Che proveresti tu se ti fiorisse
la terra sotto i piedi, all'improvviso?

Tanto accadrà, benché non sia d'aprile.
Usciamo. Non coprirti il capo. È un lento
sol di settembre; e ancor non vedo argento
sul tuo capo, e la riga è ancor sottile.

Perché ti neghi con lo sguardo stanco?
La madre fa quel che il buon figlio vuole.
Bisogna che tu prenda un po' di sole,
un po' di sole su quel viso bianco.

Bisogna che tu sia forte; bisogna
che tu non pensi a le cattive cose . . .
Se noi andiamo verso quelle rose,
io parlo piano, l'anima tua sogna.

Sogna, sogna, mia cara anima! Tutto
tutto sarà come al tempo lontano.
Io metterò nella tua pura mano
tutto il mio cuore. Nulla è ancor distrutto.

Sogna, sogna! Io vivrò de la tua vita:
in una vita semplice e profonda
io rivivrò. La lieve ostia che monda
io la riceverò da le tue dita. [. . .]


## 52. Croce (1866–1952): *Breviario di estetica*

Alla domanda: «Che cosa è l'arte?» si potrebbe rispondere celiando (ma non sarebbe una celia sciocca): che l'arte è ciò che tutti sanno che cosa sia. E, veramente, se in qualche modo non si sapesse che cosa essa è, non si potrebbe neppure muovere quella domanda, perché ogni domanda importa una certa notizia della cosa di cui si domanda, designata nella domanda, e perciò qualificata e conosciuta. Il che riceve una riprova di fatto nelle idee giuste e profonde, che si odono sovente manifestare intorno all'arte da coloro che non fanno profes-

In its abandoned state the dear place will still
smile if you smile.

I shall tell you how sweet is the smile
of certain things that forgetfulness has saddened.
How would you feel if the ground
beneath your feet suddenly blossomed for you?

That will happen, though it isn't April.
Let's go out. Don't cover your head. It's a mild
September sun; and I don't yet see silver
in your hair, and the part in it is still narrow.

Why do you refuse with that weary look?
A mother does what her good son wants.
You need to have a little sunshine,
a little sunshine on that pale face.

You need to be strong; you need
to stop thinking about bad things . . .
If we walk over to those roses,
I'll speak softly, your soul will dream.

Dream, dream, my dear soul! All,
all will be as in those far-off days.
I shall place in your pure hands
all of my heart. Nothing is destroyed yet.

Dream, dream! I shall live on your life:
in a simple, profound life
I shall revive. The light Host that cleanses
I shall receive from your fingers. [. . .]

## 52. Croce (1866–1952): *Breviary of Esthetics*

To the question, "What is art?" one could reply jokingly (but it wouldn't
be a foolish joke) that art is that thing of which it can be said that everyone knows what it is. And truly, if to some degree we didn't know what it
was, we couldn't even ask that question, because every question posits a
certain knowledge of the thing being asked about; it's designated in the
question, and thus described and known. This is factually verified by the
correct, profound ideas we often hear stated about art by those who make
no profession of philosophy or theory, by laymen, by artists not fond of

sione di filosofia e di teoria, dai laici, dagli artisti non amanti del ragionare, dalle persone ingenue, perfino dalla gente del popolo: idee
che talvolta sono implicite nei giudizi che si recano intorno a singole
opere d'arte, ma che tal altra prendono addirittura forma di aforismi
e di definizioni. Accade di pensare che si potrebbe fare arrossire, sempre che si volesse, ogni orgoglioso filosofo, il quale stimasse di avere
«scoperto» la natura dell'arte, mettendogli sotto gli occhi e facendogli
risonare agli orecchi proposizioni scritte nei libri più comuni e sentenze della più ordinaria conversazione, e mostrandogli che già con-
tengono, nel modo più chiaro, la sua vantata scoperta.

E il filosofo avrebbe ben motivo, in questo caso, di arrossire, se cioè
avesse mai nutrito l'illusione d'introdurre, con le proprie dottrine,
qualcosa di tutto suo originale nella comune coscienza umana, qualcosa di estraneo a questa coscienza, la rivelazione di un mondo affatto
nuovo. Ma egli non si turba e tira diritto per la sua via, perché non i-
gnora che la domanda sul che cosa sia l'arte (come, del resto, ogni domanda filosofica sulla natura del reale, o, in genere, ogni domanda di
conoscenza), se anche nelle parole che si adoperano prende aspetto
di problema generale e totale, che si pretenda risolvere per la prima
volta e per l'ultima, ha sempre, effettivamente, un significato cir-
costanziato, riferibile alle particolari difficoltà che si fanno vive in un
particolare momento della storia del pensiero. Certamente, la verità
corre per le strade, come l'*esprit* nel noto proverbio francese, o come
la metafora, «regina dei tropi» secondo i retori, che il Montaigne
ritrovava nel «babil» della sua «chambrière». Ma la metafora della
cameriera è la soluzione di un problema espressivo, proprio dei sentimenti che agitano in quel momento la cameriera; e le ovvie affer-
mazioni, che di proposito o per incidente tuttodì si ascoltano sulla
natura dell'arte, sono soluzioni di problemi logici, quali si presentano a
questo o quell'individuo che non fa professione di filosofo e che pure,
come uomo, è anche lui, in qualche misura, filosofo. E come la
metafora della cameriera esprime di solito una breve e povera cerchia
di sentimenti rispetto a quella del poeta, così l'ovvia affermazione del
non filosofo risolve un lieve problema rispetto a quello che si propone
il filosofo. La risposta sul che cosa sia l'arte, può suonare simile in ap-
parenza nell'uno e nell'altro caso, ma si diversifica nei due casi per la
diversa ricchezza del suo intimo contenuto; perché la risposta del
filosofo, degno del nome, ha né più né meno che l'assunto di risolvere
in modo adeguato tutti i problemi che sono sorti, fino a quel momento,
nel corso della storia, intorno alla natura dell'arte, laddove quella del
laico, aggirantesi in un àmbito ben più stretto, si chiarisce impotente

logical reasoning, by simple people, even by lower-class people: ideas that are sometimes implicit in the judgments they give on individual works of art, but at other times even take the form of aphorisms and definitions. One comes to think that, whenever one wished, one could bring a blush to the cheek of every proud philosopher who deems he has "discovered" the nature of art, by placing before his eyes and dinning into his ears statements written in the most everyday books and opinions spoken in the most ordinary conversations, and showing him that they already contain, in the clearest way, his boasted discovery.

And the philosopher would have every reason to blush, in this case; that is, if he had ever fostered the illusion that he could introduce with his own doctrines something original of his own into our common human awareness, something extraneous to that awareness, the revelation of a totally new world. But he isn't upset, he continues along his way, because he knows that the question of what art is (furthermore, like every philosophical question on the nature of reality or, in general, every question about knowledge), even if in the words employed it assumes the aspect of a general, universal problem that one claims to solve for the first and last time, always actually has a circumstantial significance referring to the particular difficulties that arise at a given moment in the history of thought. Certainly, truth walks every street, just as "wit" does in the well-known French proverb, or as metaphor does (that "queen of figures of speech," according to the rhetoricians), Montaigne having found it in the "chatter" of his "housemaid." But the housemaid's metaphor is the solution of an expressive problem, proper to the emotions that are stirring the housemaid at that moment; and the obvious assertions, which intentionally or accidentally are heard daily about the nature of art, are solutions to problems of logic as they occur to this or that individual who doesn't profess to be a philosopher and yet, being a human, is to some extent also a philosopher. And just as the housemaid's metaphor usually reflects a narrow, impoverished range of feelings compared to a poet's metaphor, thus the obvious assertion made by a non-philosopher solves a lightweight problem compared to what a philosopher hopes to accomplish. The answer to the question of what art is may sound seemingly similar in both instances, but differs in the two instances in the differing richness of its inmost content; because the answer given by any philosopher deserving of the name has the purpose, neither more nor less, of solving adequately all the problems that have arisen in the course of history up to that moment, as to the nature of art, whereas the layman's answer, moving in a much narrower orbit, is clearly powerless outside of those limits. This is verified factually by the strength of the eternal

fuori di quei limiti. Il che ha la sua riprova di fatto nella forza dell'eterno procedere socratico, nella facilità onde gli addottrinati lasciano confusi e a bocca aperta, con l'incalzare delle loro domande, i non addottrinati, che pure avevano cominciato col parlar bene, e ai quali, messi a rischio, nel corso dell'interrogatorio, di perdere anche quel poco sapere che possedevano, non resta altra difesa che rientrare nel proprio guscio, dichiarando che non amano le «sottigliezze».

Ecco, dunque, dove soltanto può essere collocato l'orgoglio del filosofo: nella coscienza della maggiore intensità delle sue domande e delle sue risposte; orgoglio che non va scompagnato dalla modestia, cioè dalla consapevolezza che, se l'àmbito suo è più largo, o il più largo possibile in un determinato momento, ha pur tuttavia i suoi limiti, tracciati dalla storia di quel momento, e non può pretendere a un valore di totalità, o, come suol dirsi, di soluzione definitiva. L'ulteriore vita dello spirito, rinnovando e moltiplicando i problemi, rende, non già false ma inadeguate le soluzioni precedenti, parte delle quali cadono nel numero di quelle verità che si sottintendono, e parte debbono essere riprese e integrate. Un sistema è una casa che, subito dopo costruita e adornata, ha bisogno (soggetta com'è all'azione corroditrice degli elementi) di un lavorìo, più o meno energico ma assiduo, di manutenzione, e che a un certo momento non giova più restaurare e puntellare, e bisogna gettare a terra e ricostruire dalle fondamenta. Ma con siffatta differenza capitale: che, nell'opera del pensiero, la casa perpetuamente nuova è sostenuta perpetuamente dall'antica, la quale, quasi per opera magica, perdura in essa. Come si sa, gl'ignari di codesta magia, gli intelletti superficiali o ingenui, se ne spaventano; tanto che uno dei loro noiosi ritornelli contro la filosofia è che essa disfaccia di continuo l'opera sua, e che un filosofo contradica l'altro: come se l'uomo non facesse e disfacesse e rifacesse sempre le sue case, e l'architetto seguente non fosse il contraddittore dell'architetto precedente; e come se da questo fare e disfare e rifare delle case, e da questo contradirsi degli architetti, si potesse trarre la conclusione, che è inutile costruire case! [. . .]

## 53. Pirandello (1867–1936): *Il fu Mattia Pascal*

Fui, per circa due anni, non so se più cacciatore di topi che guardiano di libri nella biblioteca che un monsignor Boccamazza, nel 1803, volle lasciar morendo al nostro Comune. È ben chiaro che questo Monsignore dovette conoscer poco l'indole e le abitudini de' suoi concittadini; o forse

Socratic procedure, by the ease with which the indoctrinated, by means of the dogged insistence of their questions, leave the non-indoctrinated confused and openmouthed, though the latter had started off by speaking well; put at risk, in the course of the interrogation, of losing even that small amount of wisdom they possessed, these laymen are left with no other defense than to crawl back into their shell, declaring that they don't like "hair-splitting."

Thus, here is the only place to which the philosopher's pride can be assigned: his awareness of the greater intensity of his questions and answers; this pride is not unaccompanied by modesty; that is, by the knowledge that, even if his scope is wider, or the widest possible at a given moment, it nevertheless has its limits, outlined by the history of that moment, and cannot claim to be universally valid, or, as the saying is, a definitive solution. The ongoing progress of the mind, renewing and multiplying the problems, makes the earlier solutions not wrong but insufficient; some of them become part of those truths which are tacitly implied, some of them need to be taken up again and supplemented. A philosophical system is like a house that, immediately after being built and decorated, needs (since it is subject to the corrosive action of the elements) more or less energetic, but assiduous, maintenance; at a certain moment, it no longer helps to restore it and prop it up; you've got to demolish it and build it up again from its foundations. But with this capital difference: in the works of the mind, the perpetually new house is perpetually sustained by the old one, which, as if by magic, endures within it. As is well known, those ignorant of this magic, the superficial or ingenuous thinkers, are alarmed by it; so much so that one of their boring refrains against philosophy is that it constantly undoes its own work, and that one philosopher contradicts the other. As if man didn't always build and raze his houses, and the new architect didn't contradict the preceding architect! And as if this building, razing, and rebuilding of houses, and this contradiction between architects, could lead to the conclusion that it's pointless to build houses! [. . .]

## 53. Pirandello (1867–1936): *The Late Mattia Pascal*

For about two years I was just as much a ratcatcher as a librarian in the library that a certain Monsignor Boccamazza left at his death in 1803 to our town. It's very clear that this monsignor must have known very little about the nature and habits of his fellow townsmen; or perhaps he

sperò che il suo lascito dovesse col tempo e con la comodità accendere nel loro animo l'amore per lo studio. Finora, ne posso rendere testimonianza, non si è acceso: e questo dico in lode de' miei concittadini. Del dono anzi il Comune si dimostrò così poco grato al Boccamazza, che non volle neppure erigergli un mezzo busto pur che fosse, e i libri lasciò per molti e molti anni accatastati in un vasto e umido magazzino, donde poi li trasse, pensate voi in quale stato, per allogarli nella chiesetta fuori mano di Santa Maria Liberale, non so per qual ragione sconsacrata. Qua li affidò, senz'alcun discernimento, a titolo di beneficio, e come sinecura, a qualche sfaccendato ben protetto il quale, per due lire al giorno, stando a guardarli, o anche senza guardarli affatto, ne avesse sopportato per alcune ore il tanfo della muffa e del vecchiume.

Tal sorte toccò anche a me; e fin dal primo giorno io concepii così misera stima dei libri, sieno essi a stampa o manoscritti (come alcuni antichissimi della nostra biblioteca), che ora non mi sarei mai e poi mai messo a scrivere, se, come ho detto, non stimassi davvero strano il mio caso e tale da poter servire d'ammaestramento a qualche curioso lettore, che per avventura, riducendosi finalmente a effetto l'antica speranza della buon'anima di monsignor Boccamazza, capitasse in questa biblioteca, a cui io lascio questo mio manoscritto, con l'obbligo però che nessuno possa aprirlo se non cinquant'anni dopo la mia *terza, ultima e definitiva* morte.

Giacché, per il momento (e Dio sa quanto me ne duole), io sono morto, sì, già due volte, ma la prima per errore, e la seconda . . . sentirete.

L'idea, o piuttosto, il consiglio di scrivere mi è venuto dal mio reverendo amico don Eligio Pellegrinotto, che al presente ha in custodia i libri della Boccamazza, e al quale io affido il manoscritto appena sarà terminato, se mai sarà.

Lo scrivo qua, nella chiesetta sconsacrata, al lume che mi viene dalla lanterna lassù, della cupola; qua, nell'abside riservata al bibliotecario e chiusa da una bassa cancellata di legno a pilastrini, mentre don Eligio sbuffa sotto l'incarico che si è eroicamente assunto di mettere un po' d'ordine in questa vera babilonia di libri. Temo che non ne verrà mai a capo. Nessuno prima di lui s'era curato di sapere, almeno all'ingrosso, dando di sfuggita un'occhiata ai dorsi, che razza di libri quel Monsignore avesse donato al Comune: si riteneva che tutti o quasi dovessero trattare di materie religiose. Ora il Pellegrinotto ha scoperto, per maggior sua consolazione, una varietà grandissima di materie nella biblioteca di Monsignore; e siccome i libri furon presi di

hoped that his bequest would in time, by its convenience, kindle a love of study in their mind. So far, I can bear witness, it hasn't been kindled. And I say this to the credit of my fellow townsmen. Even the town council showed itself so little grateful to Boccamazza for his gift that it even refused to erect a half-length statue of him, and left the books for many, many years piled up in a huge, damp storage area, from which it later removed them (imagine in what condition!) to lodge them in the out-of-the-way little church of Santa Maria Liberale, which had been deconsecrated for some reason or other. There it entrusted them, without discernment, as a favor and as a sinecure, to whatever well protected idler, who, for two *lire* a day, taking care of them, or even without taking care of them at all, could endure for a few hours the stench of mold and old rubbish.

This fell to my lot, as well; and from the very first day I conceived such a low opinion of books, whether printed or manuscript (such as certain very old ones in our library), that now I would never ever have begun to write if, as I've said, I didn't consider my case really odd and such that it can serve as a lesson to some inquisitive reader who by chance, finally making the old hopes of that good soul, Monsignor Boccamazza, come true, might find his way into this library, to which I leave this manuscript of mine, but on the condition that no one open it until fifty years after my *third, last, and definitive* death.

Because, at the moment (and God knows how it grieves me), I have died, yes, twice already, but the first time by mistake and the second time . . . you'll hear.

The idea, or rather the advice, to write came to me from my revered friend Don Eligio Pellegrinotto, the present librarian of the Boccamazza Library, to whom I shall entrust this manuscript as soon as it's finished, if ever.

I'm writing it here, in the little deconsecrated church, by the light coming through the skylight in the dome above; here, in the apse reserved for the librarian and closed off by a low wooden railing with little pilasters, while Don Eligio puffs and pants beneath the task he has heroically undertaken to put a little order in this veritable Babel of books. I'm afraid he'll never finish it. No one before him had thought about finding out, even roughly, by giving a cursory glance at the spines, what sort of books that monsignor had donated to the town: it was assumed that all, or nearly all, must treat of religious matters. Now Pellegrinotto has discovered, to his greater consolation, a very great variety of subject matter in the monsignor's library; and since the books were taken from here and there in

qua e di là nel magazzino e accozzati così come venivano sotto mano, la confusione è indescrivibile. Si sono strette per la vicinanza fra questi libri amicizie oltre ogni dire speciose: don Eligio Pellegrinotto mi ha detto, ad esempio, che ha stentato non poco a staccare da un tratto molto licenzioso *Dell'arte di amar le donne,* libri tre di Anton Muzio Porro, dell'anno 1571, una *Vita e morte di Faustino Materucci, Benedettino di Polirone, che taluni chiamano beato,* biografia edita a Mantova nel 1625. Per l'umidità, le legature de' due volumi si erano fraternamente appiccicate. Notare che nel libro secondo di quel trattato licenzioso si discorre a lungo della vita e delle avventure monacali.

Molti libri curiosi e piacevolissimi don Eligio Pellegrinotto, arrampicato tutto il giorno su una scala da lampionajo, ha pescato negli scaffali della biblioteca. Ogni qual volta ne trova uno, lo lancia dall'alto, con garbo, sul tavolone che sta in mezzo; la chiesetta ne rintrona; un nugolo di polvere si leva, da cui due o tre ragni scappano via spaventati: io accorro dall'abside, scavalcando la cancellata; do prima col libro stesso la caccia ai ragni su pe'l tavolone polveroso; poi apro il libro e mi metto a leggiucchiarlo.

Così, a poco a poco, ho fatto il gusto a siffatte letture. Ora don Eligio mi dice che il mio libro dovrebbe esser condotto sul modello di questi ch'egli va scovando nella biblioteca, aver cioè il loro particolar sapore. Io scrollo le spalle e gli rispondo che non è fatica per me. E poi altro mi trattiene.

Tutto sudato e impolverato, don Eligio scende dalla scala e viene a prendere una boccata d'aria nell'orticello che ha trovato modo di far sorgere qui dietro l'abside, riparato giro giro da stecchi e spuntoni.

—Eh, mio reverendo amico,— gli dico io, seduto sul murello, col mento appoggiato al pomo del bastone, mentr'egli attende alle sue lattughe. —Non mi par più tempo, questo, di scriver libri, neppure per ischerzo. In considerazione anche della letteratura, come per tutto il resto, io debbo ripetere il mio solito ritornello: *Maledetto sia Copernico!*

—Oh oh oh, che c'entra Copernico!— esclama don Eligio, levandosi su la vita, col volto infocato sotto il cappellaccio di paglia.

—C'entra, don Eligio. Perché, quando la Terra non girava . . . [ . . . ]

the storehouse and jumbled up just as they came to hand, the confusion is indescribable. Through the proximity of one book to another, friendships have been formed that are specious beyond all words: Don Eligio Pellegrinotto has told me, for example, that he has labored not a little to detach from a very licentious work called *On the Art of Loving Women,* in three books, by Anton Muzio Porro, of 1571, a *Life and Death of Faustino Materucci, Benedictine of Polirone, Whom Some Call Blessed,* a biography published in Mantua in 1625. Because of the damp, the bindings of the two volumes had fraternally pasted together. Note that in the second book of that licentious opus there's a lengthy discussion of the life and adventures of monks!

Many a curious and delightful book has Don Eligio Pellegrinotto, climbing all day up a lamplighter's ladder, fished out of the library shelves. Every time he finds one, he throws it elegantly onto the big table in the middle; it makes the little church echo; a cloud of dust rises, from which two or three spiders escape in alarm; I run over from the apse, straddling the railing; first, with the book itself, I hunt the spiders on the dusty table; then I open the book and start to riffle through it.

In that way I've gradually acquired a taste for that kind of reading. Now Don Eligio tells me that my own book should be modeled on the ones he unearths in the library; that is, it should have their particular flavor. I shrug my shoulders and reply that that's no job for me. And then, something else holds me back.

All sweaty and dusty, Don Eligio comes down from the ladder and comes to take a breath of air in the little garden he has found a way to create here behind the apse, enclosed all around with brushwood and thorns.

"Ah, my revered friend," I say to him as I sit on the little wall, my chin resting on the knob of my stick, while he attends to his lettuces. "This doesn't strike me as the right time anymore to write books, even for fun. In consideration of literature, too, as for all the rest, I must repeat my usual refrain: *A curse on Copernicus!*"

"Oh, oh, oh, where does Copernicus come in?" exclaims Don Eligio, straightening up, his face flushed under his big, ugly straw hat.

"He comes in, Don Eligio. Because, in the days when the Earth didn't revolve . . ." [. . .]

## 54. Deledda (1871–1936): *Canne al vento*

Tutto il giorno Efix, il servo delle dame Pintor, aveva lavorato a rinforzare l'argine primitivo da lui stesso costrutto un po' per volta a furia d'anni e di fatica, giù in fondo al poderetto lungo il fiume: e al cader della sera contemplava la sua opera dall'alto, seduto davanti alla capanna sotto il ciglione glauco di canne a mezza costa sulla bianca *Collina dei Colombi.*

Eccolo tutto ai suoi piedi, silenzioso e qua e là scintillante d'acque nel crepuscolo, il poderetto che Efix considera più suo che delle sue padrone: trent'anni di possesso e di lavoro lo han fatto ben suo, e le due siepi di fichi d'India che lo chiudono dall'alto in basso come due muri grigi serpeggianti di scaglione in scaglione dalla collina al fiume, gli sembrano i confini del mondo.

Il servo non guardava al di là del poderetto anche perché i terreni da una parte e dall'altra erano un tempo appartenuti alle sue padrone: perché ricordare il passato? Rimpianto inutile. Meglio pensare all'avvenire e sperare nell'aiuto di Dio.

E Dio prometteva una buona annata, o per lo meno faceva ricoprir di fiori tutti i mandorli e i peschi della valle; e questa, fra due file di colline bianche, con lontananze cerule di monti ad occidente e di mare ad oriente, coperta di vegetazione primaverile, d'acque, di macchie, di fiori, dava l'idea di una culla gonfia di veli verdi, di nastri azzurri, col mormorio del fiume monotono come quello di un bambino che s'addormenta.

Ma le giornate eran già troppo calde ed Efix pensava anche alle pioggie torrenziali che gonfiano il fiume senz'argini e lo fanno balzare come un mostro e distruggere ogni cosa: sperare, sì, ma non fidarsi anche; star vigili come le canne sopra il ciglione che ad ogni soffio di vento si battono l'una contro l'altra le foglie come per avvertirsi del pericolo.

Per questo aveva lavorato tutto il giorno e adesso, in attesa della notte, mentre per non perder tempo intesseva una stuoia di giunchi, pregava perché Dio rendesse valido il suo lavoro. Che cosa è un piccolo argine se Dio non lo rende, col suo volere, formidabile come una montagna?

Sette giunchi attraverso un vimine, dunque, e sette preghiere al Signore ed a Nostra Signora del Rimedio, benedetta ella sia, ecco laggiù nell'estremo azzurro del crepuscolo la chiesetta e il recinto di capanne quieto come un villaggio preistorico abbandonato da secoli. A

## 54. Deledda (1871–1936): *Reeds in the Wind*

All day long Efix, the servant of the Pintor ladies, had worked at reinforcing the primitive dike he himself had built a little at a time over many years and with great labor, down at the far end of the little farm along the river; and as evening fell, he was observing his handiwork from above, seated in front of the hut beneath the embankment that was blue-green with reeds halfway up the white Hill of the Doves.

There it all lies at his feet, silent and sparkling with water here and there in the dusk, the little farm that Efix considers more his own than his mistresses': thirty years of possession and labor have really made it his, and the two prickly-pear hedges that enclose it from top to bottom, like two gray snakes crawling from tier to tier from the hill to the river, seem to him like the ends of the world.

The servant wasn't looking beyond the little farm for the additional reason that the parcels on either side had once belonged to his mistresses: why recall the past? A useless regret. Better to think of the future and hope for the aid of God.

And God was promising a good year; at least He was covering with blossoms all the almond and peach trees in the valley; and the valley (between two rows of white hills, with blue distant views of mountains to the west and of sea to the east), covered with springtime vegetation, with streams, with brush, with flowers, suggested a cradle full of green cloths and blue ribbons, with the monotonous murmur of the river, like that of a baby falling asleep.

But the days were already too hot, and Efix was also thinking about the torrential rains that swell the undammed river and make it leap like a monster and destroy everything. One should hope, yes, but also not be too confident; one must be as vigilant as the reeds on the embankment, which at every puff of wind beat their leaves one against the other as if to warn one another of danger.

That's why he had worked all day and was now, as he awaited night (while he wove a rush mat so as to waste no time), praying to God to make his work worthwhile. What is a small dike unless God, with His will, makes it strong as a mountain?

Seven rushes through one osier, therefore, and seven prayers to the Lord and Our Lady of Perpetual Help, blessing on her! Down there at the furthest blue of the twilight, see the little church, and the enclosure of huts quiet as a prehistoric village deserted for centuries! At that hour, while the moon was emerging like a large rose from the bushes on the hill, and the euphorbias were shedding their scent along the river, Efix's

quell'ora, mentre la luna sbocciava come una grande rosa fra i cespugli della collina e le euforbie odoravano lungo il fiume, anche le
padrone di Efix pregavano: donna Ester la più vecchia, benedetta ella
sia, si ricordava certo di lui peccatore: bastava questo perché egli si
sentisse contento, compensato delle sue fatiche.

Un passo in lontananza gli fece sollevar gli occhi. Gli sembrò di ri-
conoscerlo; era un passo rapido e lieve di fanciullo, passo d'angelo che
corre ad annunziare le cose liete e le tristi. Sia fatto il volere di Dio: è
lui che manda le buone e le cattive notizie; ma il cuore cominciò a
tremargli, ed anche le dita nere screpolate tremarono coi giunchi ar-
gentei lucenti alla luna come fili d'acqua.

Il passo non s'udiva più: Efix tuttavia rimase ancora là, immobile, ad
aspettare.

La luna saliva davanti a lui, e le voci della sera avvertivano l'uomo
che la sua giornata era finita. Era il grido cadenzato del cuculo, il zir-
lio dei grilli precoci, qualche gemito d'uccello; era il sospiro delle
canne e la voce sempre più chiara del fiume: ma era soprattutto un
soffio, un ansito misterioso che pareva uscire dalla terra stessa: sì, la
giornata dell'uomo lavoratore era finita, ma cominciava la vita fanta-
stica dei folletti, delle fate, degli spiriti erranti. I fantasmi degli antichi
Baroni scendevano dalle rovine del castello sopra il paese di Galte, su,
all'orizzonte a sinistra di Efix, e percorrevano le sponde del fiume alla
caccia dei cinghiali e delle volpi: le loro armi scintillavano in mezzo ai
bassi ontani della riva, e l'abbaiar fioco dei cani in lontananza indicava
il loro passaggio.

Efix sentiva il rumore che le *panas* (donne morte di parto) facevano
nel lavar i loro panni giù al fiume, battendoli con uno stinco di morto,
e credeva di intraveder l'*ammattadore,* folletto con sette berretti entro
i quali conserva un tesoro, balzar di qua e di là sotto il bosco di mandorli, inseguito dai vampiri con la coda di acciaio.

Era il suo passaggio che destava lo scintillio dei rami e delle pietre
sotto la luna: e agli spiriti maligni si univano quelli dei bambini non
battezzati, spiriti bianchi che volavano per aria tramutandosi nelle nu-
volette argentee dietro la luna: e i nani e le *janas,* piccole fate che du-
rante la giornata stanno nelle loro case di roccia a tesser stoffe d'oro
in telai d'oro, ballavano all'ombra delle grandi macchie di filirèa, mentre i giganti s'affacciavano fra le roccie dei monti battuti dalla luna,
tenendo per la briglia gli enormi cavalli verdi che essi soltanto sanno
montare, spiando se laggiù fra le distese d'euforbia malefica si nascon-
deva qualche drago o se il leggendario serpente *cananèa,* vivente fin
dai tempi di Cristo, strisciava sulle sabbie intorno alla palude. [. . .]

mistresses were praying, too: lady Ester, the eldest (blessings on her!), was surely remembering him, a sinner: that was enough to make him feel contented, rewarded for his labors.

A footstep in the distance made him raise his eyes. He thought he recognized it; it was a rapid and light child's step, the step of an angel hastening to announce happy and sad tidings. May the will of God be done! It's He that sends good and bad news. But his heart began to tremble, and his blackened, chapped fingers trembled, too, along with the silvery rushes gleaming in the moonlight like trickles of water.

The footstep was no longer heard; all the same, Efix still remained there waiting motionlessly.

The moon rose in front of him, and the voices of evening informed the man that his day's labor was over. It was the rhythmic call of the cuckoo, the chirping of early crickets, a few moans from birds; it was the sighing of the reeds and the ever more distinct voice of the river: but, above all, it was a breathing, a mysterious panting that seemed to issue from the earth itself; yes, the workingman's day was over, but the fantastic life of goblins, fairies, and wandering spirits was just beginning. The ghosts of the barons of old were descending from the ruins of their castle on the territory of Galte, up on the horizon to Efix's left, and were following the banks of the river in pursuit of boars and foxes: their weapons sparkled among the low alders on the bank, and the faint barking of their hounds in the distance indicated their passage.

Efix heard the sounds that the *panas* (women who died in childbirth) made while washing their clothes down by the river, beating them with a dead man's shinbone, and he thought he glimpsed the *ammattadore*, a goblin with seven caps among which he keeps a treasure, leaping here and there below the stand of almond trees, pursued by the vampires with steel tails.

It was his passing that awakened the glittering of the boughs and stones in the moonlight; and the evil spirits were joined by those of the unbaptized babes, white spirits that flew through the air changing into the little silvery clouds behind the moon; and the dwarfs and the *janas*, little fairies who during the day remain in their rock houses weaving gold cloth on golden looms, but were now dancing in the shade of the big *filirea* shrubs, while the giants appeared amid the mountain rocks touched by the moonlight, holding by the bridle the enormous green horses they alone can ride, and looking to see whether, over yonder, among the stretches of baleful euphorbia, some dragon lay hidden, or whether the legendary serpent *cananea,* living ever since the time of Christ, was crawling over the sands around the swamp. [. . .]

## 55. Saba (1883–1957): 4 liriche

### (A) Ritratto della mia bambina

La mia bambina con la palla in mano,
con gli occhi grandi colore del cielo
e dell'estiva vesticciola: «Babbo
—mi disse— voglio uscire oggi con te».
Ed io pensavo: Di tante parvenze
che s'ammirano al mondo, io ben so a quali
posso la mia bambina assomigliare.
Certo alla schiuma, alla marina schiuma
che sull'onde biancheggia, a quella scia
ch'esce azzurra dai tetti e il vento sperde;
anche alle nubi, insensibili nubi
che si fanno e disfanno in chiaro cielo;
e ad altre cose leggere e vaganti.

### (B) Mezzogiorno d'inverno

In quel momento ch'ero già felice
(Dio mi perdoni la parola grande
e tremenda) chi quasi al pianto spinse
mia breve gioia? Voi direte: «Certa
bella creatura che di là passava,
e ti sorrise». Un palloncino invece,
un turchino vagante palloncino
nell'azzurro dell'aria, ed il nativo
cielo non mai come nel chiaro e freddo
mezzogiorno d'inverno risplendente.
Cielo con qualche nuvoletta bianca,
e i vetri delle case al sol fiammanti,
e il fumo tenue d'uno due camini,
e su tutte le cose, le divine
cose, quel globo dalla mano incauta
d'un fanciullo sfuggito (egli piangeva
certo in mezzo alla folla il suo dolore,
il suo grande dolore) tra il Palazzo
della Borsa e il Caffè dove seduto
oltre i vetri ammiravo io con lucenti
occhi or salire or scendere il suo bene.

## 55. Saba (1883–1957): 4 lyric poems

### (A) Portrait of My Little Girl

My little girl with the ball in her hand,
with her big, sky-colored eyes,
and her little summer dress, said to me:
"Daddy, I want to go out with you today."
And I thought: Of all the phenomena
that are admired in the world, I know to which
I can liken my little girl.
Of course, to the foam, the sea foam
that is white on the waves; to that wake
which issues, blue, from housetops and is dispersed by the wind;
and to the clouds, the indifferent clouds
that are formed and dissolved in the bright sky;
and to other things that are light and wandering.

### (B) Midday in Winter

At that moment when I was already happy
(God forgive me for that boastful, fearful
word!), what nearly drove my brief joy
to the verge of tears? You'll say: "A certain
lovely creature who was passing by
and smiled at you." No, it was a toy balloon,
a deep-blue wandering balloon
in the blue of the air, and my native
sky shining as never before in the bright,
cold winter midday.
A sky with a few little white clouds,
and the windows of the houses blazing in the sun,
and the thin smoke from one or two chimneys,
and over everything, every divine
thing, that sphere which had escaped
from a boy's careless hand (he was weeping,
surely, amid the crowd, in his grief,
in his great grief) between the building
of the Stock Market and the café in which I was seated,
and where, looking out the window, I admired with gleaming
eyes his treasure as it now rose, now descended.

(C) Guarda là quella vezzosa,
guarda là quella smorfiosa.

Si restringe nelle spalle,
tiene il viso nello scialle.

O qual mai castigo ha avuto?
Nulla. Un bacio ha ricevuto.

(D) Sovrumana dolcezza
io so, che ti farà i begli occhi chiudere
come la morte.

Se tutti i succhi della primavera
fossero entrati nel mio vecchio tronco,
per farlo rifiorire anche una volta,
non tutto il bene sentirei che sento
solo a guardarti, ad aver te vicina,
a seguire ogni tuo gesto, ogni modo
tuo di essere, ogni tuo piccolo atto.
E se vicina non t'ho, se a te in alta
solitudine penso, più infuocato
serpeggia nelle mie vene il pensiero
della carne, il presagio

dell'amara dolcezza,
che so che ti farà i begli occhi chiudere
come la morte.

(C) Look at that charming girl over there,
look at that simpering girl over there.

She's shrugging her shoulders,
she has her face in her shawl.

Now, what punishment did she receive?
None. She got a kiss.

(D) There's a superhuman sweetness
I know of that will make you close your lovely eyes
as if in death.

If all the saps of springtime
had entered my old trunk
to make it blossom anew even once,
I wouldn't feel as very good as I do
just from looking at you, from having you near,
from following your every gesture, your every
way of being, your every small action.
And if I don't have you near, if I think of you
in profound solitude, with greater heat
there creeps through my veins the thought
of flesh, the foretaste

of the bitter sweetness
which I know will make you close your lovely eyes
as if in death.